Cultural Overstretch?

Within a few years the Europan Union will be enlarged from 15 to 28 member states, including Turkey. *Cultural Overstretch?* investigates whether these new countries culturally fit into the European Union.

A definition of the cultural identity of the EU is necessary to determine whether EU accession countries culturally fit into the EU. Jürgen Gerhards reconstructs the EU's value order and blueprint of an ideal society using EU legislation. After determining the blueprint of an ideal society, he then proceeds by testing whether citizens in member states and accession countries support the EU concepts and whether significant country differences exist. In addition to a mere description Gerhards explains the cultural differences by referring to modernization theory and closes with a discussion of the political consequences of a possible cultural overstretch of the European Union.

Cultural Overstretch? will prove valuable reading for students and researchers of European Studies, Sociology and Political Studies.

Jürgen Gerhards is Professor of Sociology at the Free University in Berlin.

Routledge/European Sociological Association Studies in European Societies
Series editors: Thomas P. Boje, Max Haller, Martin Kohli and Alison Woodward

Cultural Overstretch?

Differences between old and new
member states of the EU and Turkey

Jürgen Gerhards

Routledge
Taylor & Francis Group

LONDON AND NEW YORK

First published 2007
by Routledge
2 Park Square, Milton Park, Abingdon, Oxon OX14 4RN

Simultaneously published in the USA and Canada
by Routledge
270 Madison Ave, New York, NY 10016

Routledge is an imprint of the Taylor & Francis Group, an informa business

© 2007 Jürgen Gerhards

Translated by Zacc Ritter

Typeset in Sabon by
HWA Text and Data Management, Tunbridge Wells
Printed and bound in Great Britain by
Biddles Ltd, King's Lynn, Norfolk

British Library Cataloguing in Publication Data
A catalogue record for this book is available from the British Library

Library of Congress Cataloging-in-Publication Data
Gerhards, Jürgen, 1955–
Cultural overstretch : the enlargement of the European Union and the
cultural differences between old and new member states and Turkey /
Jürgen Gerhards.
    p.   cm.
  1. Multiculturalism–European Union countries. 2. Social values–European
Union countries. 3. Culture conflict–European Union countries.
  4. National characteristics, European. 5. European cooperation–Social
  aspects. 6. European Union. I. Title.
HN377.G464 2007
306.44´6089943504–dc22   2007004841

ISBN10: 0–415–43549–8 (hbk)
ISBN10: 0–203–94486–0 (ebk)

ISBN13: 978–0–415–43549–9 (hbk)
ISBN13: 978–0–203–94486–8 (ebk)

Contents

Figures

Tables

Preface

Many individuals and institutions contributed to this study. The VW-Foundation funded the project and the translation of the German manuscript into English. A fellowship at the Swedish Collegium for Advanced Study in the Social Sciences provided the ideal environment to put my ideas down on paper. Christian Fröhlich and David Glowsky helped with cross-reference research, data analysis and with the designs for tables and figures. Mike Steffen Schäfer and Silke Hans commented on some of the chapters.

Special thanks go to Inga Ganzer, who checked and formatted the entire manuscript, and to Zacc Ritter for translating the manuscript from German into English. I would also like to thank Joana Schenke for her very in-depth revision of the translation.

The book is a translation of the German revised version of *Kulturelle Unterschiede in der Europäischen Union* which was published in 2005 by Verlag für Sozialwissenschaften. The German book was written in collaboration with Michael Hölscher, now at Oxford University, who, unfortunately, could not contribute to the English version. Special thanks go to Michael for his collaboration.

Jürgen Gerhards
Berlin, January 2007

1 Research question and conceptual framework

A brief outline of European Union expansion

European integration is characterized by increasing institutionalization and a gradual enlargement of member states. In 1951, the European Coal and Steel Community was established by six members. Within a few years, these members decided to integrate other sectors of their economies. In 1957 they signed the Treaties of Rome, creating the European Atomic Energy Community and the European Economic Community with the goals of removing trade barriers and forming a common market. Additional sectors were gradually included, such as a customs union, a monetary union, and a common currency for a subset of EU countries. With the Treaty of Maastricht in 1993, the EU extended its sphere of influence to the fields of foreign and domestic policy and to the security sector.

This broadening of European cooperation in multiple sectors corresponds to the expansion of European institutions, which are increasingly assuming more responsibilities and gaining greater independence. In fact, EU member states have ceded part of their national sovereignty to the EU. In that EU law supersedes national law, member states and their citizens are directly subject to the decisions made by the EU. The European Commission oversees the implementation of its decisions, and the European Court of Justice has the ability to sanction member states who do not fully comply (Lepsius 1990). A number of additional indicators illustrate how sovereignty rights have been conferred from the member states to central institutions of the EU. For instance, the number of decisions made by the European Council and the European Commission is continuously rising, the number of Councils of Ministers is increasing (Knill 2001), and intermediary organizations and interest groups increasingly direct their attention to the European level (Fligstein and Stone Sweet 2002, Stone Sweet *et al.* 2001, Wessels 1997).

Alongside this deepening institutional process, the development of the European Union is also characterized by the continuous expansion in the number of member states. Great Britain, Denmark and Ireland joined the European Community (EC) in 1973; Greece became a member in 1981, Spain and Portugal in 1986, and Austria, Sweden and Finland in 1995. The

EU's expansion to the east adds another dimension, both qualitatively and quantitatively.[1] On May 1st 2004, ten countries joined the EU (Cyprus, the Czech Republic, Estonia, Hungary, Lithuania, Latvia, Malta, Poland, Slovakia and Slovenia), and Bulgaria and Romania followed in 2007. Turkey maintains its 1963 associate member status, but has been knocking on the EU's door ever since. In December 2004, the European Council decided that the EC would begin accession negotiations with Turkey. Meanwhile, Croatia and Macedonia have also become accession candidates. Entering into accession negotiations has typically meant that the country in question will ultimately accede into the Union. Within the next few years, the "EU-15" will have absorbed at least 12 new member states. Seeing as all of the new countries must be integrated into the EU's institutional system, the dramatic increase in member states demands a fundamental reordering of EU institutions. Most of the new EU member states' economic capacity pales in comparison to the older EU members. This difference in economic capacity is measured by so-called convergence indicators, which the Deutsche Bank, among others, regularly produces.[2] Table 1.1 provides an overview of the economic gap between the EU-15 member states and the accession and acceding countries for 2003 (Deutsche Bank Research 2003). Throughout the remainder of the text, we refer to the first 15 EU member states as the "old members" or the "EU-15." We refer to the countries that acceded on May 1st 2004 either as "Enlargement I" or "Accession I" and to Bulgaria and Romania, who joined the EU on January 1st 2007, as "Enlargement II" or "Accession II."

Precise and comparable convergence indicators do not exist for Turkey, but individual indicators show that Turkey is at a similar economic level as Romania or Bulgaria. Comparing GDP per capita and purchasing power parity between these three countries and the EU-15, for example, Turkey has 23 percent of the EU-15 average, while Bulgaria and Romania are at

Table 1.1 Economic differences between EU-15, Enlargement I and Enlargement II countries in 2003*

EU-15	100
Enlargement I	
Slovenia	75.5
Estonia	71.3
Czech Republic	70.6
Slovakia	69.4
Latvia	69.2
Hungary	69.0
Poland	67.4
Lithuania	66.3
Enlargement II	
Bulgaria	63.1
Romania	61.8

* Mean of EU-15 = 100%

25 percent. With regard to the proportion of employees in the agricultural sector, Turkey and Romania trail the rest of the field, at 33.2 and 37 percent, respectively (Commission of the European Community 2003: 48). The costs and benefits for member and accession countries resulting from eastward expansion are hard to calculate (Bertelsmann Stiftung/Forschungsgruppe Europa 1998, Tang 2000). Most analysts assume that all participating economies will profit from the enlargement in the long run. It is also expected that these long-term benefits will have short-term costs, a burden that will be unevenly distributed to different social groups (Vobruba 2001).

The goal of this study

The question of whether the new members will fit into the European Union is mainly discussed in the economic realm, but sociologists do not understand societies in solely economic terms. On the contrary, they assume that society is made up of multiple subsystems. This is a highly apposite issue for the EU, seeing as how it has become much more than a purely economic union. Step-by-step the EU has attempted to create a European society; factors above and beyond the economic sphere will consequently determine the success of integrating accession countries into a unified Europe (Bach 2000b). In this book, we focus on cultural similarities and differences between EU member states and accession countries. We contend that future problems in European integration will encompass both economic and cultural differences (Fuchs and Klingemann 2002). Citizens of different European countries may have differing attitudes on how society should be organized: What kind of role should the church play in society? To what extent is the employment of women desirable? What are the attitudes of citizens regarding the ideal form of government? How much social inequality is to be tolerated and interpreted as just? What kind of responsibilities regarding welfare should the state bear? What kind of economic system do the citizens desire?

Citizens' beliefs concerning the ideal form of society are referred to as "societal culture." These beliefs are decisive for the institutional stability of the EU in that an enlarged EU will not be stable if its institutions are not compatible with the beliefs of its citizens. Because all EU members states and accession countries are democracies, it is likely that the political elites will be responsive to citizens' beliefs. These officials are dependent on the citizens in that they need approval to be elected.

In the following chapters, we investigate the citizens' attitudes regarding the ideal form a society should have in both the EU-15 and in the accession countries. We ask whether and to what extent the accession countries fit within the culture required by the EU. Our analysis is structured by three research questions, outlined below.

The normative reference point: the EU's cultural self-image

The question of how well accession countries fit into the culture of the EU-15 member states requires a normative reference point. If one is committed to the notion of value neutrality in science, then such a normative reference point cannot be scientifically defined. How then, can this dilemma of defining a normative, cultural point of reference be solved? From a sociological perspective, the entire process of European unification can be understood as an attempt to establish a coherent European value system. The various institutions of the European Union can thus be interpreted as value manufacturers that have developed a definitive set of beliefs as to what constitutes European society. In other words, the EU maintains a blueprint of an ideal society, which it attempts to realize through its policies. This blueprint manifests itself in primary and secondary European legislation and in the drafted EU constitution. This societal ideal serves as a normative guideline both to the member states as well as to the EU and supplies a reference point from which to judge how well the accession countries fit into the EU mold (Sandholtz and Stone Sweet 1998, Stone Sweet 2004, Jachtenfuchs 2002). We will first reconstruct this value system that the EU promotes, differentiating between different spheres of values – religion, family, economy, politics etc. – and thus reconstruct the ideals that the EU has developed.

Description: the culture of EU citizens

In the second part of our analysis, we test whether citizens of the member and accession countries support the EU's blueprint of an ideal society. Additionally, we want to determine whether there are significant differences among the countries. The empirical basis for this part of the study are secondary analyses of representative surveys. We analyze the extent to which the citizens of Western, Central and Eastern European countries and of Turkey accept the EU's ideals for every aforementioned value sphere. Contingency tables are used to depict the empirical results. Moreover, with the help of discriminant analysis, we test whether the old members' values differ from the various groups of accession and acceding countries.[3]

Explaining differences in citizens' value orientations

Descriptive evidence reveals that significant cultural differences exist between European countries. For example, citizens of member states versus those of accession countries differ significantly in their support of separation of church and state or of religious tolerance. After acknowledging these cultural differences, we proceed by posing the question of how they can be explained. For sociologists, countries in and of themselves do not constitute relevant analytical categories; rather, one must break countries down into social variables by investigating what lies below the surface of these countries. Emile Durkheim was the first to formulate the dictum that social facts must be explained by social facts. Adam Przeworski and Henry Teune (1970) then specified this concept methodologically. Following this logic, we attempt to decipher the particular social characteristics of the EU-15 and accession countries, which may influence the values of their citizens. There are three significant groups of variables that help to explain the citizens' values:

- A society's degree of modernization: The countries analyzed differ in terms of economic modernization and wealth. Economic modernization and wealth influence citizens' value orientations, according to social scientists from Karl Marx to Daniel Bell and Ronald Inglehart. In the following chapters, we comment more closely on how the degree of modernization in a society influences value orientations in certain ways.
- A country's cultural-religious tradition: Max Weber was among the first to show that religious beliefs influence citizens' value orientations. For example, the basis of capitalism is formed by a system of merit, asceticism, and a rational lifestyle. These characteristics have a religious origin in that they are concepts of ascetic Protestantism. Several of Weber's successors adopted and elaborated the idea that a country's cultural-religious tradition influences the beliefs of its citizens. Our comparative project is steeped in this background. We assume that the different religions in the EU-15 and accession countries have developed a variety of ideas as to what constitutes an ideal society. These beliefs, in turn, influence those who are members of the religious communities. For each value sphere, we categorize the beliefs that exist in the respective religion and then empirically test whether these beliefs have an impact on the citizens' value orientations.
- A country's political-institutional system: Lastly, we assume that a country's political-institutional system influences citizens' values. For example, the countries' concepts regarding family models are different. This, in turn, is propagated by particular policies and encouraged by political measures. In the former socialist states, for example, married women with children were strongly encouraged both by ideological and social-political measures to seek employment. On the other hand, some of the old member states, like Western Germany, fostered the concept of a housewife. We assume that particular political systems play a significant role in determining citizens' attitudes.

We empirically test these different hypotheses using regression analysis to help determine the explanatory power of different groups of variables for specific value orientations.

Conceptual framework

We would like to put our own analysis into context and clarify the pros and cons of our approach in comparison to alternative approaches. It is especially necessary to clarify one's own approach in scientific disciplines, like sociology, in which there is a lack of consensus concerning definitions, methods and theories. We will clarify our premises and conceptual framework by answering some central questions.

Defining culture

There are only a few social scientific concepts as vague as culture. This study is not able to provide a final clarification of what culture is. We understand terms to be nominal definitions which specify what conceptual substance should be covered by a certain word. Correspondingly, we define the term culture in a particular manner in order to fit our aims, thereby taking earlier considerations given to this topic into account (Gerhards 2000a). We define culture as a system of values, divided jointly among actors, and used to interpret the world. Such a definition contains three elements: 1) values as a specific interpretation of the world, 2) objects which are interpreted by values, and 3) subjects or bearers of culture.

Values as a specific interpretation of the world

We consider culture to be composed of a system of relatively stable values. Nonetheless, one might say that we are not getting closer to a definition for culture, as values are not much easier to define.[4]

- Values can be distinguished from interests and needs, in that values can be justified (Thome 2003). This notion is bound to Clyde Kluckhohn's classic definition (1951: 395), in which values are defined as a "conception of the desirable."

    > The term "desirable," however, goes beyond the idea of wish or want to bring in considerations with moral content – principles, ideals, virtues, and the like – in which "want" is modified by 'ought.' ... This emphasis of desired values is indicated by replacing terms such as "I want" with "I ought."
    >
    > (Deth and Scarbrough 1995: 26)

    Hans Joas defines his conception of values similarly (1997: 30ff.). In his critique of Michael Hechter's Rational Choice-Theory (Hechter 1993) Joas emphasizes that values are not identical to preferences, but rather to *evaluated* preferences. As Clyde Kluckhohn (1951: 396) has already pointed out, "A value is not just a preference, but is a preference which is felt and/or considered to be justified."

- Values are fairly stable over time; they do not change over night. Several studies have shown that values are acquired during socialization and, consequently, remain relatively stable (see Inglehart 1971, Meulemann and Birkelbach 2001, Kohn and Schooler 1982). Fritz Heider (1958) showed that a balanced system proves to be more pleasant than an unbalanced system, which is characterized as being very stressful. Changing values causes a cognitive imbalance, which one tries to avoid.
- Values are abstract orientations. In this regard, they vary from norms and from concrete, normative preferences, yet simultaneously influence such norms and concrete beliefs. A value, such as equal gender rights, can have substantial influence on a particular political position like preferring a liberal pro-choice law. Why is this the case? The theory of cognitive consistency shows that people's values tend to harmonize with their norms and deeds (Osgood 1960). An inconsistency among values, norms and deeds leads to stress, a condition most people try to avoid.

Objects interpreted by values

Attitudes of desirable values might also refer to different *objects*. Referencing Karl R. Popper, Jürgen Habermas (1981: 114ff.) differentiates three worlds to which people generally refer: nature as the external environment, the subjective inner world and the social world as a sphere of interactions among people. For this study, we are interested in the values that refer to the social world. Following the classical description of modern society, we assume that society is made up of different spheres or subsystems like religion, family, economy and politics. In order to analyze cultural similarities and differences in various societies, the subfields, such as an economic, political or family culture, must be distinguished. Consequently, we differentiate among the cultures of the various societal subsystems. When determining the number of subsystems or spheres of values and their structural characteristics, sociological theory provides various suggestions. Because we intend to study these subsystems empirically, we do not base our theory on Parsons' structural functionalism, Luhmann's system theory, Münch's inter-penetration theory or Schluchter's post-Weberian typology. Instead, we investigate the value spheres that the EU itself defines as relevant; those spheres that it tries to influence through policy, namely religion, family, economy, welfare and politics.

It also makes sense to differentiate between spheres of values, if one analyzes culture from the citizens' point of view. Citizens live in different social spheres, such as family, job and politics. Values that are important in one field might prove irrelevant in another. For example, religious orientation may not have a substantial relevance in one's professional life, and an economic merit system will probably not play an important role in the family sphere.

Subjects of culture

In addition to the different objects to which values can refer, we also differentiate among various subjects or bearers of culture. Sociologists are not primarily interested in values only important to one particular person. Rather, we take interest in values shared among several actors, which can be called "shared or collective evaluations" (Deth and Scarbrough 1995: 34) or socially generalized values (Gerhards 2000a).

- The subjects of culture can be collective actors and institutions. For example, governments have general notions about how the economy should be structured, what a modern family should look like and what kind of responsibilities the government should take on. Institutions can also be understood as vehicles for ideas and culture in that they try to implement desirable values through their policies. In the past few decades, neo-institutionalists, in particular John Meyer, have pointed to the cultural level of organizations and institutions (Meyer *et al.*1997). Markus Jachtenfuchs (2002) has successfully analyzed the EU using this perspective. The culture of an institution manifests itself in self-produced texts, whether those texts are party platforms, laws or public statements. In order to reconstruct cultural elements out of texts, content analysis is used, which allows the EU to be understood as a cultural enterprise. The EU maintains very particular notions regarding ideal economic and familial structure. It possesses a blueprint of an ideal society, which it attempts to realize through certain policies (Sandholtz and Stone Sweet 1998, Stone Sweet 2004). The EU can only partially succeed in this aim, due to the fact that its policies infringe on several national institutions upon which the EU can only have indirect influence. Our research does not focus on the degree of realization of this EU blueprint.[5] Instead, we reconstruct the EU's blueprint and its position regarding ideal society by interpreting EU primary and secondary law as well as the constitutional draft. The EU's beliefs concerning the preferred form of government, the role of religion in society, the ideal familial structure or economic system constitute a normative reference point that can be used to determine the degree to which member states and accession countries match the EU's self-image.
- The subject of culture can also be citizens or a subgroup or class of citizens in any given society. Depending on the value sphere, citizens from Eastern Europe might have different notions from those from Western Europe. For example, these two groups may differ in their understanding of the social responsibilities of the state, the organization of the economy (market economy or state economy), the role religion should play in society

or the degree to which the employment of women is desirable. From comparative studies we know that citizens from various societies typically have different beliefs regarding the legitimate way to organize society (Gerhards 2000b). Whereas the preferred method for reconstructing the culture of institutions is textual content analysis, the instrument of choice for reconstructing the culture of citizens is survey research. Here, our concept of culture is identical to the concept of political culture developed and applied by Gabriel A. Almond and Sidney Verba:

> When we speak of the political culture of a society, we refer to the political system as internalized in the cognitions, feelings, and evaluations of its population. ... The political culture of a nation is the particular distribution pattern of orientation toward political objects among the members of the nation.
>
> (Almond and Verba 1963: 13, see also Kaase 1983)

To summarize, our definition culture is:

- relatively stable and abstract concepts of a desirable society
- which refer to different social spheres
- and are shared among society's citizens and formulated by societal institutions and collective actors.

How to define "cultural mismatch" and "cultural overstretch"

In the subsequent empirical analysis, we compare the attitudes of citizens in the EU-15 and accession states against the ideal societal blueprint formulated by EU institutions. For the aforementioned spheres of values, we analyze the citizens' attitudes as well as the EU blueprint. By contrasting these two levels of culture, we can determine whether a mismatch exists and to what extent this mismatch translates into an "overstretch." Thus "mismatch" and "overstretch" arise from the discrepancy between how the citizens' value attitudes should be and how they actually are. In the next sections, we explain why we have chosen the EU blueprint as the normative reference point and why the countries' culture is measured via the attitudes of their citizens (see Table 1.2).

The EU blueprint of an ideal society as a normative reference point

In recent years several attempts have been made to define Europe's cultural identity. The possible admission of Turkey into the EU in particular has led to an extensive debate over European cultural boundaries and EU identity. Two basic positions can be distinguished in these debates: substantialist and constructivist. We adopt an intermediate or "empirical substantialist" position in this book.

Table 1.2 The research design of the study

| Culture | Cultural spheres | | | | |
	Religion	Family and gender roles	Economy	Democracy and civil society	Welfare state
EU blueprint					
Attitudes of the citizens					

We designate the term historical "substantialists" to authors who argue that Europe's cultural uniqueness stems from its singular history. These scholars believe that Europe's uniqueness results from its history, including Jewish-Greek-Roman antiquity, the Renaissance and Enlightenment and, finally, a modern understanding of science. Accordingly, societies that do not share these historical roots, like Turkey, are not part of Europe (Wehler 2002). Other scholars define Europe's cultural identity by its Christian tradition: "The European identity relates to its specific character directly and indirectly derived from the religion that formed Europe as a cultural unit, namely Christianity" (Brague 1996: 45, also Gebhardt 1996, Maurus 1998, Rémond 1998, Schilling 1999). Religion plays a central role in Samuel Huntington's attempt to define the boundaries between civilizations. He describes Europe's boundaries thus:

> Beginning in the North, it runs along what are now the borders between Finland and Russia and the Baltic states (Estonia, Latvia, Lithuania) and Russia, through western Belarus, through Ukraine separating the Uniate west from the Orthodox east, through Romania between Transylvania with its Catholic Hungarian population and the rest of the country, and through the former Yugoslavia along the border separating Slovenia and Croatia from the other republics.
>
> (Huntington 1996: 158)

Historians Hans-Ulrich Wehler (2002) and Heinrich August Winkler (2002) oppose to various degrees the admission of Turkey into the EU. "Due to its geographic location, historic past, religion, culture and mentality, Turkey is not a part of Europe" (Wehler 2002: 9). Both authors particularly emphasize that Muslim Turkey and Christian Europe do not belong together.

These authors' definition of Europe's cultural identity contains both empirical and normative dimensions. There is no question that the old members have a Christian tradition. Declaring, however, that countries with a different religious heritage cannot be EU members is a normative claim that cannot be empirically legitimated. The EU guarantees its citizens religious freedom; therefore the fact that Turkey is not a Christian country is not a good reason for denying EU membership. In any case, a normative standpoint cannot be used to decide the matter of EU membership if one is committed to the notion of value neutrality in science. These aforementioned "substantialist" authors, however, attempt to do exactly that.

In contrast, we designate the term "constructivist" to those authors who believe that substantialist criteria will not persist. Constructivists contend that the "substantive evidence" of a European culture is socially constructed. According to this school of thought, European identity and EU membership criteria are contingent on subjective formulations. Wolfgang Burgsdorf (2004) shows that Europe's territorial boundaries have been rather flexible and correspondingly concludes that Europe's territorial boundaries are not historically grounded. He demonstrates that determining boundaries through reference to antiquity is not plausible because ideas from antiquity also spread throughout the Mediterranean region. Consequently, parts of modern Turkey would be included in this definition and other parts of what is now the EU would in fact be excluded. Finally, he emphasizes that Christianity cannot serve as a reference point to define Europe's cultural identity. The Apostle Paul grew up in a region of Turkey that is part of the near East, not Europe. Moreover, Christianity maintains at least as many anti-Enlightenment traits as Islam. Burgsdorf and other constructivist authors conclude that it is impossible to determine Europe's culture and that defining the borders of Europe is a subjective endeavor. "One time, the former French foreign minister, François-Poncet, declared that there are no compelling historical, geographical or cultural reasons, which can be used to determine the EU's boundaries clearly. History does not make political decisions" (Burgsdorf 2004: 31).

The position taken in this book can be described as "empirical substantialism" or as constitutional positivism. This perspective differs from constructivism in that it assumes that substantially definable values that constitute European identity exist. It differs from historical substantialism in that European values are not defined by the author. Instead, the normative question is translated into an empirical one; values that the EU itself defines as meaningful are decisive for determining Europe's identity. Article I-1, Paragraph 2 of the constitutional draft states that "the Union remains open to all European states that hold its values and are prepared to support them collectively." We reconstruct these EU values from primary and secondary law as well as the constitutional draft. We differentiate various spheres of values – religion, family, gender roles, economy, politics etc. – and determine the attitudes that the EU has developed in respect to each sphere.

Ascertaining a European identity in reference to European law and, most importantly, to the constitutional draft is justifiable for various reasons. First, in contrast to politicians' non-binding statements on talk shows, European law is binding and member states must adhere. Second, the primary law, constituted from the treaties, is legitimized by the member state governments' espousal of it. The adoption of these EU treaties by national governments is further legitimated in that these countries are democratic and their governments are elected by the people. Our reference to the constitutional draft, however, necessitates a special rationale following the developments of May 2005, when the French and Dutch rejected the European constitution in two referenda. Since then, several political options on how to proceed have been expressed. Some politicians call for a new approach to the constitution, such as translating it into an addendum to the Nizza Treaty. Others favor the idea of splitting the EU into two tracks, in which the more advanced countries more rapidly conform to EU concepts than do other countries. It remains unclear which strategy will ultimately come out of the so-called constitutional crisis. The fact that the constitutional draft was not ratified does not exclude the possibility of using it to reconstruct the European value system. The sections of the constitutional draft we interpret largely summarize *existing* treaties and legal systems into one unified text. The second part of the constitutional draft contains, for example, the basic EU laws which are already in force. In this respect, the values that are codified in the constitutional draft are already enforced and still important.

The measurement of a country's culture through its citizens' value orientations

In order to contrast the EU's convictions of an ideal society with the citizens' value orientations, we investigated survey results. Determining a country's culture by means of measuring its citizens' value orientations requires justification, due to the fact that multiple attempts to determine a country's culture have been previously undertaken. Culture is commonly described by reference to a country's particular history or history of ideas. Seen from a systematic, cultural comparative perspective this approach is plagued by three problems.

- A comparison among multiple entities is possible only if the point of comparison is kept constant, for example, the same instruments are used in all of the investigated countries. This is generally not the case in many philological and historical studies because most case studies deal with only one or two countries. Consequently, no reliable comparison is possible, especially between 27 different countries.
- Moreover, in philological-historical culture studies, it is often unclear what the analyzed material actually represents. Sociologists focus on cultural elements that influence society. A study concerning the similarities and differences between Western and Eastern European philosophical thought might be of interest for philosophers, but may only mirror an elite discourse that has little bearing on society at large.
- Finally, some cultural analyses are historically oriented and can therefore only be considered relevant if they can also show that a historical

perspective furthers the understanding of Europe in the present and future. Hans-Ulrich Wehler (2002) and Heinrich August Winkler (2002) conclude that there is a factual difference between Turkey and the EU by noting their different histories and prior military conflicts. This different historical heritage and earlier wars between the Muslim Ottoman Empire and Christian Europe do not necessarily mean that the EU should not accept Turkey as a member. According to this logic, Germany, who twice overran half the world in the last century, would also not be considered as belonging to a unified Europe. On the contrary, Western Germany was purposefully integrated into the Western alliance in order to prevent a future German *Sonderweg*. An argument relying on historical hostility is therefore only convincing when the different, historical experiences still exist today and still influence the present cultural orientation of a country.

If we define the culture of a country by the citizens' current value orientations, then we are more likely to be dealing with a contemporary rather than a historical measurement of culture. The fact that the citizens' value orientations in all of the countries are measured by the same standardized survey satisfies the demand that the study be truly comparative. Furthermore, because the survey was carried out in a representative manner, we are able to draw conclusions for a country's entire population (rather than just for an academic or political elite). We determine the culture of a country by describing the citizens' value orientations. Why, then, are these citizens' values considered as something important for their society?

Human behavior, not value orientations, is generally the focal point of sociological interests. A basic explanatory model for human behavior begins with the decision-making process of individuals (Coleman 1990). Both the preferences of the agent and situational restrictions and opportunities characterize decision-making processes. One must consider both sides of the preference/value orientation and the restrictions and context of any given situation in order to completely explain human behavior.[6] In analyzing the citizens' value orientations, we only investigate the abstract, *evaluated* preferences of the citizens. For example, we ask whether citizens prefer a separation of church and state or whether they desire religion to play an influential role in state affairs. Do they prefer a traditional family, where the man is employed and the woman takes care of the children, or do they prefer that both husband and wife are employed and split up household responsibilities? Our study focuses on the generalized, evaluated preferences of the citizens. Numerous studies demonstrate that people's value orientations influence their concrete preferences and actions. Moreover, recent microeconomic studies have, via experiments, revealed that people's value orientations strongly influence their behavior, such as the excellent work by Ernst Fehr and his associates (Fehr and Gächter 2002, Fehr and Rockenbach 2003, Henrich *et al.* 2001).[7]

Although generalized preferences in the form of values are important for explaining human behavior, they only constitute one aspect of a complete explanation. An analysis of restrictions and opportunities is the second step required to attain a more complete picture, but we do not consider this in our analysis. In this regard, we cannot infer the possible actions of citizens from our values analysis. We can, however, assume that the citizens' opportunities to realize their preferences are highly favorable, because the societies in question are all democracies in which the political elite depend on voter support. It is the more likely in democratic societies that the elites will orient themselves towards the citizens' wishes and values. In dictatorships, the elites are forced to orient themselves towards the citizens' values to a far lesser extent. For example, let us assume that the majority of citizens in a democratic society support an Islamic theocracy. It is very likely that a party will emerge which adopts these citizens' desires and integrates them into its party platform. This will, consequently, make the party more attractive to those voters and increase its chances of being elected.[8] If the party succeeds in winning positions in government, it can then have a hand in realizing the citizens' convictions by altering the structure of society. In this case, the citizens' values would play a decisive role in the restructuring of society. Through this logic, one can argue that the citizens' cultural orientations have a strong impact on the structure of their society. Empirical studies support this theoretical argument. In their seminal study, Benjamin I. Page and Robert Y. Shapiro (1983) demonstrate that citizens' attitudes influence politicians' decisions (see the overview in Burstein 1998, 2003). Naturally, the citizens' value orientations do not immediately precipitate concrete policies, nor do they lead to direct structural changes. The path of citizens' values is substantially filtered in the political process (Almond *et al.* 2003: 42).

A second argument for the importance of the citizens' value orientations to society is found in political culture research, whose tradition stems from Gabriel A. Almond and Sidney Verba's *The Civic Culture* (1963). This perspective assumes that political institutions are stable only when there is congruence between institutions and citizens' value orientations. Ronald Inglehart (1988) further developed this argument both theoretically and empirically. He considers the term congruence to encompass the citizens' support for the basic values of the political system, for the political regime and for the politicians' actual performance (Fuchs 2002).

Political culture research experienced a significant renaissance during the period when former socialist societies were making the transition to democracy (Fuchs and Roller 1998, Merkel 1995 and 1999, Rohrschneider 1999, Rose *et al.* 1998). The basic assumption was that the implementation of democratic institutions would only lead to stabilization if the citizens also supported these institutions. As a result of socialization in an anti-democratic system, the question of whether democratization brings about the adequate value orientations is a central question in various empirical studies of transformation research (Franzen *et al.* 2002).

Congruence between societal institutions and citizens' value orientations is important not only for the stability of the political system, but also for the economy. The institutional transfer of the economic system in former socialist societies has been quite successful. It is, however, unknown whether citizens' attitudes and values actually support the new capitalistic institutions or whether the socialization under a former command state economy will lead citizens to reject the new market economy. Economists label the consequences of such a rejection as "costs":

> When changes in formal rules are in harmony with the prevailing informal rules, the incentives they create will tend to reduce transaction costs and free some resources for the production of wealth. When new formal rules conflict with the prevailing informal rules, the incentives they create will raise transaction costs and reduce the production of wealth in the community.
>
> (Pejovich 2003: 5)

It can therefore be argued that citizens' value orientations form a relevant basis for structural stability and structural change in society. This statement holds true both in the rational-choice perspective, which emphasizes the particular "constraints" of democracies, and in a theoretical perspective, which is interested in the conditions of institutional stability. We assume that the greater the divergence of value orientations between different countries is, the more likely conflict will ensue and the more difficult integration will prove to be.

How can one explain cultural differences among different countries?

We aim not only to describe cultural similarities between EU member states and accession countries, but also to explain possible differences. Three important societal factors significantly influence citizens' value orientations.

First, modernization and value orientations: Karl Marx was one of the first authors to assume that there is causal relationship between people's values and their economic living conditions. In his critique of Hegel and German idealism, he tried to work out that the consciousness does not determine the being, but rather that the being determines the consciousness (Marx 1972, Marx and Engels 1969). Accordingly, economic factors gain a particular meaning. Some scholars have argued that Marxist explanations have been falsified by history: since most capitalist societies were wealthier than socialist societies, the Marxist assumption that a country's economic well-being is determined by the ratio of property to means of production has been proven false. This evidence, however, does not falsify the assumption that economic development and well-being influence citizens' value orientations. This abstract central theorem lies at the core of several modernization theories.

To describe the complete modernization theory with its multiple nuances and critiques (Berger 1996, Inglehart 2001, Knöbl 2003, Zapf 1998) would transcend the framework of this book. Describing modernization theory is further complicated because it does not have a coherent theoretical structure, but is rather an overarching term used for a multiplicity of theorems which describe the development of traditional societies into modern and post-modern societies.

Even today we are uncertain which factors promote modernization and how causal relationships among various factors are structured. The result of the modernization process is a historical, one-time growth of the economy and of citizens' well-being. Angus Maddison (1995: 21) has impressively substantiated this fact by calculating the per-capita GDP from 1820 to 1992. Regardless of how one explains the growth and increase in wealth in modernizing societies, when describing this phenomenon, many different theorists concur that modernizing societies can be described, if not explained, by a set of characteristics that together form a syndrome (Norris 2002: 20ff.).

Daniel Bell (1979, 1996) articulates two phases of the modernization process. He describes the first phase as industrialization, during which modern (industrialized) societies are distinguished from traditional societies. Traditional societies are characterized by a specific set of features: the agricultural sector is the main sector of production, families are the central units of production and consumption and the degree of mechanization in agricultural production is marginal. The extended family forms the central societal unit and the level of education and urbanization is low. Industrialization is characterized by the industrial production of goods as the dominant form of production, and factories and formal organizations make up the dominant units of production. Goods and services are exchanged via markets and the degree of product mechanization is high. Levels of education and urbanization also rise. The emergence of societies with these features leads toward an overall, substantial improvement in the level of wealth and well-being. Bell's second phase of modernization is described as post-industrialization. Inglehart (1997) uses the term post-modernization. In this type of society, the dominant sector of production is the service sector. Technological development and scholarship gain increasing importance and the level of education in society increases substantially. Post-industrial societies are welfare state societies, in which most of the population obtains a historically unique high level of disposable income and social security.

Alongside this modernization process are specific value orientations. David McClelland (1961) has shown that a strong merit orientation is typical for modern, industrialized societies, which he describes as "achieving societies." In addition to this merit orientation, individual responsibility, competition and self-determination increase in significance. Other authors – like Karl Marx – assume that the secularization process is connected to economic modernization. If economic living conditions improve, the need for religion to compensate for the adversity in the world will decrease, religion as the "opium for the people" decreases in meaning. Post-industrial societies are linked with another set of specific value orientations that partially replace the values common in modern societies. Referring to economic attitudes, Bell emphasizes that industrialization-phase values like merit, competition, thriftiness and waiver of consumption are replaced by a hedonistic orientation (Bell 1979): feelings of duty are replaced by a search for excitement, free time becomes more important than work and rational planning is overcome by emotional orientations. Ronald Inglehart (1997) makes a similar argument, in which the increased possibility of fulfilling material needs leads to a change from materialistic to post-materialistic values. These values include desires for self-development and participation.

What do these considerations mean for our analysis? The societies under investigation in this book differ in their degree of economic modernization and societal welfare associated with modernization. We assume that the degree of modernization has an influence on the citizens' value orientations. We will empirically test the degree to which this assumption is met.

A second important societal factor that significantly influences citizens' value orientations is the religious heritage of a country. Whereas Karl Marx is the classical thinker who formulated the effect of the economy on values, Max Weber worked out the influence of religion on people's value orientations. "Material and ideal interests, not ideas, hold direct sway over the people's behavior. But: The 'world view,' which was created by 'ideas,' quite often determines the path, in which the dynamic of interests move forward" (Weber 1988: 252). In this well-known quotation, Weber formulates his opinion regarding the powerful role of world views and values on people's actions. In his comparative religious studies, Weber attempts to show that the spirit of capitalism is of a religious origin, which namely stems from the Protestant ethic. According to Weber, this ethic has a causal impact on the capitalistic mindset because Protestantism defines work and professional values as important, which are also important in a capitalistic economy.

The belief that a country's religious tradition strongly influences the behavior of its population has been formulated theoretically and empirically by a number of Weber's successors. Paramount among historical, comparative researchers are Shmuel Eisenstadt (1992, 2000), Wolfgang Schluchter (1988, 1991) and Björn Wittrock (2001). In the field of international politics, Samuel P. Huntington (1996) describes the political, post-1989 world order in his controversial work, *The Clash of Civilizations*. Huntington assumes that international cleavages after the end of the East-West conflict will be determined by cultural differences, which are determined by the different world religions. In particular, the conflict between the Western world, which has a Christian tradition, and the Arab world, which has an Islamic tradition, will earmark the future of international conflicts.

The field of development sociology has also rediscovered "culture" as an independent variable of analysis. Lawrence E. Harrison (2000: 296) even assumes that the long-standing, predominant dependence theory is being gradually replaced by a cultural paradigm. An abundance of empirical evidence exists which substantiates that one can attribute a country's economic development to structural dependence (Landes 2000, Porter 2000). In the past 30 years, some countries have developed substantially despite unpropitious economic pre-conditions, while other countries have stagnated or even declined in their economic growth. Ghana and South Korea, for example, faced similar economic situations in the 1960s. Thirty years later, however, South Korea has achieved a per-capita GDP that is 15 times greater than that of Ghana (Huntington 2000: XIII). Several analysts ascribe this economic developmental gap to differences in economic culture, which is, in turn, influenced by differences in religious orientations.

The concept of culture has also experienced a renaissance in the field of comparative politics. Ronald Inglehart constantly emphasizes and empirically proves that the development and stability of democracies is dependent on cultural factors. Seymour Martin Lipset and Gabriel Salman Lenz (2000) demonstrate how family culture, on the one hand, and religion, on the other, can explain the degree of corruption in different countries. Finally, cultural factors play an important role when looking at why certain ethnic minorities are more successful than others in achieving higher-status positions within the social structure of the USA (Glazer 2000, Patterson 2000).

Attempts to test Huntington's thesis by means of data from the World Values Survey are particularly interesting for our research interests (Esmer 2002, Inglehart and Baker 2000, Inglehart *et al.* 2002, Norris and Inglehart 2002). We tie our analysis to the aforementioned cultural comparative studies and assume that the different religions that exist in the EU member states and in the accession countries have created concrete beliefs as to what constitutes an ideal society. These beliefs influence members of religious communities. For each of the value spheres (religion, family and gender roles, economy, democracy and civil society, welfare state) we reconstruct the beliefs of the different religions. We then empirically test whether or not these beliefs are influential factors for the citizens' own beliefs. Unlike some anecdotal socio-cultural works, we will be in the position to empirically test whether and to what degree the citizens' values are influenced by the different religions. Furthermore, we can determine the relative explanatory power of religion in comparison to economic modernization factors.

The political-institutional structure of a society is a third important factor that significantly influences citizens' value orientations. We assume that a country's political-institutional structure has an influence on the citizens' value orientations. Since the countries investigated in this study have different institutions, we assume that this deviation can partially explain the citizens' value orientations. Authors who emphasize the importance of national institutions have criticized modernization theory, which assumes a convergence of modernized societies (Skocpol and Amenta 1986, Thelen 1999). For example, Peter Flora and Jens Alber (1981) show that a country's degree of industrialization cannot explain whether a country will introduce a social insurance scheme. Comparative research on industrial relations, welfare states, democracy and familial relations has shown that different nation states have developed their own institutional systems. This has a formative influence on multiple dependent variables. The literature in this field is so vast that we are not able to detail specific studies, but comparative analyses that investigate the influence of different institutions on citizens' values are rather rare. Nevertheless, we consider such an approach to be plausible. The countries differ in the degree to which the state encroaches upon the economy and in the type of welfare system the state maintains; we assume that a country's institutions influence the citizens' attitudes regarding the economy and other value spheres. In each chapter of this book, we will specify which institutional characteristics have what kind of effect on citizens' value orientations.

Methodology

Our empirical analysis employed three data sets.

Content analysis

We reconstruct the EU's cultural blueprint with the help of the EU primary and secondary legislation. We differentiate different spheres of values – religion, family life and gender roles, economy, welfare state and politics – and determine which notions the EU has developed regarding these spheres. The majority of the legislative texts are rather confined, and the law is hierarchically constructed. This construction allows for the division of more important issues from less important ones. We can therefore limit ourselves to a qualitative content analysis. By means of citations and references from these texts, we make our interpretations plausible throughout the text.

Citizen surveys regarding value orientations

We measure the culture of EU societies by means of its citizens' value orientations. For our analysis, the most important data set is the European Values Study of 1999–2000.[9] The first European Values Study (EVS) was carried out in 1981 under the auspices of the European Values Systems Study Group initiative headed by Jan Kerkhofs and Ruud de Moor. With the help of an advisory committee consisting of Gordon Heald, Juan Linz, Elisabeth Noelle-Neumann, Jacques Rabier and Helene Riffault, surveys were carried out in 20 West European societies aiming to describe values and their influence on political and social life. This survey was repeated in another 14 countries and was labeled the World Values Survey (WVS) from 1981 to 1984. The second wave of the EVS was carried out from 1990 to 1993. The coordination committee consisting of Ruud de Moor, Jan

Kerhofs, Karel Dobbelaere, Loek Halman, Stephen Harding, Felix Heunks, Ronald Inglehart, Renate Koecher, Jacques Rabier and Noel Timms merged the EVS team with the WVS initiators. This committee organized a round of surveys in 42 countries throughout the world.

The WVS was repeated in 1995–97 and this time paid special attention to the political culture in new democracies. The European research group did not participate in this project. The third wave of the European Values Study took place in 1999–2000 and is part of the larger World Values Survey. This last wave of the European Values Study is the best data set for our purposes because it includes most of the EU member states and accession countries (Halman 2001). Additionally, the EVS has the advantage of being relatively up to date.[10] The data set is accessible at the Central Archive for Empirical Social Research in Cologne under the number 3811. The national samples of at least 1,000 randomly chosen interviewees are representative for each society. People at least 18 years of age were questioned in face to face interviews. The countries that participated in the 1999–2000 EVS, the primary researcher for each country, the number of interviewees and the response rates are shown in Table 1.3.

Several scholars have criticized the determination of national culture based on citizen surveys, and we briefly expand on two problem areas. First, survey researchers assume that interviewees from different countries similarly interpret a survey's questions and, as a result, that the answers are comparable among countries. Critics argue that cultural differences between countries might influence how a question is understood. In this case, the question does not measure the same perceptions and results are non-comparable findings. In an effort to neutralize this problem as much as possible, research teams are composed of international members and questions are carefully re-translated. Researchers try to discover and then neutralize possible divergent meanings that could lead to discrepancies by translating and re-translating the questions. One hopes that if the members of the research groups from all surveyed countries work together, that they can neutralize culturally specific meanings of questions. Second, our study relies on secondary analysis of survey data, because the surveys were not specifically created for our research interests. We must therefore use questions that we did not create and that were created, at least in part, for different research purposes. As a result, incongruities may arise between the dimensions derived from theoretical questions and data for measuring these dimensions. Some questions in the survey do not correspond to dimensions of the EU blueprint of an ideal society. But without the appropriate questions, the citizens' preferences cannot be operationalized and measured. For most of the theoretical dimensions, however, the European Value Study contains suitable questions.

Overall, we will be able to sketch a rough picture of the culture in both the EU member states and in the accession countries. In describing the culture of different societies, one must accept a certain level of abstraction

Table 1.3 Basic information about the European Values Study 1999/2000

Country	Principal investigator	Number of respondents	Response rate (in %)
Austria	Paul M. Zulehner	1,522	77.0
Belgium	Karel Dobbelaere, Yesak Billiet	1,912	n.a.
Bulgaria	Georgy Fotev, Atanas Atanasov, Mario Marinov	1,000	88.0
Croatia	Josip Baloban	1,003	n.a.
Czech Repubulic	Ladislav Rabušic	1,908	65.0
Denmark	Peter Gundelach	1,023	57.0
Estonia	Andrus Saar	1,005	13.1
Finland	Juhani Pehkonen	1,038	n.a.
France	Jean-François Tchernia	1,615	42.0
Germany	Wolfgang Yesgodzinski, Hans-Dieter Klingemann	2,036	42.0
Great Britain	Helmut Anheier, Stephen Harding	1,000	80.0
Greece	Yesmes Georgas, Kostas Mylonas, Aikaterini Gari	1,142	82.0
Hungary	Miklós Tomka	1,000	87.5
Iceland	Fridrik H. Jonsson, Stefan Olafsson	968	65.5
Ireland	Tony Fahey, Bernadette C. Hayes, Richard Sinnott	1,012	62.0
Italy	Renzo Gubert	2,000	68.0
Latvia	Brigita Zepa	1,013	n.a.
Lithuania	Stanislovas Juknevicius, Rasa Alisauskiene	1,018	75.0
Luxembourg	Pol Estgen, Michel Legrand	1,211	73.0
Malta	Anthony M. Abela	1,002	n.a.
Netherlands	Wil Arts, Yescques Hagenaars	1,003	39.6
Northern Ireland	Bernadette C. Hayes, Tony Fahey, Richard Sinnott	1,000	68.4
Poland	Aleksandra Yessinska-Kania, Mira Marody, Joanna Konieczna	1,095	73.0
Portugal	Jorge Vala, Alice Ramos, Manuel Villaverde Cabral	1,000	n.a.
Romania	Malina Voicu, Cătălin Zamfir, Lucien Pop	1,146	n.a.
Russia	Elena Bashkirowa	2,500	72.9
Slovakia	Zuzana Kusá	1,331	95.0
Slovenia	Brina Malnar, Niko Tos	1,006	53.0
Spain	Yesvier Elzo, Francisco Andrés Orizo	1,200	n.a.
Sweden	Thorleif Pettersson, Bi Puranen	1,015	41.0
Turkey	Yilmaz Esmer	1,206	n.a.
Ukraine	Olga N. Balakireva	1,195	66.0

and observe the societies from a distance to achieve a complete overview. In using a high level of abstraction, however, one loses sight of individuals and micro-situations. In other words, a wide-angle perspective is used at the price of less precision. In this respect, a comparative description of different societal cultures is always an approximation at best.

Macro-indicators

We not only intend to describe the cultures of different countries, but also attempt to explain the discovered differences. We can derive many of our independent variables from the survey data. For example, we test whether the different religions have an influence on citizens' family values by using the citizens' membership of different religious denominations as an independent variable in the statistical analysis. We cannot, however, operationalize all independent variables at the individual level. In these cases, we use macro-variables.

We assume that the degree of modernization plays a role in the citizens' value orientations. Two different indicators are commonly used to measure modernization levels. Each year, the United Nations Development Program releases the Human Development Index (HDI) for almost every country in the world. The HDI is made up of the real GDP per capita, the educational level and the average life expectancy. In addition to the HDI, the GDP at purchasing power parity (PPP) per capita is an alternative way to measure the degree of economic modernization. Compared to using GDP as a measurement, the HDI has the advantage of going beyond a purely economic measurement and is therefore a more sensitive indicator for measuring general societal welfare. We primarily use the HDI in our analysis. Both values – GDP and HDI for the year 2000 – are recorded in Table 1.4 (Human Development Report Office 2000).

We assume that the political-institutional structure of a country has an influence on citizens' value orientations. For example, countries differ in the degree to which the separation of church and state is institutionalized. We assume that this has an influence on the citizens' attitudes. We attempt to classify the countries according to their institutional separation of church and state and to introduce this variable in the explanatory analysis. In regard to family values, we presume that a country's gender equality policy influences the values that the citizens themselves place on equal rights between the sexes. We measure the country's equality policies with the UN's Gender Empowerment Measure (GEM). Similar to the Human Development Index, the GEM is determined by the United Nations Development Program for multiple countries. The index consists of three variables: the proportion of men and women in parliament, the proportion of men and women in leading positions in the political community and in the economy, and the income gap between men and women. A country receives a value of 1 in the index for complete equality between men and women and 0 for absolute inequality. Unfortunately, the values for France, Luxembourg, Malta and Bulgaria are not available in this index.

In regard to economic values, we assume that the citizens' socialization in a socialist command economy or a market economy plays a role in their beliefs concerning the ideal economic order. Correspondingly, we classify each country as a "market or socialist economy," using the number of years a country maintained a socialist regime as an indicator. Independent of a country's socialist past, we assume that the degree to which states intervene in the economy influences the citizens' beliefs concerning the economy. Greater state intervention in the economy usually leads to regulated competition, and the incentive of individual performance decreases. Different indicators can be used to measure state influence, like Gwartney and Lawson's (2003) size of Government indicator. The values for the different macro-indicators we use in our analysis are listed in Table 1.4.

Table 1.4 Macro indicators used for the description of different societies

	Gross Domestic Product (PPP US$)	Human Development Index (HDI)	Gender Empowerment Measure (GEM)	Size of government economy (EFW)	Years under socialist rule (SOZANNO)
EU-15					
France	24.223	0.928	–	2.3	0
Great Britain	23.509	0.928	0.656	6.2	0
Germany	25.103	0.925	0.756	4.5	0/44
Austria	26.765	0.926	0.710	3.4	0
Italy	23.626	0.913	0.524	4.6	0
Spain	19.472	0.913	0.615	4.6	0
Portugal	17.290	0.880	0.618	5.1	0
Netherlands	25.657	0.935	0.739	4.5	0
Belgium	27.178	0.939	0.725	3.5	0
Denmark	27.627	0.926	0.791	3.6	0
Sweden	24.277	0.941	0.794	3.0	0
Finland	24.996	0.930	0.757	4.1	0
Ireland	29.866	0.925	0.593	6.1	0
Greece	16.501	0.885	0.456	6.4	0
Luxembourg	50.061	0.925	–	4.5	0
Enlargement I					
Estonia	10.066	0.826	0.537	5.4	51
Latvia	7.045	0.800	0.540	5.2	51
Lithuania	7.106	0.808	0.531	5.6	51
Poland	9.051	0.833	0.512	3.5	42
Czech Republic	13.991	0.849	0.537	4.6	30
Slovakia	11.243	0.835	0.533	3.5	30
Hungary	12.416	0.835	0.487	4.8	40
Slovenia	17.367	0.879	0.519	2.9	45
Malta	17.273	0.875	–	5.9	0
Enlargement II					
Romania	6.423	0.775	0.405	4.0	26
Bulgaria	5.710	0.779	–	4.0	20
Turkey	6.974	0.742	0.321	7.1	0

Summary

We assume that the success of EU expansion is not only a question of economic convergence, but also depends on cultural factors. In the following chapters, we analyze the cultural differences between the EU member states and accession countries. The normative reference point for our analysis is formed by the EU's cultural self-conception – its blueprint of an ideal society as defined in primary and secondary legislation. We compare the EU beliefs regarding an ideal society with those of the citizens from the different countries and measure the citizens' values with the help of representative surveys. In addition to this descriptive analysis, we attempt to explain the cultural similarities and differences. Three variables – a society's degree of modernization, religious tradition and political-institutional structure – are the central explanatory factors.

2 Religion in a wider Europe

Religion strongly influences people's behavior and is a central element in societal culture. The influence of religion is evident through directly related actions such as: praying, attending church, eating particular foods or the way the calendar year is arranged. Religious orientations also influence non-religious activities, such as: voting behavior, economic behavior and moral attitudes toward questions, e.g. abortion and homosexuality (Pickel 2001). They can provoke conflicts and even civil wars, such as those between Muslims and Hindus in India and Pakistan, between Catholics and Protestants in Northern Ireland, and the continuing tensions in the Balkans. The United States is an example of a modernized country in which this strong relationship between religion and politics holds true: American presidents typically end their public addresses with "God bless America."[1]

Some political scientists and political actors emphasize the importance of religion for a common European culture (Kallscheuer 1996, Rémond 1998, Zulehner and Denz 1994). For these actors, the central issue surrounding Turkey's accession into the EU is not economic, but cultural-religious. Those opposing the accession of Turkey try to demonstrate that today's EU members are, due to completely divergent histories, fundamentally different from Turkish citizens. Paramount among these differences is religious orientation – people in the EU are predominantly Christian, those in Turkey, Muslim. Therefore, Europe and Turkey are not culturally similar enough to be included in the same common Union (Wehler 2002). In drawing the borders of his cultural map of the world, Samuel Huntington (1996) is even stricter about the West. Not only does he exclude Muslims, but also Orthodox Christians. Huntington views the spreading of Protestantism and Catholicism as the central criteria for defining Europe's border (Huntington 1996: 251ff.).[2] The fact that Turkey is not a Christian country and that the majority of Bulgaria's and Romania's citizens have Orthodox Christian beliefs, however, is not a sufficient reason to exclude these countries from the EU. The EU guarantees freedom of religion for all its citizens, which includes the freedom to be Muslim or Orthodox Christian. The decisive factor is whether these different religious denominations prove to be incompatible with the EU value system.

First, we reconstruct the EU's blueprint of religion. What kind of role should religion play in the European community? Second, we investigate whether and to what degree citizens' religious cultures deviate from this blueprint and vary from one another. Third, we classify countries according to their overall religious orientations to pursue our fourth research aim: how to explain the differences in religious attitudes.

The EU's blueprint of religion

Our basis for reconstructing the blueprint of religion of the EU comes from interpreting the laws, directives, regulations and recommendations released by EU institutions. There are two levels of analysis: EU primary legislation, consisting of founding and enlargement treaties, protocols and the constitutional draft, and secondary legislation, consisting of directives, regulations and guidelines. These two levels are distinguished by the degree of legal commitment required. Gerhard Robbers (2003a, 2003b) has collected, summarized and published all EU legally binding rules concerning religious issues, although he did not consider the constitutional draft in his analysis. The EU blueprint of religion can be summarized as follows.

The EU as a secular value community

The EU regards itself as a value community that does not prefer a specific religious orientation and consequently leaves religious aspects undefined. There are no statements in the primary or secondary legislation that bind the EU to a particular religion. Although all of the old EU member states have a Christian tradition, the constitutional draft does not contain any references to Christianity or to the Christian God.

In the constitutional draft, religion is referred to once in the preamble: "The European Union draws inspiration from the cultural, religious and humanist inheritance of Europe." Nevertheless, this reference does not refer to a specific religion. In fact, the text proceeds to explicate that this European inheritance has led to an anchoring of individual rights and the principle of the constitutional state. Thus, the values and goals defined in Part I of the EU's constitutional draft are solely secular, emphasizing "respect for human dignity, liberty, democracy, equality, the rule of law and respect for human rights" (European Convention 2003: Article 2). This secular self-perception has been controversial in discussions regarding the constitution and in individual national debates. Representatives of the Catholic Church, and political parties and heads of state who are closely associated with the Catholic Church or represent a predominantly Catholic population (e.g. Spain, Poland) substantially criticized the fact that there is no mention of God or Christianity in the constitutional draft. Over the past several years, the Pope has held numerous talks with European politicians encouraging a reference to Christianity in the constitution. In Germany, the Christian

Democratic Union (CDU) has been the most outspoken party in favor of a Christian reference in the EU constitution.[3] Despite all of these efforts, there have been no changes in the constitutional draft.

Individual and collective religious freedom and tolerance vis-à-vis religious plurality

The fact that the EU defines itself as a secular value community also means that the EU protects its citizens' religious freedom. In Part I of the constitutional draft, the EU defines its central values as pluralism, tolerance and non-discrimination. In Part II, which includes the Union's Charter of Fundamental Rights, it specifies general principles regarding religious orientation. In addition to freedom of speech and opinion, Article II-70 also guarantees freedom of religion. "This includes freedom to change religion or belief and freedom, either alone or in community with others and in public or in private, to manifest religion or belief, in worship, teaching, practice and observance" (European Convention 2003: Article II-70). The guarantee of freedom for individual and collective religious practices indicates the expectation that every religion adhere to the concept of tolerance. Correspondingly, the EU declares all religions to be of equal value, respects religious diversity (Article II-82) and prohibits any discrimination based on religion (Article II-81). Following Rosa Luxemburg's thesis that freedom always includes the freedom of different-minded individuals, the EU defines religious freedom by ensuring minority rights. This includes demanding tolerance of religious diversity. The EU is therefore legitimized to apply necessary measures to ensure adherence to the principles of religious freedom and religious plurality (non-discrimination). There are two references to religious issues in Part III of the constitutional draft that describe the duties of EU institutions. Article III-118 states that the EU should "combat discrimination based on ... religion." The Council of Ministers may establish, by unanimous vote, measures required for combating religious discrimination through European law or framework law after obtaining the consent of the European Parliament (Article III-124).

The principles of religious freedom and tolerance in the different fields of law

The basic principles of the EU's blueprint of religion appear in various legal fields and are codified as legally binding in EU secondary legislation. We now address several of these aspects (see Robbers 2003b).

- In the 2000 Council directive regarding "equal treatment in employment and occupation," discrimination due to religious beliefs is forbidden:

> Discrimination based on religion or belief (...) may undermine the achievement of the objectives of the EC Treaty, in particular the attainment of a high level of employment and societal protection, raising the standard of living and the quality of life, economic and social cohesion and solidarity, and the free movement of persons.
>
> (Robbers 2003b: Council Directive 2000/78)

There are exceptions to equal treatment of religion in the workplace in cases for which religious orientation creates an extraordinary occupational demand. For example, the European Court of Justice ruled that a very strict Catholic hospital had the right to fire a doctor who campaigned for the legalization of abortion.

- The EU protects different religious practices in various directives. The following three examples are characteristic of these directives. First, every member state may decide if and to what extent Sunday should be a day of rest. Second, the meat regulations of the EU allow for member countries to exceed the normal slaughter quota of sheep and goats when preparing for religious festivals. Third, a directive states the necessary to ensure that animals do not suffer when being slaughtered. Exceptions can also be made for religious practices: the inflation of an organ, typically forbidden, is allowed when a particular religion demands that this be done.
- Broadcasting of church services may not be interrupted by advertisements or tele-shopping. This also holds true for other religious programs lasting under 30 minutes.
- Finally, the EU has specific tax and tariff regulations for religious items, such as crosses or rosaries.

All of these concrete directives and regulations stem from the basic principles mentioned above. The EU considers itself a secular value community that does not have any specific religious basis. It nevertheless protects religious freedom for individuals and religious communities and defines the boundaries of every religious community through the principles of tolerance and non-discrimination. The EU recognizes and protects the unique societal position of religion. In summary, the EU views itself as a federation of secular societies that maintains an institutionalized separation of politics, society and religion.

The religious orientations of citizens

In this section, we describe the similarities and differences between the religious orientations of citizens in different member states and accession countries. Using survey analysis, we accomplish this task in two steps. First, we present basic information on religious similarities and differences not connected with the EU blueprint. In the second step, we use the EU's blueprint of religion as a benchmark to test whether and to what extent citizens in different countries support the EU concept of religion.

Basic information on citizens' religious orientations

Religiosity can be distinguished using various dimensions, such as integration into church and individual religiosity (see Jagodzinski and Dobbelaere 1993). Integration into church and other religious institutions refers to membership and participation in church activities, whereas individual religiosity describes the subjective feeling of religiosity independent of church organizations. This difference becomes particularly meaningful in the debate concerning the secularization process. Some scholars assume that the decline of integration into church in Western societies was not accompanied by a similar decline in individual religiosity. On the basis of an empirical study, Wolfgang Jagodzinski and Karel Dobbelaere prove that the importance of religion in the 1960s and 1970s declined enormously (1993). Detlef Pollack and Gert Pickel (2003) confirm this result by using East and West Germany as examples.[4]

Integration into religious institutions and institutionalized religiosity

Table 2.1 depicts the rate of citizen membership in different religious denominations using data from the European Values Study. The EVS data for some countries deviates from the results of other surveys and data found in the Encyclopedia Britannica. But the Encyclopedia Britannica information is not particularly reliable. For example, the values given for Germany clearly diverge from the data available at the Federal Office of Statistics. Reliable information on membership rates in religious denominations in European countries does not appear to be available.

With the exception of Greece, citizens of the old EU-15 countries and of the Enlargement I countries are primarily Catholic or Protestant. A substantial proportion of these two groups lack any religious affiliation at all. Citizens of the Enlargement II countries (Bulgaria and Romania) are primarily Orthodox Christians, and Bulgaria also has a Muslim minority. Turkey deviates from this pattern in that it is a primarily Muslim country and therefore does not belong to the Christian religious community.[5] Membership of religious denominations does not, however, indicate participation in church activities or integration in church institutions. To use Germany as an example, many citizens are members of a church, but at an increasing rate, no longer participate in the church's activities. A well proven indicator for measuring citizens' integration into "their" church is attendance at religious services.[6] Table 2.2 shows that attendance at religious services varies significantly in different countries.[7]

A look at the aggregate categories shows that the attendance rate in the old EU countries is lowest. Rates in the Enlargement I and II countries

Table 2.1   Membership in religious denominations (in %)

	Roman Catholic	Protestant	Christian Orthodox	Muslim	Not belonging to a religious denomination	Other
EU-15	42.1	24.2	6.2	0.6	23.6	3.3
Ireland	89.0	2.0	0.2		6.9	1.9
Portugal	85.9	0.3			11.4	2.4
Italy	81.5	0.3	0.1		17.9	0.3
Spain	80.8	0.9		0.3	18.0	
Austria	80.6	5.2	0.7	0.2	12.5	0.9
Luxembourg	65.1	0.2	0.4	0.6	30.4	3.3
Belgium	55.3	1.2	0.4	3.1	35.7	4.4
France	52.7	1.3	1.2	0.1	42.6	2.1
Denmark	0.8	87.1		0.5	10.1	1.6
Finland	0.1	84.2	1.1		11.7	2.9
Sweden	1.6	68.9	0.5	0.4	25.3	3.3
Great Britain	13.8	57.4	0.2	0.9	15.0	12.7
Western Germany	39.3	41.3	0.5	2.1	14.2	2.7
Eastern Germany	3.4	28.0	0.3	0.2	66.0	2.1
Netherlands	22.1	10.1		1.1	55.0	11.8
Greece	1.5		93.8		4.0	0.7
Enlargement I	54.1	7.1	3.6	0.2	33.5	1.5
Malta	97.7	0.9			1.3	0.1
Poland	94.1	0.3	0.3	0.1	4.6	0.7
Lithuania	75.1	1.3	3.0		19.5	1.2
Slovenia	66.4	0.3	1.6	1.1	30.0	0.6
Slovakia	64.2	11.2	0.8		23.1	0.8
Estonia	0.4	13.1	9.8	0.1	75.8	0.8
Czech Republic	29.8	3.8	0.1		64.9[a]	1.4
Hungary	39.2	16.2	0.2		42.3[a]	2.0
Latvia	19.6	17.0	16.8	0.1	40.8	5.8
Enlargement II	3.9	1.4	73.0	4.2	16.2	4.2
Bulgaria	7.5	2.0	85.6	8.3	2.5[a]	2.5
Romania	0.3	0.7	60.5		29.9	0.2
Turkey		0.1	0.1	97.5	2.3	0.1

a   Significant differences exist for Czech Republic and Hungary depending on which data set is used (ISSP 1998, WVS 1995–7). The ISSP data shows that only 43.5% in Czech Republic and 27.2 % in Hungary do not belong to a religious denomination at all. In turn, the number of Roman Catholics in both countries rises by approx. the same amount. Additionally, in Bulgaria the number of respondents without religious affiliation according to the ISSP and the WVS is higher than the number given in the EVS (ISSP: 12.8%, WVS: 33.2%). We decided to use the EVS data because we have no additional information to assume which of the data sets is most accurate.

are somewhat higher, while Turkey has the highest rate of attendance. A look at the country differences shows that the level of church integration does not depend on membership levels, but rather on the dominance of different religious denominations.[8] Countries with a very high proportion of Catholics have higher rates of church attendance, with the exceptions of

Table 2.2 Attendance at religious services (in %)

	At least once a month	Less than once a month	Never
EU-15	30.6	36.2	33.2
Ireland	74.6	17.6	7.7
Italy	53.6	32.5	13.9
Portugal	53.2	31.0	15.8
Austria	42.9	40.6	16.5
Spain	36.0	32.5	31.5
Greece	33.6	61.7	4.6
Finland	12.5	59.4	28.2
Denmark	11.9	45.4	42.7
Western Germany	34.7	41.5	23.7
Luxembourg	30.4	36.3	33.3
France	12.3	27.2	60.4
Eastern Germany	13.4	29.4	57.2
Great Britain	18.7	26.2	55.1
Netherlands	25.1	26.9	48.1
Belgium	27.8	25.9	46.3
Sweden	9.1	45.2	45.7
Enlargement I	37.0	34.9	28.1
Malta	87.2	8.9	3.9
Poland	78.1	16.0	5.9
Slovakia	49.8	27.1	23.1
Lithuania	28.9	53.5	17.5
Estonia	10.8	50.9	38.3
Latvia	15.1	50.4	34.6
Slovenia	30.7	39.2	30.1
Czech Republic	12.7	31.1	56.1
Hungary	17.9	38.1	44.0
Enlargement II	34.2	49.2	16.7
Romania	46.4	46.1	7.5
Bulgaria	21.9	52.3	25.8
Turkey	41.2	26.5	32.3

France and Luxembourg. Orthodox Christian and Muslim countries have the next highest attendance rates, while Protestant countries or countries with a high level of non-affiliated citizens have the lowest level of attendance. The different compositions of religious denominations in the four groups of countries lead to these previously described differences in the aggregate.

Individual religiosity

People can still be religious even if they are not members of a religious denomination and do not attend religious services. We can measure "individual religiosity" using two questions: whether one believes in God (possible answers being "yes" and "no"), and if one would characterize oneself as a religious person (possible answers being "a religious person," "not a religious person," and "a convinced atheist") (see Figure 2.1 and Table 2.3).

Both indicators reveal similar results.[9] Taking the aggregate figures, the degree of religiosity is approximately the same between the old EU member states and Enlargement I countries. Enlargement II countries, and particularly Turkey, show the highest rate of religiosity. The differences correspond to the dominance of various religious denominations in these countries. Muslim,

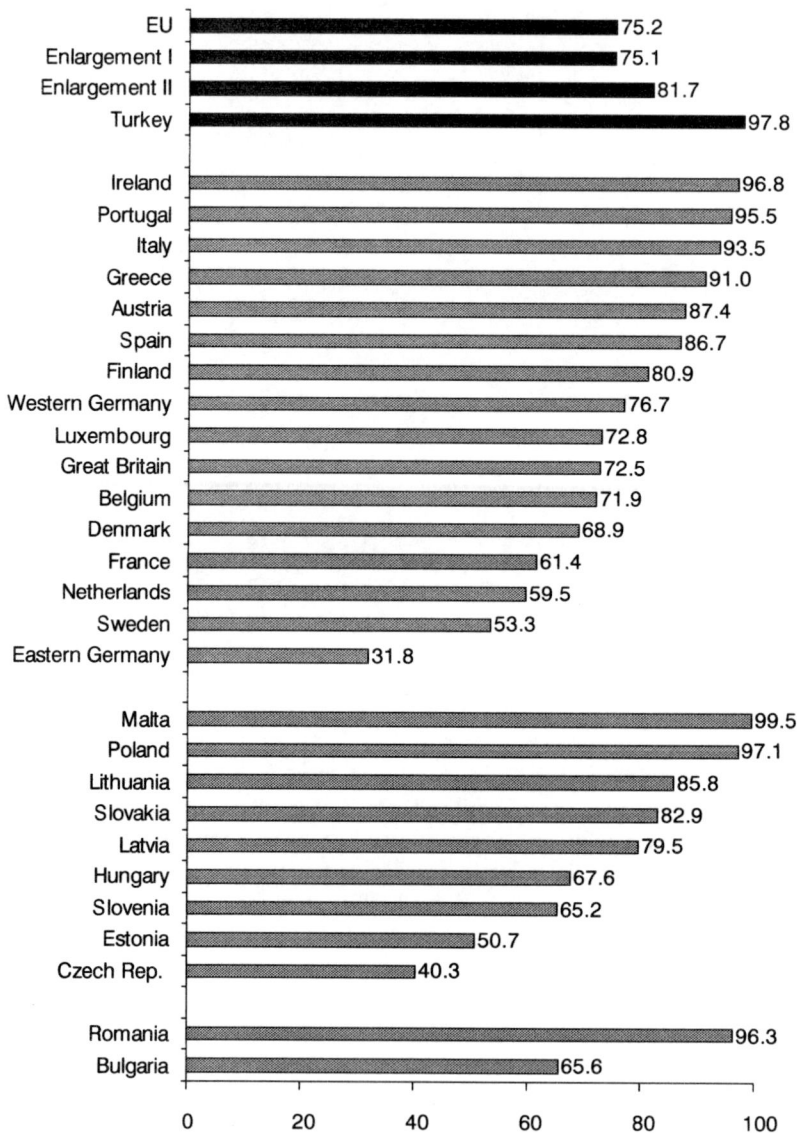

Figure 2.1   Percentage of people who say they believe in God

Table 2.3 Percentage of people describing themselves as religious

	Religious person	Not a religious person	Convinced atheist
EU-15	63.7	29.9	6.5
Portugal	87.6	9.3	3.1
Italy	85.8	11.5	2.7
Austria	80.9	17.4	1.8
Greece	79.7	15.7	4.6
Denmark	76.5	18.1	5.4
Ireland	76.4	22.3	1.2
Belgium	65.0	26.6	8.4
Finland	64.1	32.7	3.2
Western Germany	62.1	33.5	4.4
Luxembourg	62.1	30.2	7.7
Netherlands	61.4	32.2	6.5
Spain	58.9	34.6	6.5
France	46.3	39.1	14.6
Great Britain	41.5	53.2	5.4
Sweden	38.8	54.6	6.6
Eastern Germany	29.4	48.9	21.7
Enlargement I	69.8	25.8	4.5
Poland	93.9	4.5	1.6
Lithuania	84.2	13.9	1.9
Slovakia	81.7	13.9	4.4
Latvia	76.8	20.3	2.8
Malta	75.3	24.5	0.2
Slovenia	70.1	21.3	8.6
Hungary	57.5	36.9	5.6
Czech Republic	44.6	46.6	8.8
Estonia	41.2	52.0	6.8
Enlargement II	68.8	27.6	3.6
Romania	84.8	14.4	0.8
Bulgaria	52.0	41.5	6.6
Turkey	79.7	18.8	1.5

Orthodox Christian and Catholic countries demonstrate very high levels of religiosity. Protestant countries and countries with above average levels of citizens lacking religious affiliation have a lower level of individual religiosity. The results are similar to those regarding the rate of church attendance, which we confirmed with a correlation analysis. The statistical relationship between the regularity of attending church and believing in God as well as between attending church and judging oneself to be religious amounts to 0.51 (Pearson's correlation, p-value: 0.01). This evidence refutes the thesis that decreased institutionalized religiosity is replaced by individual religiosity. Pollack and Pickel (2003) arrive at similar results. Additionally, it is important to note that secularization (see Hervieu-Léger 1999), commonly described as a European phenomenon, does not appear to be especially significant in the sense of declining institutionalized or individual religiosity. In almost every country (the most significant exception being East Germany), the majority of people belong to a religious denomination, believe in God and do not describe themselves as atheists.

In summary, the citizens of EU member states are mostly Catholic or Protestant, and the religious structure of the EU will shift with the accession of Bulgaria and Romania (predominantly Orthodox Christian countries) and, in the future, Turkey (a completely Muslim country). Comparing levels of individual religiosity, Catholics, Muslims and Orthodox Christians attend church most often and demonstrate the strongest degree of individual religiosity. Due to the fact that the EU sees itself as a secular value community which does not favor any particular religious belief, Orthodox Christian and Muslim countries with higher levels of religiosity should still be able to join and be completely compatible with EU criteria. It would not be acceptable, however, if the citizens in these countries did not support the separation of religion and society or did not support the principle of tolerance toward other religions. The following section tests whether this proves to be the case.

Differences between the EU blueprint of religion and the religious beliefs of citizens

In this section, we investigate two questions: whether people support a separation of religious and secular spheres, and whether they prove to be tolerant toward other religions.

Separation of religious and the secular spheres

Concerning separation of religious and secular spheres, we distinguish between three dimensions.

On the individual level, the separation of sacred and secular worlds arises in the division between religious and non-religious lifestyles. First, we operationalize this dimension using the question "how important is God in your life," with a 10–point scale ranging from "not at all important" to "very important" as possible answers. In Table 2.4, the mean values and percentage rates for "very important" (value 10 on the scale) are indicated. Second, we operationalize the general attitude toward the separation of religion and personal life conduct using the question of how important religion is in a person's life. This question has four possible answers: "not at all important," "not important," "quite important" and "very important." Again, we provide mean values and the percentage rates of the answer "very important."

Both questions yield similar results, in that the importance of God and religion increase as one moves further away from the EU core. Whereas God and religion do not have a particularly strong significance in EU-15 citizens' conduct of life, the importance increases for Enlargement II citizens, especially for Romania, and particularly for Turkey. In these countries, there is no significant separation of religion and personal conduct of life. On the

Table 2.4 Separation of religion and personal conduct of life

	Importance of God in life (mean)	Importance of God in life ("very important")	Importance of religion in life (mean)	Importance of religion in life ("very important")
EU-15	**5.7**	**18.4**	**2.42**	**17.9**
France	4.3	8.3	2.17	10.6
Great Britain	4.9	13.8	2.19	12.6
Western Germany	5.5	9.1	2.24	9.3
Eastern Germany	3.2	4.5	1.62	3.8
Austria	6.6	26.0	2.60	21.4
Italy	7.4	33.1	2.97	33.0
Spain	5.9	18.1	2.29	14.9
Portugal	7.8	36.7	2.97	28.2
Netherlands	4.9	11.1	2.27	16.5
Belgium	5.3	18.7	2.43	20.7
Denmark	4.0	6.6	2.05	7.9
Sweden	4.0	8.9	2.24	10.8
Finland	5.7	14.7	2.35	12.1
Ireland	7.7	39.8	3.07	37.6
Greece	7.3	30.6	2.90	32.9
Luxembourg	5.4	14.9	2.34	14.8
Enlargement I	**6.1**	**27.3**	**2.51**	**23.1**
Estonia	4.1	7.0	1.90	5.4
Latvia	5.6	15.0	2.19	10.7
Lithuania	6.5	26.5	2.60	12.2
Poland	8.3	52.3	3.25	44.9
Czech Republic	3.7	9.6	1.84	8.3
Slovakia	6.6	29.9	2.64	26.8
Hungary	5.2	20.6	2.34	19.0
Malta	9.1	67.8	2.23	67.1
Slovenia	5.0	14.9	3.56	12.2
Enlargement II	**6.9**	**35.4**	**2.84**	**34.1**
Romania	8.6	56.0	3.25	51.3
Bulgaria	5.1	14.4	2.42	16.3
Turkey	9.3	80.9	3.73	81.9

disaggregated level, one can see that these results correspond to the strength of different religious denominations in the countries.

The European Values Study poses three yes or no questions concerning the relevance of religion for resolving societal problems: Does the church give adequate answers to individual moral problems, domestic and familial issues, and social problems facing the country?[10] We interpret the answers to the three questions as indicators with which to measure the degree of separation between religion and society. If the respondent believes that religion provides adequate answers to and solutions for societal issues, then his subjective separation of the religious and societal spheres is less substantial.

Table 2.5 Separation of religion and society (in %)

Church gives adequate answers to ...	... moral problems	... problems of family life	... social problems
EU-15	39.0	31.5	27.8
France	35.3	27.3	20.9
Great Britain	32.5	30.2	26.5
Western Germany	53.6	41.6	35.8
Eastern Germany	34.6	26.7	15.3
Austria	37.8	28.5	30.7
Italy	61.8	47.7	43.5
Spain	39.9	35.1	28.9
Portugal	56.0	45.0	36.8
Netherlands	35.2	29.6	37.0
Belgium	36.2	32.6	27.1
Denmark	20.0	15.0	11.5
Sweden	25.6	18.3	16.9
Finland	42.0	39.9	29.9
Ireland	31.8	29.0	28.4
Greece	43.1	30.6	31.0
Luxembourg	33.0	24.2	23.4
Enlargement I	56.5	53.0	32.8
Estonia	44.7	30.1	14.1
Latvia	58.2	47.9	26.3
Lithuania	81.3	78.8	54.2
Poland	65.6	64.4	40.5
Czech Republic	36.8	32.1	16.7
Slovakia	68.2	63.8	29.7
Hungary	44.8	38.9	23.3
Malta	66.6	75.0	57.0
Slovenia	44.9	42.8	33.8
Enlargement II	63.6	54.8	32.8
Romania	80.7	78.5	52.2
Bulgaria	44.5	28.8	13.9
Turkey	76.2	67.2	43.7

The results are similar to those in Table 2.4. The majority of citizens in old member states do not expect the church to solve societal problems. This is noticeably different for citizens in accession countries.[11] Once more, the further away a country is from the EU core, the more popular the notion that religion can solve societal problems. Turkey shows the lowest degree of separation between religion and society. There are, however, substantial differences between countries within the aggregate categories. Countries with a large population of Muslims have the lowest degree of separation of society and religion, followed by those countries with a large number of Orthodox Christians, then by countries with a large Catholic population. Protestant countries and countries with a significant amount of non-religious citizens show the highest degree of separation of church and society.

Results from the European Values Study also allowed us to test the extent to which citizens believe the spheres of religion and politics should be separated. First, people were asked whether they think politicians who do not believe in God are unfit for public office. They were then asked whether they believe it would be better for their country if more people with strong religious beliefs held public office.[12] Interviewees could choose from five answers ("disagree strongly," "disagree," "neither agree nor disagree," "agree," "agree strongly"). We combined the "agree" and "agree strongly" responses in Table 2.6, which shows mean values and percentages.[13]

The results for both questions show the expected results, with the EU-15 member states manifestly expressing a preference for the separation

Table 2.6 Separation of religion and politics

	Politicians should believe in God		It would be better for the country if more people with strong religious beliefs held public office	
	(mean)	*(% of approval)*	*(mean)*	*(% of approval)*
EU-15	2.08	12.2	2.41	18.8
France	1.70	9.2	1.98	12.7
Great Britain	2.10	9.7	2.46	16.7
Western Germany	2.24	17.6	2.74	29.7
Eastern Germany	1.96	7.7	2.26	15.9
Austria	2.14	15.1	2.64	26.6
Italy	2.40	15.0	2.68	22.2
Spain	2.21	9.5	2.54	16.4
Portugal	2.26	14.5	2.69	25.4
Netherlands	1.56	1.7	2.17	11.8
Belgium	1.70	9.1	2.15	17.8
Denmark	1.53	3.7	1.66	5.6
Sweden	1.72	4.0	2.09	8.8
Finland	2.25	11.9	2.41	15.4
Ireland	2.40	16.2	2.65	24.1
Greece	3.07	37.3	3.04	32.0
Luxembourg	2.11	13.1	2.45	20.0
Enlargement I	2.43	18.4	2.82	31.3
Estonia	2.41	13.9	2.77	25.0
Latvia	2.64	22.2	3.19	43.8
Lithuania	2.62	20.4	3.10	36.8
Poland	2.35	15.9	2.79	29.3
Czech Republic	2.06	6.3	2.23	9.5
Slovakia	2.51	22.0	3.01	37.0
Hungary	2.11	12.4	2.52	23.1
Malta	3.06	41.7	3.59	64.5
Slovenia	2.10	10.7	2.16	12.3
Enlargement II	3.06	38.7	3.31	47.2
Romania	3.46	52.0	3.76	64.7
Bulgaria	2.67	24.9	2.86	28.9
Turkey	3.52	62.3	3.42	57.1

of religion and politics. There is less support for such separation in the Enlargement I and II countries, particularly in Romania. This concept is most clearly rejected by Turkish citizens, who believe that religion should guide political actions and assume that religion provides the correct solution for many everyday political problems. In this regard, Turkey and Romania fit the EU's blueprint of religion the least.

Tolerance toward other religious communities

The EU expects its members, regardless of their religious denomination, to tolerate other religions. The European Values Study poses only one question that can be used to operationalize tolerance toward other religious communities. In almost all countries, respondents were asked whether they would be opposed to having a Muslim as a neighbor. A fitting equivalent was, unfortunately, not asked in Turkey. Respondents in all countries were asked whether they would oppose having Jewish neighbors. We therefore use this question as a measurement of citizens' religious tolerance.[14]

Figure 2.2 shows that there is widely-accepted tolerance toward Jews in the old EU member states. The Enlargement I and II countries also show high levels of tolerance toward Jews, although about one-fifth of the population expresses non-tolerance. The situation is noticeably different in Turkey, where 60 percent of the interviewees are opposed to having Jewish neighbors. These results must be carefully interpreted, in that the question regarding tolerance towards Jews may also measure anti-Israel sentiments regarding Israel's policies toward Palestinians. Yet the following empirical evidence also supports our thesis that the indicator measures general tolerance towards other religious denominations. Pearson's correlation coefficient of attitudes towards Jews and Muslims as neighbors, a question not posed in all countries, amounts to 0.47 (p-value: 0.01). We can also show through secondary analysis of the World Values Survey from 1990 and 1995–7 that the level of religious tolerance in Turkey is very low. In both of these surveys, respondents were asked whether they had anything against a Muslim living in their neighborhood. This same question was asked in Turkey, and the word "Muslim" was replaced by "Christian." Both surveys show that Turkey has the lowest level of religious tolerance for all countries under analysis. The percentages of respondents in Turkey who did not want a Christian living in their neighborhood were 54.7 and 49.1 percent in the 1990 and 1995–7 surveys, respectively.

We now turn to a summary of the descriptive evidence. The EU considers itself a secular value community, favoring the separation of societal and religious spheres and expecting reciprocal tolerance among religious groups. The old EU citizens strongly support these beliefs, whereas citizens of the 2004 accession countries accept these concepts to a lesser degree. Romania visibly deviates from these beliefs. Moreover, a significant proportion of Turkish citizens express a desire for a closer relationship between religion,

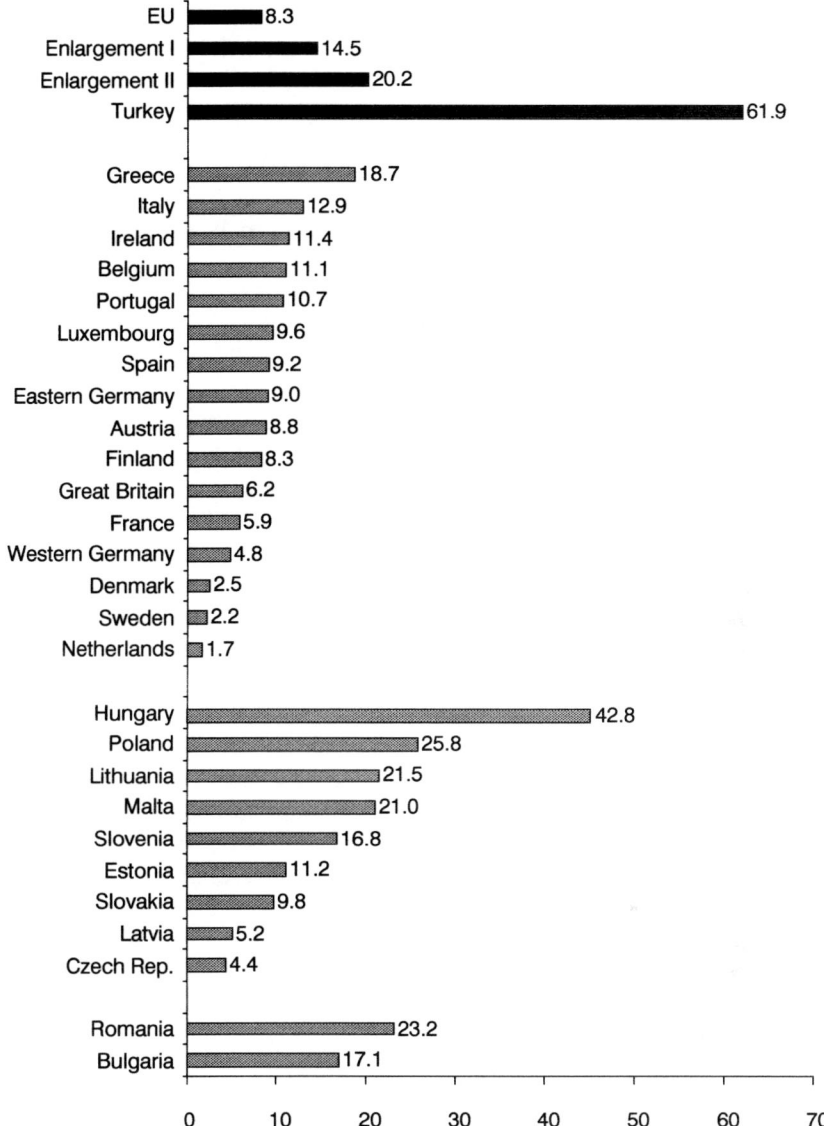

Figure 2.2   Intolerance against other religious denominations (in %)

society and politics.[15] The admission of new countries will change the overall religious culture in the EU, and the proportion of those who do not share the EU's concept of a clear separation of the sacred and the secular spheres will increase.

In addition to the differences on the aggregate level, there are significant variations within individual country groups. Countries with large Protestant populations most strongly support the EU blueprint of religion, countries with substantial Catholic and Orthodox populations adopt a middle ground, and Muslim Turkey shows less support.

Classification of different countries in regard to their religious attitudes

More precise analysis of whether and to what degree European citizens share the EU's ideas of separating religious and secular spheres and tolerance toward other religious denominations becomes possible with advanced statistical methods. Discriminant analysis provides an ideal method and offers two kinds of insights. First, such analysis can determine the degree to which individual respondents agree with the EU blueprint. Second, discriminant analysis can estimate the effect that certain variables have on the degree of support for EU beliefs.

As previous results have shown, predominantly Protestant Western countries support the EU ideal the most, particularly in Denmark, the Netherlands, Sweden and East Germany. Citizens of Catholic France also show high levels of support for the EU's blueprint due to its strong secular tradition. We use these five countries as the "benchmark countries" that conform to the EU position, comparing them with other countries to determine their proximity to the EU's blueprint.

Table 2.7 shows information on the differentiation between the benchmark countries and other European countries. The correlations of the indicators with the discriminant function are listed in the upper third of the table. High values indicate that variables have a strong influence on the separation between the two groups.[16] The variable "how important is God in your life" is the single most important explanatory factor. Two other very strong effects are "separation of religion and personal conduct of life" and "separation of religion and politics," each with a correlation coefficient around 0.7. The two groups are more similar in regard to the other two dimensions, "separation of religion and society" and "tolerance toward other religious affiliations." All correlations have the expected positive sign. Eigenvalue and canonical correlation are used as measures of goodness of fit in discriminant analysis and show how well the analysis is able to differentiate between the groups. Higher values indicate that variables have a higher effect on the differentiation between benchmark and non-benchmark countries. Another indicator for the quality of an analysis is the percentage of respondents classified correctly, 63.2 percent in our case. Considering that a random assignment to one of the two groups would lead to an average of 50 percent correct classification, the improved ability to predict based on the discriminant function is certainly acceptable, but by no means excellent.[17] It is important to note that the benchmark countries most closely represent the EU position. We do not postulate that such a position is non-existent in other countries. In this respect, misclassifications are partially preprogrammed. We return to this issue below.

Table 2.7 Religious values: differentiation between benchmark countries and other countries

	EU-position[a][b]
Separation of religion and personal conduct of life	
Importance of religion in life	0.630
Importance of God in life	0.849
Separation of religion and society	
The Church gives adequate answers to moral problems	0.459
The Church gives adequate answers to problems in the family life	0.480
The Church gives adequate answers to social problems	0.325
Separation of religion and politics	
Politicians who do not believe in God are unfit for public office	0.759
It would be better for the country if more people with strong religious beliefs held public office	0.713
Tolerance of other religious denominations	
Not wanted as neighbors: Jews	.392
Eigenvalue	0.121
Canonical correlation	0.329
Group centroids	
Group to classify	0.166
EU-position (benchmark countries)	–0.731

Classification results[c]	Groups (predicted)	
	1	2
1 Group to classify	60.3% (9,556)	39.7% (6,289)
2 Benchmark countries	24.0% (863)	76.0% (2,729)
Classified correctly	63.2%	

a   Benchmark countries: Denmark, Eastern Germany, France, Netherlands, Sweden.
b   Pooled within-group correlations between discriminating variables and canonical discriminant function.
c   In order to take all countries into account equally, cases were weighted by sample size.

The mean values of the discriminant function of the benchmark countries (–0.731) and the rest of the countries (0.166) reveal a clear difference. All variables show a positive correlation with the discriminant function, with high positive values signifying a strong religious orientation, while negative values indicate less emphasis placed on religion. As the classification results show, about one-quarter of the interviewees from the benchmark countries are placed in the incorrect group, and more importantly, about 39 percent of the interviewees from the non-benchmark countries are incorrectly classified. This illustrates the rigidity in choosing the benchmark countries.

We are not so much concerned with the results on the individual level, seeing as our interest is in the differences amongst countries, not individuals. Therefore, we aggregated the values for individuals on the country level, obtaining two closely related measures. These measures show the extent to which citizens from these countries support the EU blueprint. The results are found in Table 2.8.

Table 2.8 Closeness of countries to the EU blueprint (benchmark countries)

	Percentage of citizens in the group of benchmark countries	Average probability of citizens to be classified in the group of benchmark countries
EU-15	**54.2**	**0.49**
Denmark	86.8	0.65
Sweden	76.9	0.61
Eastern Germany	74.7	0.60
France	74.1	0.59
Netherlands	68.3	0.57
Belgium	65.0	0.54
Great Britain	59.0	0.51
Luxembourg	57.5	0.51
Finland	52.2	0.48
Western Germany	52.4	0.47
Spain	49.3	0.47
Austria	48.4	0.46
Italy	30.0	0.38
Portugal	26.8	0.38
Ireland	30.5	0.38
Greece	24.3	0.32
Enlargement I	**40.7**	**0.40**
Czech Republic	73.0	0.58
Slovenia	59.1	0.51
Estonia	59.8	0.50
Hungary	50.6	0.44
Latvia	40.2	0.40
Slovakia	34.0	0.36
Poland	23.3	0.33
Lithuania	20.5	0.30
Malta	6.9	0.21
Enlargement II	**27.6**	**0.31**
Bulgaria	47.9	0.45
Romania	8.9	0.19
Turkey	7.2	0.15

Within each group, countries are sorted by the average probability that their citizens hold benchmark group values.

A look at the four aggregate categories results in the same ordering of countries as was derived from the descriptive evidence.[18] The 15 old member states show the most support for the EU religious blueprint, and on average half of the interviewees agreed with the blueprint. People in Enlargement I countries support the EU position to a lesser extent, while only around one-quarter of the interviewees from Enlargement II countries support the EU blueprint. Very few Turkish citizens share the EU's position, with only 7 percent classified with the benchmark countries. Within aggregate groups, clear country differences also exist. Italy, Portugal, Ireland and Greece have different convictions from other old member countries. In Catholic and Orthodox Christian countries with a relatively strong connection to the church, only a minority of the population supports the EU blueprint. Contrastingly, the majority of citizens from the new EU member states Slovenia, Estonia and especially the Czech Republic support this blueprint.[19] The Czech response becomes less astonishing when one considers that more than half of the population does not hold any religious affiliation. And although two-thirds of the population in Slovenia is Catholic, ties to the church are minimal. The countries with the largest Catholic populations among the accession countries (Poland, Lithuania and especially Malta) support the EU ideal to a much lesser extent. Even though both of the Enlargement II countries are predominantly Orthodox Christian, clear differences exist between Bulgaria and Romania. Whereas Bulgaria has a moderate position with a slight majority against the EU's religious blueprint, Romanians (along with citizens of Malta and Turkey) support the blueprint the least.

By and large, the discriminant analysis confirms our interpretations of the descriptive results. The overall cultural pattern of the EU regarding religious conceptions will change as accession countries become members. Consequently, the proportion of those who do not identify with the EU's blueprint, characterized by religious tolerance and the separation of religious and secular spheres, will increase.

Explaining differences in religious orientations

This section attempts to explain differences in the religious orientations of citizens. As we emphasized in the introduction, a country must be broken down into the social factors that form the structure of that particular country. We differentiate between four dependent variables: three dimensions regarding the separation of religious and secular spheres, and one dimension regarding the citizens' tolerance toward other religious denominations.[20]

- Separation of religion and personal conduct: By analyzing the survey questions on the importance of God and of religion in one's overall life, we measure the attitudes toward the separation of religion and personal conduct. We have created a quite reliable additive scale out of these two variables (Cronbach's Alpha = 0.85).[21]
- Separation of religion and society: To measure attitudes regarding the separation of religion and society, we used three questions that highlight the relevance of religion in solving societal problems (family, social and moral problems). We again combined these questions to create an additive scale (Cronbach's Alpha = 0.82).
- Separation of religion and politics: We also formed an additive scale from the survey questions that measure the separation of religion and politics. This scale is also sufficiently reliable (Cronbach's Alpha = 0.77).

- Tolerance towards other religions: We measure this dimension using the question on whether one would accept a Jew in one's neighborhood.

In addition to these four dependent variables, we differentiate between three groups of independent variables.

First, we look at religious denominations and integration into the church. As already noted in this chapter, attitudes concerning the separation of religion and the secular sphere and tolerance toward other religions vary depending on the degree of integration into a church or a religious institution and the particular religious denomination.

We assume that *all* religious communities are predisposed to spreading their convictions beyond the field of religion. We presume, then, that people with no religious affiliation support separation between religious and secular spheres and are tolerant toward other religions to a greater degree than members of religious communities. We also assume that the degree of integration into a particular church, measured by attendance, influences beliefs on the separation of religious and secular spheres.[22] The less people are involved in the daily practices of their church, the more likely they are to support a separation between religion and the secular world.

It is very controversial as to whether different religions as entire entities can be characterized by a particular belief concerning the relationship of religion and the wider world and, more importantly, by a particular belief on the desired position between religion and the state. Theologians and scholars debate as to whether beliefs concerning the relationship of religion and the secular sphere can be textually derived from the Bible or the Koran. This debate is not particularly surprising, in that the Bible and the Koran are both extremely ambiguous texts whose longevity can be attributed to this very fact; ambiguity allows for different interpretations of the text. It is not our task to judge the accuracy of different interpretations of the Bible or the Koran, but rather to formulate a hypothesis and test whether it can be empirically confirmed. We start from the *hypothesis* that Islam is a religion in which the separation between the religious and secular spheres is less apparent than in the other faiths under analysis.[23] Unity of religion and politics has existed since Muhammad became the simultaneous religious and political leader of the first Muslim community in the seventh century AD. The Koran is both a secular and religious book of laws. The sharia sets guidelines for social-political life. And although the Koran does not demand a particular form of government, religion and politics appear to be more closely interwoven in Islam than is the case in Christianity.[24] Separation between church and state appears to be more anchored in the Christian tradition, though to varying degrees depending on the particular denomination.

The Orthodox Christian faith maintains a greater association between church and state than the other Christian denominations. Starting with Constantine the Great, the emperor had a strong influence on the relationship between the church and state, which were considered as two sides of one

Christianity. The emperor accorded the force of law to church ordinance. The Roman Catholic Church, on the other hand, followed Augustine's model for a separation between the earthly and divine orders. The church claimed "potestas directiva" instead of "potestas directa" for worldly matters. The church declared precepts concerning the secular world, but never made particular decisions. Following Samuel Huntington, it can be expected that the support for separation between religious and secular spheres increases in the following manner: Muslims, Orthodox Christians, Catholics, then Protestants (Huntington 1996).

Muslims, Orthodox Christians and Catholics are more integrated into their religious institutions than are Protestants and people with no religious affiliation. We can therefore not use the contingency tables to discern whether the degree of church integration forms the basis for rejecting separation between the religious and secular spheres or whether this is related to the content of the different religions. We can, however, test this in a multivariate regression analysis.

The second group of independent variables focus on the degree of modernization. Several scholars claim that societal modernization has an impact on the separation of religion from society and politics. The more modernized a society, the greater the support for separation of religion and society. The degree of societal modernization is expressed by multiple factors, such as economic welfare and educational levels.

Emile Durkheim formulated the thesis that educational levels influence the separation between religion and society (Durkheim 1983: 177). Education increases the potential for self-reflection and the likelihood of a scholarly and secular outlook on the world. As levels of education rise, so does the likelihood that traditions will be questioned rather than automatically accepted. We assume that more educated interviewees are more likely to support a separation of religion and society, whereas people with lower levels of education will not support such a separation. We operationalize the interviewees' education by using their highest completed level of education. Because national educational certificates are difficult to compare, the EVS created an approximate comparative classification ranging from 0 "inadequately completed elementary education" to 8 "highest education – upper-level tertiary certificate."

A second assumption of modernization theory is that economic conditions as a determinant of quality of life influence a person's religious interpretation of the world. This theory stems from the religious sociology of Karl Marx and Friedrich Engels, who incorporated Friedrich Feuerbach's theory of religion. The growth and persistence of religion is explained in terms of worldly factors: "All religion is nothing more than the phantasmagoric reflection in people's minds of those external powers that rule their daily existence, a reflection in which the earthly powers assume the form of heavenly ones" (Engels 1973: 294). Marx and Engels perceive "phantasmagoric products" such as religion as compensation for the trials and tribulations people experience in their daily lives. These trials are of a double nature: they consist not only of natural threats like plague or flood, but also of societal impediments like economic conditions for survival.[25] In order to endure the burdens imposed by nature and society, humans invented religion. Religion gives a supernatural interpretation to this earthly veil of tears:

> Religious misery is at one and the same time the expression of real misery and a protest action against it. Religion is the sigh of the burdened creature, the soul of a heartless world, just as it is the mind of mindless conditions. It is the opium of the masses. True happiness will only emerge when the illusory happiness of religion is eradicated.
>
> (Marx 1972: 378)

With this last remark, Marx indicates the conditions under which religion loses its power and persuasiveness: As earthly happiness waxes, the need for religion wanes. Earthly happiness consists mainly of securing living conditions and economic welfare. From this presumed link, we derive the following hypothesis: With less existential and material needs – i.e. greater prosperity – the need for religiosity decreases. We assume that greater societal economic well-being increases the likelihood that material needs are met, which in turn leads to a greater separation of religion and society. We measure the degree of a country's economic modernization by the level of its Human Development Index. Unfortunately, it is not possible to measure the relative economic well-being of all the interviewees from all countries at the individual level.

The third set of independent variables concerns the institutional separation of religion and politics. Different countries vary in the degree to which the church and state are institutionally separated. The scale ranges from countries that maintain a strict separation (France and Turkey) to states that have an institutionalized state church (England, Sweden, Denmark).[26] We assume that the institutional separation of church and state also influences citizens' attitudes toward the separation of religion and the secular world (see Chaves and Cann 1992, Pollack and Pickel 2000, Pollack 2003). In order to test this hypothesis, we must first classify the countries in regards to the institutionalized degree of separation between church and state. This task is neither theoretically nor empirically simple. A number of typologies refer to the national legislation in each country that defines the relationship between the church and the state (see overview in Minkenberg 2003). Gerhard Robbers (1995) separates Europe into three different models: the state church system and the systems of strict and basic separation between religion and politics. Maurice Barbier (1995) developed a similar typology with four models that range from secular to non-secular. Mark Chaves and David Cann (1992) attempt to incorporate economic, i.e. church tax, and political dimensions, such as the state naming church personnel, in their typology in addition to legal regulations regarding the relationship between the church and state. Countries are classified with the help of a 7-point scale.

Detlef Pollack and Gert Pickel's study is the only one that also includes East European countries (see Pollack and Pickel 2000, Pollack 2003). These authors construct an 8–point scale using five dimensions (existence of a state church, existence of theological faculties at state universities, religious instruction in public schools, existence of military and penitentiary spiritual guidance, and fiscal preferential treatment of churches). A value of 7 indicates a very slight separation of church and state, whereas a value of 0 signifies a complete separation. The authors classify those countries that are part of our analysis in the following way: Austria (5), the Czech Republic (6), Denmark (7), France (2), Germany (7), Great Britain (6), Hungary (5), Ireland (5), Italy (6), the Netherlands (4), Poland (4), Portugal (6), Spain (5) and Sweden (8). Additionally, we classify Turkey as (1), because we know that the separation of religion and the state is strictly implemented.

We assume that the degree of institutional separation of church and state influences the extent to which the citizens support the separation of these spheres. We measure the degree of institutional separation with Pollack and Pickel's scale. In a multivariate regression analysis we analyze the influence of the different independent variables on the four dependent variables. This analysis is performed in two steps. Because we only have information regarding the degree of institutional separation of church and state for 15 of the 27 countries, we first conduct the analysis for these 15 countries. Institutional separation of church and state has a slight effect on the separation of religion and conduct of life, but the effect goes in a different direction than we expected (the standardized regression coefficient Beta is 0.05). The institutional separation of church and state has no significant effect on attitudes toward the separation of religion and society. The effect on attitudes toward the separation of religion and politics (Beta = 0.06) has the expected effect. Consequently, our hypotheses are neither clearly supported nor refuted. This result could be expected on the basis of our descriptive analysis (see the second part of this chapter). The citizens of Scandinavian countries (Denmark, Sweden and Finland) with a strong church–state connection, support a separation between religion and the secular world. On the other hand, Turkey belongs to those countries where the separation of church and state is significantly institutionalized (Jung 2003), but the citizens' acceptance of this separation is slight. Our result corresponds with other studies that analyze the influence of institutional separation of religion and the state either on citizens' religiosity (Pollack 2003) or on support for democracy or for certain policies (Minkenberg 2003). No noteworthy effect exists on any of the dependent variables.

In the second step of our analysis, we excluded the variable, "institutional separation of church and state." By doing so, we were able to consider all 28 countries. Table 2.9 shows the results of four multivariate regression models.

Table 2.9 Explaining attitudes toward separation of religion and personal conduct of life, religion and society, religion and politics, and tolerance toward other religious denominations: linear regressions

	Separation of religion and personal conduct of life	Separation of religion and society	Separation of religion and politics	Tolerance towards other religious denominations
Religion[a]				
Protestants	−0.153	−0.105	−0.070	0.023
Roman Catholics	−0.339	−0.161	−0.093	−0.020*
Orthodox Christians	−0.222	−0.056	−0.174	−0.022
Muslims	−0.284	−0.080	−0.108	−0.183
Integration into church	−0.496	−0.367	−0.360	−0.047
Level of modernization				
HDI	0.049	0.164	0.218	0.143
Education of respondent	0.079	0.084	0.134	0.121
R^2	**0.570**	**0.260**	**0.320**	**0.100**

The models represent standardized beta-coefficients from the ordinary least squares (OLS) regression analysis.
If not indicated differently, coefficients are significant at the 1% level. * = significant at 5% level.
a   Category of reference: people who do not have a religious affiliation.

A look at the explained variance for all four dependent variables shows that the chosen independent variables are able to explain quite well the attitudes regarding the separation of religion and personal conduct of life, religion and society as well as religion and politics. This is less the case when explaining tolerance toward other religious denominations.

Educational levels and economic development, variables derived from modernization theory, both influence the separation of religion from the secular world as well as tolerance toward other religions. This confirms our theoretical assumptions. The more educated an interviewee and the more modernized his country, the more likely he is to support a separation of religious and secular spheres and advocate tolerance toward other religions.

All religious affiliations, with the exception of Protestants, exhibit less tolerance toward other religions than people having no religious affiliation. This is particularly the case for Muslims. Likewise, all of those affiliated with a religion accept a separation of religion and the world to a lesser degree. One *may not* assert that Orthodox Christians and Muslims differ from Catholics and Protestants; the results are too inconsistent to reach this conclusion. Less important is the religious denomination to which a respondent belongs than is the degree to which he is integrated into his religious community.[27] The degree of integration in a specific church or religious institution has a much greater degree of influence on views about the separation of the religious and secular spheres than does the religious denomination to which the interviewee belongs. This is an extremely interesting discovery. Regarding

Turkey's accession into the EU, some authors like Samuel Huntington (1996) and Hans-Ulrich Wehler (2002) assume that a separation of church and state is *inherent* to the Christian tradition and that this is not the case for the Muslim faith.

> The co-existence of church and state or, more generally, the state and religious communities is so self-evident for modern people that they are unconscious of the fact that this is a particular characteristic of Christianity. Even today, Muslim and East Asian countries still do not recognize this fact.
>
> (Campenhausen 2002: 98)

Our analysis does not support this statement. The fact that Turkey and the Enlargement II Orthodox Christian countries support the EU religious concepts to a lesser degree has little to do with the inherent substance of their dominant religious systems. Rather, this orientation is influenced by the degree of modernization and the strength of integration into the church. Because the degree of modernization is slight in these countries and the degree of integration into religious institutions, particularly in Turkey, is very high, the citizens of these countries show less support for the EU's blueprint.

Conclusion

The EU blueprint of an ideal European society includes ideas about the role of religion in European societies. The EU favors a separation of religious and secular spheres and expects its citizens to tolerate other religious communities. If one distinguishes among the old and new EU member states, the Enlargement II countries and Turkey, it then seems that the old member states support the EU position the most and country groups support it to an ever decreasing degree in chronological order of accession. This result includes support for all four groups of dependent variables. Within country groups, differences between individual nations are to some extent substantial. This is particularly true for the Protestant countries as well as for the Czech Republic and France, where the interviewees strongly support the EU's blueprint. In the other Catholic, Orthodox Christian and, above all, Muslim countries, the separation of religion and the secular world is supported to a significantly lesser degree.

We examined the questions of how one can explain the differences in the degree to which people accept religious tolerance and a separation between religion and the secular world using a multiple regression analysis. We have shown that support for the EU position has less to do with belonging to a specific religion and depends more on the degree of integration into a religious institution. Furthermore, the degree of societal modernization significantly influences the level of support for the EU's blueprint of religion.

The more modernized a society, the more likely its citizens are to support a separation of religious and secular spheres as well as advocate religious tolerance. Thus, in countries that are less modernized and where the level of integration into religious institutions is high, the support for the separation of religious and secular spheres and for religious tolerance is substantially lower. Turkey is the most fitting example of this configuration.

We restricted this chapter to an analysis of religious beliefs. Differences in religious attitudes among countries become especially relevant if religious beliefs influence attitudes in other societal fields (Zulehner and Denz 1994). Whether and to what degree religious beliefs influence value orientations in other domains (family, economy, politics etc.) is investigated in the following chapters.

3 Family values, gender roles and support for the emancipation of women

Family is an important societal sphere in people's lives in almost all societies; for many, it is the most important. Such an assertion may come as a surprise from a comparative book emphasizing societal differences, but empirical evidence overwhelmingly supports this statement. The European Values Study asked citizens from different countries how important different aspects of their life (work, politics, religion, family, leisure time, friends and acquaintances) were to them. Respondents could choose between the following alternatives: "very important," "quite important," "not important" or "not at all important;" 85.5 percent consider family "very important;" for comparison, only 7.8 percent give the same worth to politics. Country values for the family sphere vary from 66.8 percent in Lithuania to 97.2 percent in Turkey.

Despite the overall importance placed on family, the exact type of family people prefer might differ from country to country. Do they favor a multi-generational family? Should a family include children and if yes, how many? Should the relationships between men and women remain monogamous and be institutionalized through marriage? How should the division of labor between men and women be organized? A cursory view of historical family research shows that families had very different forms in the past and that there were distinct differences among countries (Ehmer *et al.* 1997, Mitterauer 1999, Mitterauer and Ortmayr 1997, Mitterauer and Sieder 1991, Rosenbaum 1982, Sieder 1987). The historical heterogeneity of families in different countries persists today. For example, the average age of marriage for people living west of the north–south axis from St Petersburg to Triest is significantly higher than for people living east of this axis (Mitterauer 1999: 314, Oesterdiekhoff 2000). This "European marriage pattern" has not changed.

As in other chapters of this book, we do not analyze actual differences in family structures, but focus on what kinds of beliefs people have regarding an ideal family. These familial conceptions held by the majority of a state's population constitute a country's family culture. The structure of this chapter is similar to that of Chapter 2. First, we reconstruct the EU blueprint of family and gender roles. Then, with the help of secondary survey data analysis, we investigate the extent to which citizens of member states and accession countries support this EU family model. Finally, we pursue the causal question of how one can explain the country differences in terms of family structure. This chapter incorporates ideas from a previous article (Gerhards and Hölscher 2003). Throughout the chapter, we make use of a database (European Values Study) that was not available at the time of the previous analysis. The advantage of this survey over the International Social Survey Programme, the data set used for the aforementioned article, is that the EVS is more current and includes more countries, like Turkey.

The EU blueprint of family and gender roles

We used treaties, directives, regulations and recommendations that the EU institutions enacted into law as the material with which to reconstruct the EU blueprint of an ideal family. Many of these documents were incorporated into the constitutional draft. Part II of the constitutional draft includes basic EU rights and comprises the Charter of Fundamental Rights, already in force. Article II-93, Paragraph 1 states "The family shall enjoy legal, economic and social protection." Familial relationships refer both to man–woman and parent–child. Normative beliefs regarding childhood are only very vaguely written out in EU law. The EU defines childhood as a particular stage of life demanding a special amount of protection. In Article 3, Part I of the constitutional draft, the EU names the protection of children's rights as a goal. Article II-84 states that children shall have the right to such protection and that care is necessary for their well-being. More specifically: "The minimum age of admission to employment may not be lower than the minimum school-leaving age." Additionally, "young people admitted to work must have working conditions appropriate to their age" (Article II-92). Due to the general character of these statements and to the fact that the surveys analyzed do not contain any questions that would allow for an operationalization of EU concepts regarding children, we are forced to drop this dimension from our analysis. Consequently, we concentrate solely on the relationship between men and women.

The EU very clearly specifies its beliefs on gender relations (Carson 2004). Since the EU emerged first and foremost as an economic community, family and gender questions are relevant to EU politicians only insofar as they concern economic matters. Consequently, EU regulations regarding the familial sphere commonly relate to the economy. Regulations concerning the personal relationships of family members do not exist. The title of Article II-93 of the constitutional draft is, fittingly, "Family and Professional Life." The article primarily regulates the reconciliation of work with family life. Since political regulations on the relationship between the economy and family affect family life, the EU pursues an *indirect* policy approach regarding the family. Through this indirect path, the EU attempts to establish its conception of an ideal family. EU politicians who express ideas on this topic usually refer to the question of equality between men and women, particularly equality in the work place (Bergmann 1999, Ostner 1993, Watson 2000). The principle of equality is institutionalized on three levels, each of which differs in its degree of legal commitment: 1) the EC primary laws, consisting of the founding treaties, protocols, supplementary treaties and the constitutional draft, 2) secondary legislation, consisting of regulations and directives, and 3) recommendations and Commission Action Plans such as the "Social Policy Agenda" or the European social policy "White Paper" (Bergmann 1999).

The constitutional draft makes three references to the principle of gender equality. In Part I, Article 3, the EU states its goal: "It ... shall promote ... equality between women and men." In Part II, Article II-81 of the Charter of Fundamental Rights, several kinds of discrimination are forbidden, and gender discrimination is paramount among the categories.

When mentioning equality between men and women, the EU primarily focuses on the business world. This is clearly expressed in Article II-83, the Charter of Fundamental Rights reads: "Equality between women and men must be ensured in all areas, including employment, work and pay. The principle of equality shall not prevent the maintenance or adoption of measures providing for specific advantages in favor of the under-represented sex." The principle of equality in the workplace is mentioned in Part III of the constitutional draft, and its specificity is astonishing for a constitution. Article III-210 states that the EU supports and complements member state activities toward equality between women and men on the labor market and equal treatment in the workplace. Article III-214 further specifies these target goals.

The principle of gender equality in the workplace has a long tradition in the EU. Article 119 in the Treaties of Rome (1957) established the principle of equal pay for men and women in the EC realm. The Treaty of Amsterdam adopted and expanded this concept in Article 141. Numerous regulations and community directives have further supplemented this article, and decisions substantiated by the European Court of Justice have made it legally binding (Bergmann 1999: 45ff., Wobbe 2001). The Court's decision on equal employment opportunities for women in the German army proves the effectiveness of this principle. The plaintiff won the right to be employed in the German army, and the German parliament had to change its constitution as a result (Wobbe 2001). The principle of equality includes equal treatment of men and women regarding access to employment, job counseling and education. This principle also guarantees equality in regard to work conditions as well as membership in employee and employer organizations. Member states have, for the most part, adopted these EU directives into their national legislation.[1]

Some scholars have criticized the fact that EU equality policies refer only to the workplace. Many women perform household chores, an activity that does not count as employment. The chances to access employment therefore remain unequal (Ostner 1993). The EU reacted to this criticism. Article

II-93 of the Basic Rights Charter of the constitutional draft broaches the compatibility of work and family. As a fundamental right, pregnant women are protected against being fired and receive paid maternity and parental leave. Additionally, the 1999 Amsterdam Treaty extended the equality principle to several other political spheres. Article 3 (accepted as Article II-83 in the constitutional draft) obliged the EC to facilitate equality of men and women in all policy spheres (Läufer 1999). At the March 2000 meeting in Lisbon, European heads of state further substantiated this for political-employment measures. In order to achieve an equal level of employed women in member states, the EU aims to create equal chances for both genders in all political spheres. Moreover, it declares the compatibility of family and work as a political goal (European Council 2000). The principle of equality is most comprehensively extended in the EC's recommendations on various societal spheres, but these recommendations are not legally binding. In order to facilitate the compatibility of work with family and household chores, the EC's 1994 "White Papers on European Social Policy" called for an improvement in the availability of childcare. Furthermore, the EC demanded a more equitable division of household chores between men and women (European Commission 1994: 47). Six years later, the recommendations of the 1994 White Papers were adopted in the "European Social Agenda" (Council of the European Union 2000), in which political goals and concepts until 2010 were laid out. Equality in businesses was one such central goal. The issue of restrictions hindering women from employment was also broached, and necessary changes were defined.

We now summarize our findings concerning the EU family blueprint. EU family policy deems equality between men and women in the workplace as the most important issue. The EU believes this goal will only become reality if an infrastructure for raising children outside the family is developed and if traditional household gender roles are removed. With this political orientation, the EU supports an egalitarian relationship between men and women, in which women are employed and the socialization of children takes place in part outside the familial environment. In this regard, EU policies show a preferred familial model that differs from the traditional, bourgeois family model.[2] One must, however, correctly assess the importance of EU family policy; although family policy has become an EU theme via the issue of gender equality, this policy sphere is not of paramount importance to the EU compared to other spheres like agricultural policy. This holds true, even though the majority of people consider family to be the most important part of their life, as was mentioned at the beginning of this chapter.

Citizens' conceptions of family and gender roles

In this section, we investigate whether and to what degree the citizens of EU member states and accession countries support the EU family and gender blueprint. The equality of men and women in the workplace is an important concept for the EU's preferred gender and family model. Moreover, the EU perceives the "ultimate goal" of gender equality to be achievable only when men and women share household chores and raise children together so that both parents may work, children must be cared for partially outside the family environment, i.e. in kindergarten or preschool.[3] Our analysis is primarily based on the European Values Study, which contains very good indicators to measure citizens' opinion on the EU family and gender blueprint. Some of the relevant questions were unfortunately not asked in all countries. To keep our analysis of the four aggregate groups, we must significantly restrict the number of indicators. This most affects our ability to reconstruct the acceptance of equal distribution of household chores and child care responsibilities between men and women.

Equal opportunity of employment for men and women is the most central part of the EU's family and gender policy. By utilizing the following questions, we are able to operationalize and empirically determine the degree to which citizens from EU member and accession states support this model quite well. Citizens were asked whether they agreed with the following statement: "When jobs are scarce, men have more right to a job than women." Possible answers are "agree," "neither" and "disagree." The question measures attitudes toward gender equality in the workplace fairly well. The question insinuates a shortage of jobs, which forces interviewees to express their actual attitude by making them answer whether their convictions toward equality would also hold under restrictive conditions.

First, we look at differences at the aggregate level. As Table 3.1 shows, there are clear and significant differences between country groups regarding their attitudes toward the employment of women. Whereas the old member states and Accession I countries express a clear support for gender equality in the workplace, slightly less than 50 percent of citizens in Accession II countries and only a third of the Turkish population express support for this concept. Of all EU countries, Turkish citizens show the lowest level of support for the EU's blueprint concerning gender equality. The results also reveal high internal variance within particular aggregate country groups. Scandinavian countries show the most clear support for gender equality. In the accession countries, a significantly higher percentage of Polish and Maltese citizens reject the EU equality model. We return to these country differences when explaining our findings. A second question for measuring attitudes toward gender equality indirectly measures convictions toward equal access to employment for men and women without suggesting the restriction of job shortages on the market. Unfortunately, this question was not asked in Turkey. Citizens were asked whether and to what degree they agreed with the following statement: "A job is alright, but what most women really want is a home and children." The possible answers range from "strongly agree" and "agree" to "disagree" and "strongly disagree."[4] We summarized the percentages of both concurrence alternatives in Figure 3.1.

Table 3.1 Attitudes towards equality of men and women in the labor market (%): "When jobs are scarce, men have more right to a job than women"

	Approval	*Disapproval*	*Neither ... nor*
EU-15	**19.7**	**69.8**	**10.5**
Sweden	2.3	93.4	4.4
Denmark	6.2	89.4	4.4
Finland	9.0	84.7	6.3
Netherlands	12.5	83.4	4.1
Ireland	16.4	75.6	8.0
Greece	19.9	72.6	7.5
Great Britain	21.0	66.9	12.1
Belgium	25.0	70.1	4.9
France	21.7	68.3	10.0
Spain	21.7	62.5	15.8
Luxembourg	23.7	66.0	10.2
Portugal	27.2	61.4	11.3
Italy	27.0	56.8	16.2
Austria	28.6	52.9	18.5
Western Germany	28.4	52.8	18.8
Eastern Germany	24.8	59.0	16.2
Enlargement I	**25.3**	**61.4**	**13.4**
Estonia	13.6	75.5	11.0
Hungary	22.7	67.9	9.3
Slovenia	17.8	67.8	14.4
Latvia	19.8	69.5	10.7
Czech Repubic	19.2	65.3	15.6
Lithuania	22.7	65.1	12.1
Slovakia	24.1	54.2	21.7
Malta	48.8	42.7	8.4
Poland	37.9	45.1	17.0
Enlargement II	**37.3**	**47.4**	**15.3**
Bulgaria	36.7	47.5	15.8
Romania	37.9	47.4	14.7
Turkey	61.9	34.4	3.8

The results on the aggregate level are similar to those found in Table 3.1. The support of the EU model for gainfully employed women shrinks with each subsequent EU accession group. Slightly less than half of the old EU citizens maintain that women would rather not be employed. This percentage rises to 70 percent in Accession I countries and to 80 percent in Accession II countries. Country differences within the aggregate categories, particularly between EU-15 countries, are significant.

Lastly, we carried out a third measurement of attitudes toward the notion of gender equality by utilizing the ideas of Ronald Inglehart and Pippa Norris (2003a). Both authors assume that attitudes toward equality in professional life are connected to a generalized belief concerning the equality of men and women. In order to measure this generalized orientation, the authors devised a scale consisting of the following five questions:

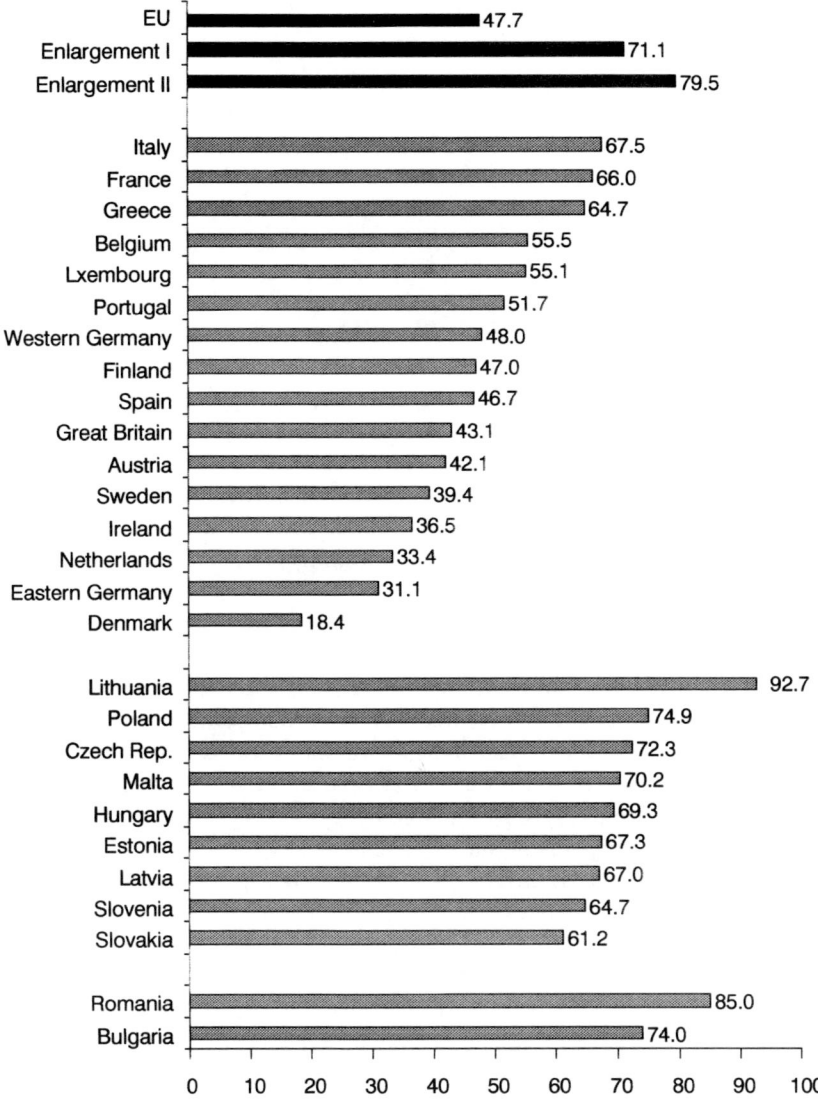

Figure 3.1 Attitudes towards being a housewife: "A job is alright but what most women really want is a home and children" (%)

- "When jobs are scarce, men have more right to a job than women." The alternative answers are "agree," "neither" or "disagree."[5]
- "If a woman wants to have a child as a single parent, but doesn't want to have a stable relationship with a man, would you approve or disapprove?" The alternative answers are "approve," "depends" or "disapprove."

- "Do you think that a woman has to have children in order to be fulfilled or is this not necessary?" The alternative answers are "needs children" or "not necessary."
- "Men make better political leaders than do women." The alternative answers are "agree strongly," "agree," "disagree" or "strongly disagree."
- "University is more important for a boy than for a girl." The alternative answers are "agree strongly," "agree," "disagree" or "strongly disagree."

The European Values Study does not include all five questions, but the 1995–6 World Values Survey does. However, far fewer EU member and accession countries participated in this latter survey. Of the old EU member states, only West and East Germany, Sweden, Finland and Spain took part, and Poland, Slovenia, Estonia, Lithuania and Latvia are the only representatives for the Accession I group. Bulgaria was the only participatory Accession II country, and Turkey also participated. Similar to Inglehart and Norris, we carried out a factor analysis of the five questions. The results are found in Table 3.2.

In Figure 3.2 high positive factor values represent substantial support for gender equality, and lower values represent less support.[6] First, we look at the aggregate level. The mean values for both accession rounds do not differ significantly, but differences between the other groups are statistically significant. Similar to the analysis of the data from the European Values Study, support of gender equality decreases with each subsequent accession group. Compared to the three other aggregate categories, Turkish interviewees show the lowest level of support for gender equality. The gap between EU member countries and both accession groups is higher than in the aforementioned results of the European Values Study. This can however be attributed to the fact that the World Values Survey fails to include some countries which took part in the European Values Study.

We now summarize the descriptive findings of our analysis. The EU sees itself as a community that considers gender equality, particularly equality in the workplace, as very important. On average, old EU member country citizens support this belief. This support decreases slightly for the Accession I

Table 3.2 Factor analysis (principal component analysis) of gender equality scale

	Factor
Men have more right to a job than women	0.69
Disapproval of woman who wants children without having a stable relationship	0.41
A woman has to have children in order to be fulfilled	0.60
Men are better politicians than women	0.74
A university education is more important for boys than for girls	0.68
% of total variance	**40.90**

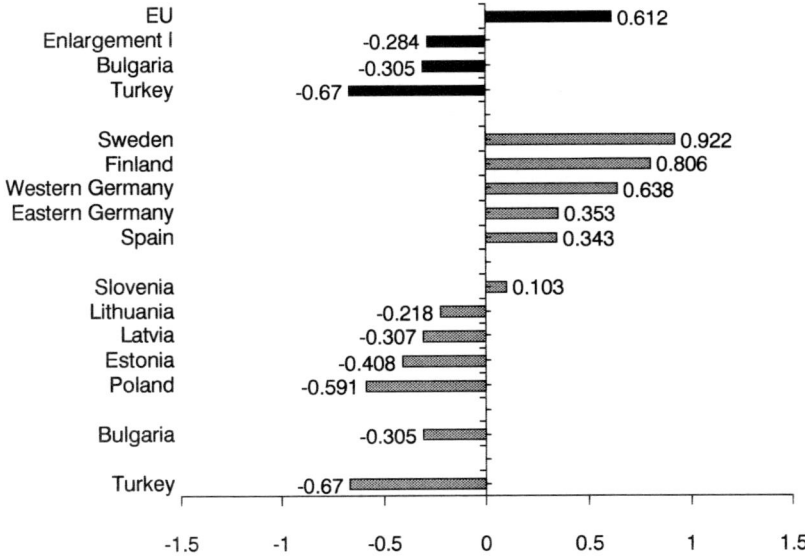

Figure 3.2 Attitudes towards gender equality (factor values of gender equality scale)

countries and even more so for the Accession II countries. Turkish citizens most clearly deviate from this belief. This aggregate level difference is slightly misleading, due to the fact that variance within the country groups is sometimes significant.

Explaining differences in the conception of family and gender roles

In this section, we attempt to explain the differences among citizens' concepts of family and gender roles. We understand the different EU member states and accession countries as representations of different social constellations. In order to determine these factors, we rely on earlier studies. Numerous empirical studies attempt to explain differences in the concepts of family and gender roles through country comparisons (Gomilschak *et al.* 2000, Haller and Hoellinger 1994, Inglehart 1997, Inglehart and Norris 2003a, Knudsen and Waerness 1999, Künzler *et al.* 1999, Gerhards and Rössel 2000). We differentiate between two dependent variables:

- "When jobs are scarce, men have more right to a job than women."
- "A job is alright, but what most women really want is a home and children," a question not posed in Turkey.

In determining the independent variables, we distinguish between three different groups of variables and an additional single variable.

The first independent variable to consider is the degree of modernization in a society. Social scientists assume that a relationship exists between the support for gender equality and the degree of modernization. The more modernized a society, the more that gender equality is supported. The degree of a society's modernization is expressed by multiple factors, like the degree of economic modernization or educational levels.

Economic modernization is connected to economic welfare. According to Ronald Inglehart, economic modernization and welfare influence people's generalized value orientations. Economic modernization affects attitudes toward family and gender roles in the following manner: greater economic wealth raises the likelihood that material needs are met. This, in turn, increases the population's preference for post-materialistic values (Inglehart 1997, Inglehart and Norris 2003a). Post-materialistic values include self-determination and gender equality. One can then expect that people living in countries with a high level of modernization will support a family model with equality of employment for women to a greater degree.[7] We measure the degree of a country's economic modernization using the Human Development Index (HDI). As mentioned above, numerous measures for determining the level of modernization are included in the HDI: per-capita GDP, level of education and average life expectancy. We unfortunately do not have the ability to measure the relative economic welfare of interviewees in all the countries at an individual level.[8]

Education is another aspect of societal modernization. Education increases the possibility of self-reflection and the likelihood of gaining a scholarly worldview. Inglehart describes the effect associated with higher levels of education as cognitive mobilization in which more education increases the likelihood that traditional concepts are not automatically accepted, but rather questioned and possibly rejected. Questioning tradition also relates to traditional gender roles. We assume that more educated interviewees are more likely to support gender equality and operationalize education by means of the highest level of completed education by the interviewee. This is measured with the help of an 8-point scale ranging from "inadequately completed elementary education" up to "university with degree/higher education – upper-level tertiary certificate."

Our second independent variable to measure support for gender equality is cultural-religious orientation. Societies are influenced by different cultural lines of tradition that shape conceptions toward family and gender (Haller and Hoellinger 1994, Inglehart and Norris 2003a). Cultural traditions are substantially influenced by religion and by the ideas embodied in the belief systems of different religions. As seen in Chapter 2, current and future EU citizens either have no religious affiliation, or are Muslims, Catholics, Protestants or Orthodox Christians. We assume that membership in one of these religions will influence attitudes toward gender equality in the following manner.

All of the religions in our analysis have at some point in time legitimized the dominance of men over women to varying degrees and continue to do so to some extent.[9] In the Christian denominations, the book of Genesis legitimizes a male dominated world. The originally equal relationship between man and woman disappeared after the fall of mankind and was transferred into a relationship in which the woman is subject to the man. The Koran states that men have superiority over women, and it also provides the right to polygamy. Men, as witnesses, carry twice the weight of women. We therefore assume that the degree of integration into a particular church/ religious institution (measured by attendance) – regardless of which one – impacts attitudes toward gender equality. The less a person is integrated into the daily practices of his or her religious institution, the more likely he or she is to support gender equality.

We assume also that differences exist among the various religious denominations regarding their interpretation of gender roles, which affects their followers' beliefs. It is highly controversial whether and to what degree different interpretations of gender roles can be traced back to particular religious texts like the Bible or the Koran. We do not judge the correctness of different interpretations. Rather, we theoretically formulate one position as a hypothesis and empirically test whether it can be confirmed by our data. We assume that the four religions under analysis in this book hold certain attitudes toward the relationship between man and wife that consequently influence their members. Islam advocates strongly a traditional gender hierarchy, in which the wife is responsible for the children and the household, while the husband is responsible for earning money and maintaining a position of power in the family. Being a wife and mother is the most important societal function for women; education and employment are subordinate (El-Saadawi 1991: 51). The public sphere is reserved for men, and women who participate in the public sphere are forced to conceal this fact. To look at Turkey for example, Swiss civil law was introduced in 1926, shortly after the establishment of the republic. This legislation placed family and marriage questions under the secularized control of the state and strengthened the role of women. Despite this strong legal protection, traditional family law, derived in part from the Islamic faith, remains central in contemporary Turkey (Nauck and Klaus 2005). Traditional Islamic law is structured in a patriarchal manner and secures the dominance of men in many spheres.

Compared to the importance of family and gender roles in the Islamic faith, Christianity has relatively little to say about gender roles (Mitterauer 1999: 325). We expect, therefore, that the preparedness of Muslims to support the EU gender equality model will be lower than that of the other religions. Of the three Christian denominations, Protestantism appears to deviate most from the patriarchal gender order. Since the Reformation, representatives of the Catholic and Protestant Church have developed differing beliefs on the family. Protestants defined this sphere of life as a mainly secular sphere and have therefore governed it less normatively (Dülmen 1990: 157–64). As compared to the Protestant Church, the Catholic Church has been oriented more toward the bourgeois model of a family in which the man is the provider and the woman is responsible for the children, household and family. This belief is still relevant for the Catholic Church today. In the newly published "Letter to the Bishops of the Catholic Church on the Collaboration of Men and Women in the Church and in the World" (Ratzinger and Amato 2004), the Vatican recognizes the role of women in the workplace, but sees motherhood a woman's most important role. We expect, therefore, that readiness to support the EU equality model by religious orientation is as follows: Muslims will show the least support, followed by Orthodox Christians and Catholics. Protestants appear to support the EU model the most.

The third set of independent variables we use to explain conceptions of family and gender relate to welfare state models and institutionalized equality. The countries under analysis differ in the degree to which national policies contain a specific family model and the degree to which political measures support this model (Kaufmann *et al.* 1997). For example, socio-political measures in former East Germany supported the employment of women with small children, but women with children in former West Germany were ideologically and structurally supported to stay at home (Wendt 1997, Wingen 1997).[10] We assume that political support for the employment of women affects citizens' attitudes toward equality. Unfortunately, there is no classification available to satisfactorily describe the equality policies of the 28 countries. Nevertheless, we want to discuss the different approaches that exist and then introduce the indicator we will use in our analysis.

A country's family policies are embedded in the type of welfare state, different types of which do exist[11] (Blossfeld and Drobnic 2001, Korpi 2001, Künzler *et al.* 1999, Lessenich and Ostner 1998, O'Connor 1993, Orloff 1993, Pascall and Manning 2000, Pfau-Effinger 2000, Roller 2000a). Almost all of these typologies relate to Gösta Esping-Andersen's 1990 classification of "liberal," "conservative" and "social democratic" welfare states. Esping-Andersen's typology has been criticized for not being sensitive enough to gender differences (see Esping-Andersen's reply to these critiques 1999). For our purposes, Walther Korpi's (2001) proposal to integrate the gender dimension into the typology of welfare states appears most suitable, as it is substantially based on empirical data. Korpi suggests a typology of gender relevant policies, characterized by two dimensions by which to classify the different countries, which results in three country groups that hold differing influences over the family concept.[12] The first family model is called a "dual earner support model," which includes low levels of support for the traditional nuclear family, preferring dual incomes. The second model is the "general family support model," in which there is substantial support for the nuclear family and less support for the dual-income model. The third family model is the "market oriented model," which supports neither dual-income nor nuclear family models. Rather, the market regulates whether daytime nurseries exist, whether the mother stays at home etc.

We assume that countries with a "dual earner support model" will most support the EU family blueprint, which is characterized by dual earners and a division of household chores. Countries with a "general family support model" will accept this blueprint the least. Countries classified as "market oriented" lie somewhere in between. We cannot use Korpi's typology for all countries in our analysis, because relevant data is not available for all countries. The Korpi classification can be used for the Western European countries excluding Portugal, Greece and Luxembourg. Classifying the former socialist countries in Central and Eastern Europe proves to be the main problem. During the period of state socialism, these countries strongly encouraged the employment of women.[13] By using secondary sources, one can therefore classify these countries as having a "dual earner support model" (see Blossfeld and Drobnic 2001, Götting 1998, Pascall and Manning 2000, Watson 2000). These countries have radically changed since the introduction of democratic market economies, however. This transformation has substantially altered gender and family policies and makes classifying these countries a difficult task. The fact that no information is available regarding family policy in Turkey or Malta poses an additional problem. Due to this overall poor database, we only consider the variable "welfare state model" in our first analysis.[14] We thereafter substitute this variable with the Gender Empowerment Measure (GEM).[15] Similar to the Human Development Index, the UNDP-sponsored GEM project conducted surveys in several countries in the world to create indicators (Human Development Report Office 2000). This index measures the degree of institutionalized gender equality with three variables. The proportion of women and men in parliament, the proportion of women and men in top business and government positions and the difference between the income for men and women. Complete gender equality results in a value of 1, and total inequality results in a value of 0. Values for France, Luxembourg, Malta and Bulgaria are missing. The GEM is certainly not an optimal operationalization with which to measure institutionalized support for gender equality, in that GEM measures "output," or the results concerning equality. The degree of equality can be, but is not necessarily, traced back to national policies. As no better measurement exists, however, we use this indicator in our analysis.

Our fourth independent variable is gender, because we assume that questions regarding gender equality affect men and women differently. We hypothesize that women support the concept of gender equality more than men do.

Table 3.3 contains the results of the regression analysis. The following comments on the results can be made:

Table 3.3 Explaining attitudes towards gender equality: linear regressions

	Women have an equal right to a job	Women want more than just home and children
Level of modernization		
HDI	0.080	0.092
Education	0.254	0.170
Religion[a]		
Protestants	0.038	−0.002+
Roman Catholics	−0.081	−0.043
Orthodox Christians	−0.055	−0.020*
Muslims	−0.140	−0.047
Integration into church	−0.081	−0.083
GEM	−0.004+	0.213
Gender[b]	0.082	0.064
R²	**0.140**	**0.147**

The models represent standardized beta-coefficients from the OLS regression analysis.
If not indicated differently, coefficients are significant at the 1% level (* = significant at 5% level, + = not significant).
a   Category of reference: people who do not have a religious affiliation.
b   Category of reference for the gender variable: men.

- The explained variance of both dependent variables shows that we can satisfactorily explain attitudes toward the employment and equality of women with the chosen independent variables.
- Both of the modernization variables (educational levels and economic development) have the strongest influences on citizens' conceptions of equality and go in the direction we expected. The higher the respondent's level of education and the more modernized his or her country, the more likely he or she is to support gender equality.[16]
- The degree of institutionalized equality clearly increases the likelihood that one supports gender equality, for at least one of the dependent variables.
- Religious membership also impacts citizens' conceptions of gender equality. Affiliation with Islam increases the probability that one rejects the EU concept of gender equality.[17] Orthodox Christians and Catholics also show a rejection of gender equality, although to a somewhat lesser degree. Protestants are more likely to support this concept. This result corresponds to our expectations. It is also evident that the degree of integration in a religious institution has a negative influence on support for gender equality, which also corresponds with our assumptions.
- Finally, our analysis shows that the gender of the interviewee influences his or her attitudes toward gender equality. As expected, women support their right to equality more clearly.

Conclusion

EU family policy primarily concerns gender equality in the workplace. The EU believes this can only be achieved when a childcare infrastructure exists outside the household and when traditional household chores are split between men and women. We reconstructed the family blueprint from EU legislation as a reference point for our empirical analysis and analyzed the extent to which citizens from EU member states and accession countries accept the EU's conception of an ideal family. When one distinguishes between old and new EU member states as well as Turkey, it becomes clear that the old members support the EU position most strongly. This support weakens with subsequent accession groups. Turkish citizens reject the EU family blueprint most strongly and express the clearest preference for a traditional, male-dominant gender order. With the help of a multiple regression analysis, we tried to account for the differences in support for gender equality. We could show that the support for the EU's family blueprint is influenced by the degree of modernization and institutionalization of equality through domestic policies. Additionally, citizens' religious affiliation, integration into a religious community and their own gender influence their attitudes toward gender equality.

A country's degree of economic modernization is an important factor in explaining differences in family and gender attitudes. Yet even if the Central and Eastern European countries and Turkey attain similar standards of living enjoyed by today's EU member states, this will not automatically lead to an immediate cultural change. Ronald Inglehart (1997) has shown that people's value orientations are acquired through socialization and are thereafter relatively resistant to change. Although economic development substantially influences the emergence and character of culture, cultural orientations are relatively immune to short-run economic changes. Looking at the development of political culture in post-WWI and post-reunification Germany as an example, one can see how slowly cultural orientations adjust to new conditions (Conradt 1980, Pickel *et al.* 1998, Fuchs 1999b, Roller 2000a). It is also uncertain as to when and if economic convergence between member states and accession countries will occur.

Our empirical findings imply possible problems for the future of the integration process, particularly for actors who place the emancipation of women as an important goal. This goal will become harder to implement with EU expansion, as there is less support for gender equality in accession countries. The EU was rather successful in carrying out this effort in the past (Wobbe 2001). Even the Western-inspired women's movement appears to be losing steam due to a lack of support in Eastern Europe, even among women (Watson 2000, Bretherton 2001). Accession countries will receive co-determination rights and seats on EU boards as they become members, and this new configuration will result in changes in the power structure in EU institutions. In the future, it may be increasingly difficult to garner political support for women's issues. If EU representatives from the new countries orient themselves with their citizens' beliefs, they will have less interest in issues of gender equality.

4 Economic concepts of an expanded EU

The EU began as an economic community, and economics is still the EU's most important policy field. The European Community started first with the European Coal and Steel Community and later became a customs union, subsequently forming a common market and a common economic and monetary union. The reasons as to why the economic integration of Europe has developed so efficiently as compared to other societal fields are twofold. First, national governments had strong and overlapping interests on which to form a common economic union. Second, it is argued that economic issues are more easily institutionalized than other societal issues:

> Europe developed in "small" steps which legitimated the belief that a common market would lead to economic success. Through a rationalization effect of the common market, all countries should gain an advantage from a growing national product. By isolating the economy from other societal and political spheres, the traditional inner and social policy order of the nation states remained stable, even though a policy of competition sometimes necessarily intruded in these spheres. Economic and socio-political adjustments were externalized to the member countries and their socio-political conflict management, which absorbed the burdens as well as the implemented new regulations and de-regulations of the old structure.
>
> (Lepsius 2003: 39)

In the first section of this chapter, we reconstruct the EU's blueprint of an ideal economy. We then analyze the degree to which citizens of the member states and accession countries accept this ideal. We use a discriminant analysis to group the countries according to their approval of the EU concepts. Finally, we explain differences and similarities between the countries.

In the first chapter, we justified the importance of citizens' attitudes for the stability of societal institutions. That general argument applies also to the economy. Research on the transformation of the societies of former socialist states that are already or will soon become part of the EU emphasizes the importance of economic culture.[1] For the transfer and implementation of Western economic institutions to be successful, the citizens' support is required. Svetozar Pejovich has formulated what he calls the interaction thesis, explaining that:

> When changes in formal rules are in harmony with the prevailing informal rules, the incentives they create will tend to reduce transaction costs and free some resources for the production of wealth. When new formal rules conflict with the prevailing informal rules, the incentives they create will raise transaction costs and reduce the production of wealth in the community.
>
> (Pejovich 2003: 5)

Wolfgang Merkel perceives the acceptance of changed economic rules by the elite and by citizens at large as central requirements for consolidating former socialist societies (Merkel 1995). These considerations integrate ideas of economic sociology, which Peter L. Berger (1991) formulates as follows: "Economic institutions do not exist in a vacuum but rather in a context (or, if one prefers, a matrix) of social and political structures, cultural patterns, and, indeed, structures of consciousness (values, ideas, belief systems)" (Berger 1991: 24).

Institutional transfer in former socialist economies has been very successful even though the economic differences between member states and accession countries are substantial.[2] What remains unknown is whether the citizens' beliefs and values support the new economic institutions. It may be that their beliefs are incompatible with the new market economy due to the fact that they were socialized in a socialist command economy.

The EU's economic blueprint

Since the economy is the central policy field of the EU, most European laws focus on economic issues. "EU law is in its substance chiefly public regulation of economic life, i.e. economic legislation" (Lane 2002: 1). It is difficult to reconstruct the EU's blueprint of an ideal economy due to the number of laws and the fact that comprehensive laws have integrated old, but still valid, treaties. We concentrate our analysis on the fundamental economic concepts of the European Union found mainly in primary and supplementary treaties and the constitutional draft. Rules are not always uniform even when the focus is restricted to these documents, possibly resulting from compromises necessary to reach consensus.

The EU's main economic goal is to improve the economic welfare of all its citizens. "The Union's aim is to promote peace, its values and the well-being of its people" (Article 3, Para. 1 of the EU constitutional draft) through "sustainable development of a Europe based on balanced economic growth" (Para. 3, Conference of Representatives 2004). This leads to two basic conclusions. First, the EU believes that the formulated goals are achievable only if a particular kind of economy is in place. Second, citizens of member states are expected to hold specific economic attitudes that help them participate in the economy as economic subjects. Together, these two dimensions form the EU blueprint of the economy. We analyze these dimensions separately. In the next section, we focus on the first dimension, namely EU concepts regarding the ideal organization of the economy. Then we discuss the second dimension which refers to the citizens' attitudes as economic subjects.

The EU concept of an economic order

The European economic model is defined in Article 2 of the EU Treaty as well as in Articles 2, 3 and 4 of the Treaty for the Founding of the European Community (ECT).[3] The model is basically defined as an open market economy committed to competition and welfare (Friedrich 2002, Hödl and Weida 2001). Three dimensions are characteristic of this model: competition, an open common market and state control of the economy.

The EU is a strong advocate of open market competition in the form of the European common market (Schmidt and Binder 1998). The goal of free competition is to create an optimal market process; the EU therefore tries to forbid cartel building and to control governmental aid and subsidizing for companies. The EU's rationale for these actions is their belief that competition and market liberalization lead to economic growth, progress and prosperity (European Commission 2000a). However, the EU's principle of generating competition through deregulation applies mainly to the *inner relationship* between European countries, more precisely, EU member states. Regarding economies beyond the EU's borders, measures include state support and promotion of European industries to prepare them for international competition. According to the Lisbon strategy of 2000, Europe wants to become the world's most dynamic and competitive economy (European Council 2000). This goal leads to the support of particular sectors like research and development or to institutional assistance to international cooperation efforts. In certain cases, this also includes the approval of European oligopolies, which are formed in order "to protect home markets against aggressive international competition" (Turek 1997: 49).[4] The tools used to achieve these goals include industrial and trade policies. Norbert Berthold and Jörg Hilpert state that "competition, industrial and trade policy often come into conflict with one another. EU treaties pre-program conflicts in these three political fields because they can be interpreted differently depending on one's interests" (Berthold and Hilpert 1996: 106).

The second major aspect of the EU's blueprint of the economy is an open common market. The opening of European markets is a central requirement for undistorted competition in the EU. After formulating the Single European Act in 1987, the European common market was launched early in 1993. The common market established the "four freedoms" and states that people, goods, services and capital should move just as freely in the EU as they do within national markets. The same freedom of movement was adopted for people outside of the labor force, such as students and retirees. The EU also agreed to mutually recognize certifications and social security rights for people moving between EU member states. The open common market is referred to several times in the aforementioned articles as well as in the preambles of the EUT and the ECT. The successful introduction of the common market was made possible after a rethinking of economic philosophy in the 1980s. The new concept emphasized the importance of market liberalization for strengthening the economy (Schäfer 2002, Thiel 1996: 125ff.).

The open market is a well-anchored principle in the national economies of all member states. Extending this national principle into a supranational space is certainly a new element, and states and economic players attempt to hinder unwanted foreign competition from within the EU.[5] The 1979 "Cassis de Dijon" verdict is worth mentioning in this regard, seeing as how the European Court made a decision on this topic before the common market was introduced. At that time, the judges of the European Court voted against a German legislator who claimed that a 20 percent alcoholic rate for liquor was not compatible with German law, in which a 32 percent minimum existed. The European Court ruled that what was allowed in one state of the EC may be sold in the markets of all other states (Fritzler and Unser 1998: 62).[6]

State control of the economy is the third aspect of the EU's blueprint of the economy. Determining the EU's position on the role of the state in regulatory policy is a difficult task. The EU speaks out against state interference in economic affairs and also encourages state intervention in some realms. When the EU discourages state interference, it can be interpreted as a "motor of deregulation" (Donges *et al.* 1997: 280, Schneider 1998). This economic-political orientation is reflected in the following decision: in Article 87, Paragraph I of the ECT, the treaties clearly reject "any aid granted by a Member State or through State resources in any form whatsoever which distorts or threatens to distort competition."[7] The European Council in Stockholm requires member states to reduce general government subsidizing (Commission 2002b: 22). The Lisbon Strategy was also adopted to strengthen this liberal economic orientation. The goal of the Lisbon Strategy is to create a climate of regulatory policy that is "conducive to investment, innovation, and entrepreneurship" and "to remove unnecessary red tape" (European Council 2000: Point 14). This suggests that the state should play a more restrained role in the economic realm.

At the same time, there are several economic spheres in which the EU allows and even enforces state intervention. The EU justifies these interventions in three separate ways. First, it is assumed that the common market only functions optimally under certain conditions, like common legal regulations. The EU attempts to guarantee these conditions either on its own terms or by means of coordinating country policies. The second reason for state intervention in economies is so that the EU can become a competitive player in the global market. Toward this aim, the EU is making targeted investments in economically relevant areas like education and giving direct support to particular industries. European economic concepts are also characterized by decisive social components, which is the basis for the third type of EU intervention. We return to this concept in greater detail in Chapter 5.

What kind of economic attitudes does the EU expect from its citizens?

The first dimension of the EU economic blueprint relates to an ideal economic system as formulated in EU documents. For the EU to achieve its ultimate goal of improving the economic welfare of its citizens, certain economic orientations must be required from them. Two value orientations are crucial in this respect: performance based on achievement, and general trust. Achievement is a direct result from the demands of the market economy. General trust is both a foundation of trade and anonymous markets as well as for European solidarity (Delhey 2004).

- Achievement orientation: Although this concept is not explicitly mentioned in the basic laws, the EU expects its citizens to be achievement-oriented. The free market, the EU's preferred economic model, puts a strong emphasis on economic competition, which relies on the achievement of individuals. If individuals lack a certain preparedness to achieve, they cannot survive under the competitive conditions of the open market.[8] An emphasis on achievement is explicitly stated in EU policies, such as the reorientation of job market policies from demand to supply policies (Schäfer 2002) or in the aforementioned Lisbon Strategy.
- General trust: Economic activity in anonymous markets has become a characteristic of modern industrial countries and requires a certain amount of trust between actors (Mummert 2001). Georg Elwert thus perceives trust as a "condition of market activities" (1987: 301). Several studies have shown that trust helps reduce transaction costs and is therefore a conducive force in the market (Dorner 2000: 40ff. and 90ff., Fukuyama 1995, La Porta *et al.* 1997, Lagemann 2001, Uslaner 2004). Economic activities often demand cooperation under conditions of uncertainty, e.g. in anonymous markets or in large organizations. This uncertainty can be slightly reduced with binding contracts, but such mechanisms are associated with a significant rise in transaction costs. Mutual trust is a cost-effective and functional equivalent. "Trust reduces transaction costs by providing information and a means to enforce contracts, so that the possibility of opportunistic behavior diminishes" (Höhmann *et al.* 2002: 5ff.). Accordingly, Höhmann *et al.* conclude that "low levels of

trust constrain market entry, enterprise growth and competition whilst encouraging unproductive forms of entrepreneurship. High levels of trust, on the other hand, encourage open and dynamic competition structures and foster enterprise growth" (Höhmann *et al.* 2002: 4).

The citizens' attitudes toward the economy

In this section, we analyze the attitudes of EU citizens toward the five dimensions of the EU economic blueprint taken from EU documents. First, we analyze trust and achievement. We then turn to the degree of acceptance for competition, the open market economy and state intervention.

Achievement and trust

There are a number of possibilities for measuring the achievement orientation of individuals. For example, Ronald Inglehart looks at how achievement oriented goals are instilled when raising children. The European Values Study poses the question as follows: "Here is a list of qualities which children can be encouraged to learn at home. Which, if any, do you consider to be especially important?" The respondent could choose up to five out of eleven presented goals, two of which are decisively achievement related ("hard work" and "determination, perseverance"). From these answers, we formed an index ranging from 0, "no achievement related goal chosen," to 2, "both chosen." Figure 4.1 illustrates the country mean values.

At the aggregate level, achievement orientation is highest among citizens of Accession II countries, followed by citizens of the new EU countries, then by Turkey. Citizens of the EU-15 countries are least achievement oriented. At the country level, extreme variations exist within individual aggregate groups. The Scandinavian countries (Sweden, Denmark and Finland) have low achievement orientation, whereas Portugal and Luxembourg show high levels. The EVS has another question we can use to measure achievement orientation. On a 5-point scale ranging from "disagree strongly" (1) to "agree strongly" (5), the interviewees evaluate the following statement: "Work should always come first, even if it means less spare time," a question directly related to achievement orientation in the professional sphere.[9] The country mean values are given in Figure 4.2. High values signify a strong achievement orientation.

The results in Figure 4.2 repeat the central findings of the first indicator. EU-15 member states have the lowest achievement orientation, Accession I countries have the highest, and Accession II countries and Turkey rank in between. Former socialist East Germany has the highest value of old (non-socialist) member states, while Malta, the only Accession I country with no socialist past, demonstrates the lowest achievement orientation in its group. Differences within the groups are noticeable, and it is also important to note the variances that exist between the two indicators.[10] For instance,

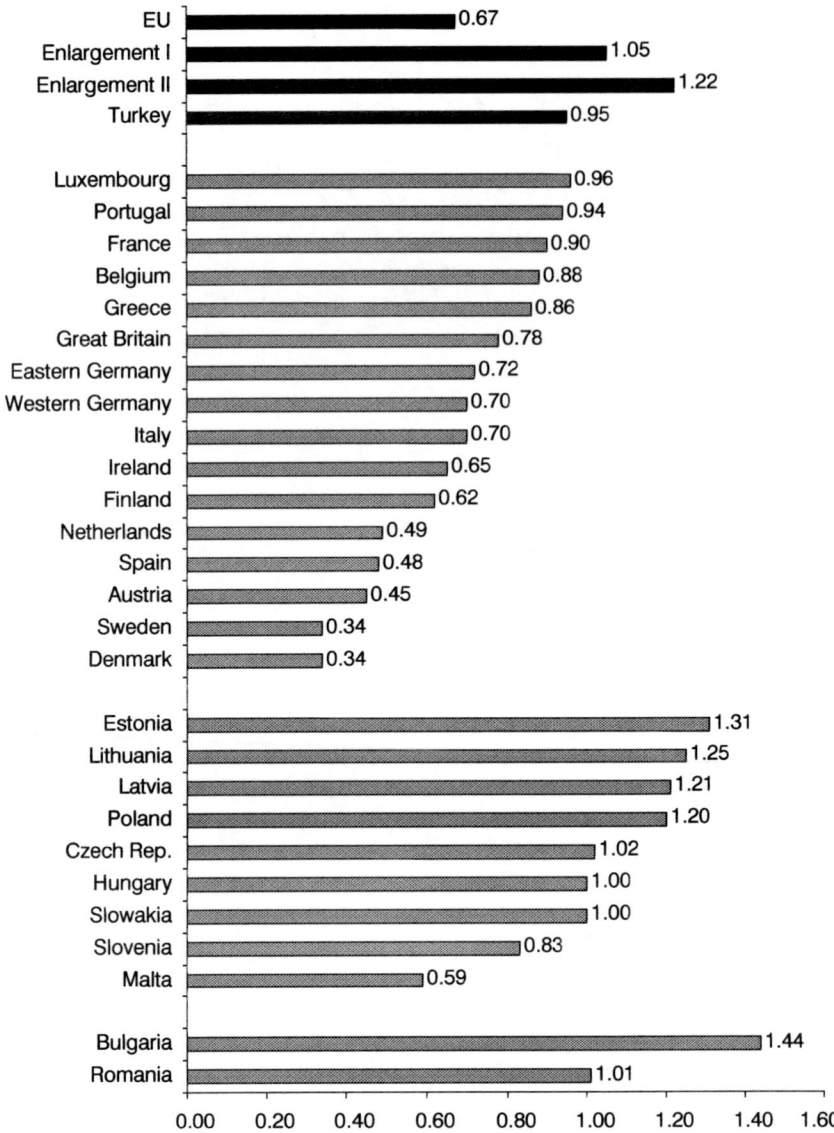

Figure 4.1 Educational goal: achievement orientation (mean of index)

particularly low values occur in the Netherlands and Great Britain, whereas Romania's and Hungary's values are quite high.

It is difficult to interpret these findings as a whole, partially because the results contradict the theoretical expectations. Contrary to almost all of our other analyses, the accession states' citizens support the EU's economic blueprint more than the citizens of the old member states do. When these countries join the EU, support for an achievement oriented culture will

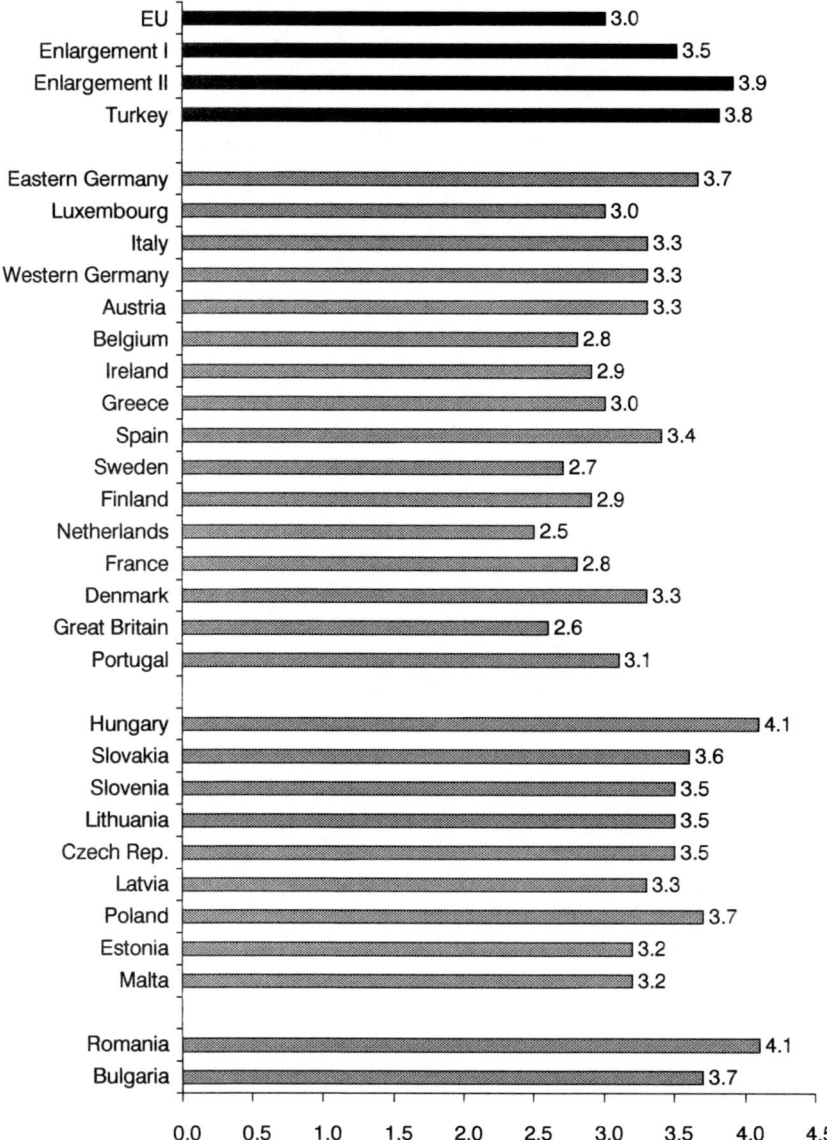

Figure 4.2　Priority given to work over leisure time (mean)

increase. Another surprising finding is that our analysis does not confirm the classical relationship between Protestantism and achievement orientation. Protestant countries like Great Britain and the Netherlands show a lower achievement orientation than Catholic countries, like Poland, and Orthodox Christian countries, like Bulgaria. Our analysis also contradicts the assumption that a socialist tradition leads to less support of achievement orientation. All ex-socialist states, including East Germany, showed levels of support above the EU average. In fact, the Accession I average (3.6) is higher than country levels for every non-socialist EU-15 member state (Luxembourg has the highest average of 3.4). The fourth section of this chapter tries to explain the country differences.

Generalized trust forms the second fundamental dimension of individual economic beliefs. We measure trust with the following question: "Generally speaking, would you say that most people can be trusted or that you can't be too careful in dealing with people?" The interviewee had to decide between these two alternatives.

Figure 4.3 shows that there are substantial country differences. The Scandinavian countries represent one extreme, with mutual generalized trust being the highest in Denmark, Sweden, Finland and the Netherlands. Turkey has the smallest amount of generalized trust. Looking at the aggregate level, the results for generalized trust follow the pattern from previous chapters of this book. Old EU members exhibit the greatest amount of mutual trust (38 percent), followed by Accession I countries (21 percent) and Accession II countries (19 percent). Only 7 percent of Turkish citizens reported mutual trust.

Attitudes toward the economic order

In analyzing the citizens' attitudes toward the EU conception of the economic order, we use the following three dimensions: competition, market openness and the role of the state.

Free and open competition in the market is a main pillar of the EU's economic concept. Two indicators exist for testing whether EU citizens support this concept. The first indicator is a direct measurement of citizens' attitudes regarding competition. On a 10-point scale, the interviewee could indicate where he or she stands given the following spectrum: "Competition is good. It stimulates people to work hard and develop new ideas" (10) versus "Competition is harmful. It brings out the worst in people" (1). Figure 4.4 displays the country mean values.

At the aggregate level, we can extrapolate that Accession I and II countries as well as Turkey are more competition-oriented than the old EU member states. But the differences between the individual countries are not very high. The majority of the citizens in all countries surveyed view competition favorably. Romania shows the strongest level of support, followed by Malta, the Czech Republic, Austria and Slovenia. Belgium, the Netherlands, Luxembourg and France are the least competition-oriented.

The second question measuring competition was posed in a more indirect manner. It reads:

Imagine two secretaries of the same age doing practically the same job. One finds out that the other earns 30 Euro a week more than she does. The better paid secretary, however, is quicker, more efficient and more

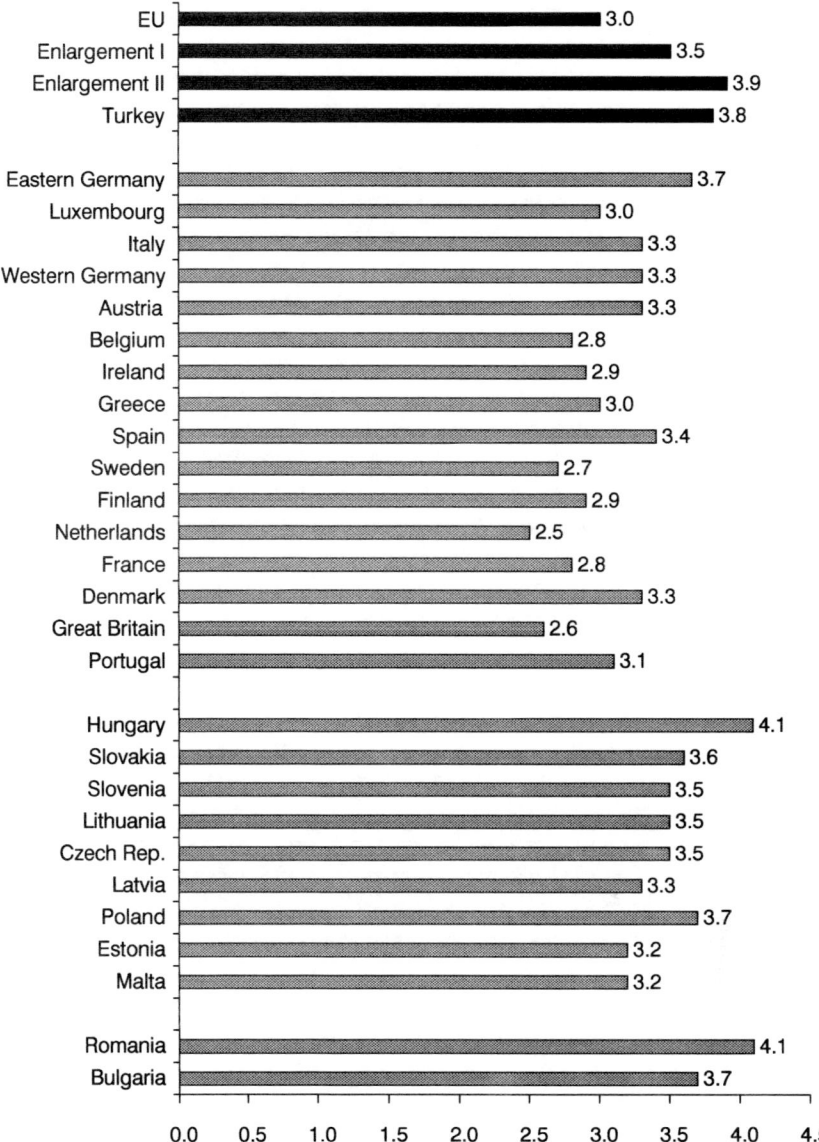

Figure 4.3 Generalized trust: "Most people can be trusted" (%)

reliable at her job. In your opinion is it fair that one secretary is paid more than the other?

In this question, competition is implied because the best "product" on the market gets the best price. If the respondent approves, this signifies that a differentiated salary is fair, which in turn signifies support for competition on the market. Figure 4.5 shows the percentage rate of the populations concurring with this statement.

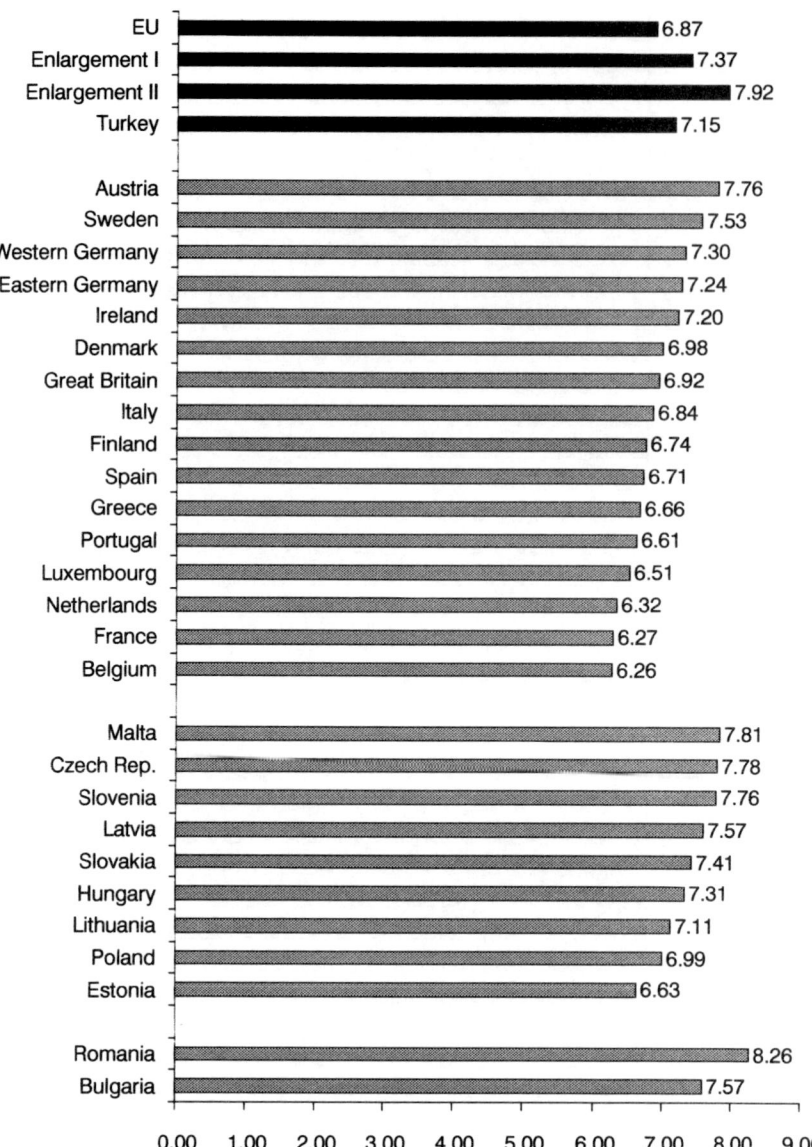

Figure 4.4 Attitudes towards competition (1): "Competition is good" versus "Competition is harmful" (mean)

The results from this question are similar to those of the first competition question. The majority of interviewees in all countries agree that the better secretary is entitled to earn more money, thereby showing support for the EU's concept of competition. Most countries who strongly supported competition in the first question also agreed with the second item. This includes the Czech Republic, Slovakia, Bulgaria, Romania, Slovenia and

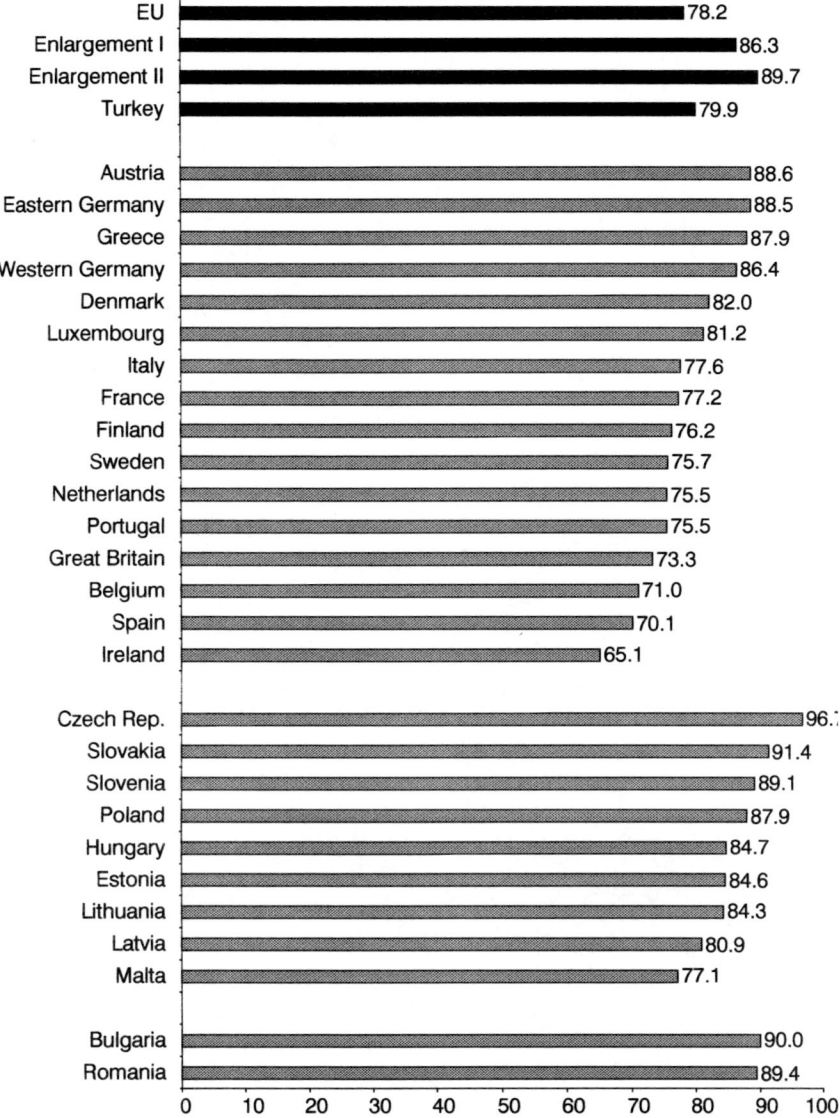

Figure 4.5 Attitudes towards competition (2): "A performance oriented salary is fair" (%)

Austria. Similarly, countries who were more skeptical of competition according to the first indicator also displayed reservations concerning the second. These countries include Belgium, the Netherlands, Spain and Portugal. The accession countries seem to support the notion of competition to a slightly greater degree, particularly in the Accession II countries.

To conclude, the majority of the citizens in all EU countries support the notion of competition, albeit to varying degrees. The accession countries show higher levels of support for competitiveness, whereas Belgium, Luxembourg, the Netherlands and Southwest European countries support this concept to a lesser degree.

The openness of markets within the common market in the fields of people, goods, services and capital forms the second element of the EU economic blueprint. The European Values Study data contains only one indicator of citizens' attitudes regarding the openness of the market, namely freedom of movement of labor. The EVS asked respondents to respond to the statement: "When jobs are scarce, employers should give priority to nationals over immigrants." Respondents could answer "agree," "disagree" or "neither" on a 3-point scale. The question is restrictively formulated, in that it implies crisis on the job market ("jobs are scarce"). If the respondent agrees with the statement, we interpret this as support for closing the market and rejecting the EU position. The percentage rate for the category "disagree" (i.e. support for the EU blueprint) is shown in Figure 4.6.

Whereas the majority in every country supported the EU's concept of competition, the situation appears entirely different for the open job market, rejected in all countries. This level of rejection varies significantly; almost 40 percent of the old EU member states support the idea of an open job market, but this support drops to 10 percent in the accession countries. Turkey lies in between these extremes with a one-third approval rating.

Clear country differences in the four aggregate groups are also present for this variable. A majority of citizens support the open job market in Sweden, the Netherlands, Denmark and Luxembourg, whereas Belgium and Estonia fall just short of a majority consensus. Estonia is the only accession country with a national average higher than that of the old EU member states.[11] Less than 5 percent of citizens in other accession countries like Lithuania, Poland and Malta support the idea of an open market.

It is important to note that the indicator refers to "immigrants" without differentiating between foreigners from other European countries and foreigners from outside the EU. It may then be that the interviewees associated the term foreigner with people from outside the EU, which would not necessarily contradict an opening of the European market. We test this assumption with a Eurobarometer question (Eurobarometer 53 from 2000).[12] This question asked whether one should differentiate among groups of people who want to work in the respondent's country. The following groups were named: Muslims, Eastern Europeans, people from crisis areas, people seeking political asylum and people from other EU countries. Respondents supporting the idea of equality gave equivalent responses for all the aforementioned groups. We built an additive index from these different questions (Cronbach's Alpha 0.89, see Hölscher 2006). It can be assumed from the high Cronbach's Alpha score that our indicator is a reliable measurement with which to measure the EU's position on the openness of the common market. Yet another data set allows us to prove the vailidity and accuracy of our question. The European Social Survey asked respondents whether their

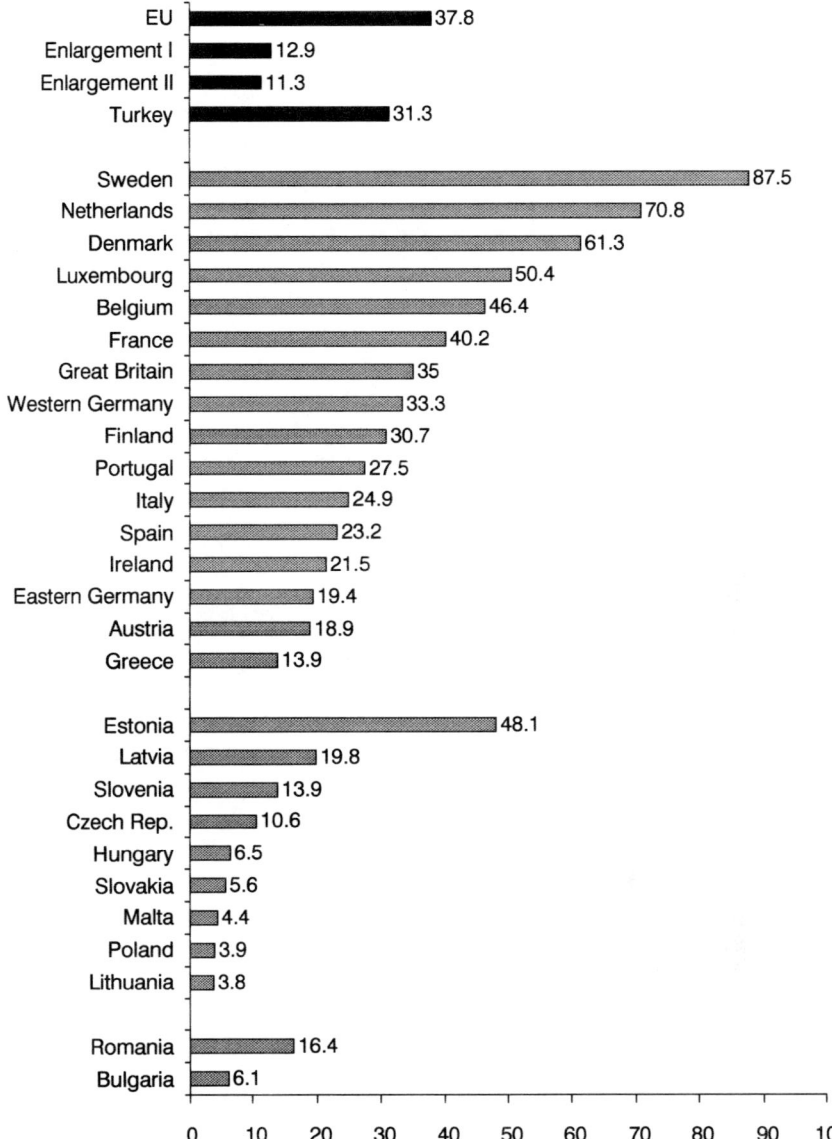

Figure 4.6 Attitudes towards an open labor market: "When jobs are scarce, employers should give priority to national citizens over immigrants" (% disapproval)

country should allow people from poorer European countries to come and live in their country. A second question asked people whether their country should allow people from poorer countries *outside Europe* to come and live in their country. We conducted a correlation analysis between the two items, and the resultant Pearson's correlation was rather high (0.84). This indicates that EU citizens do not distinguish between European immigrants and third country nationals.[13]

A third part of the EU's economic blueprint is state control of the economy. As discussed at the beginning of the chapter, the EU's position on this matter is difficult to categorize. The EU emphasizes liberalization and the deregulation of economic development to the greatest extent possible, but also uses political measures to create an economic and competition-friendly environment. One such interventionist political measure is strengthening the European economy in relation to the outside. The EVS includes the following question for measuring attitudes about state control of the economy. On a 10-point scale, the interviewee could indicate which statement they agreed with more: "the state should give more freedom to firms" (10) versus "the state should control firms more effectively" (1).

Figure 4.7 shows the mean values by aggregate groups and by countries. The data illustrates that the ambivalence of the EU is mirrored in its citizens' beliefs; no country adopted an extreme position. At the aggregate level, citizens of the old EU member states support a smaller state role the most, whereas Turkish citizens represent the other extreme. Accession I and II countries fall in between.

Familiar country differences are again present. The Scandinavian countries, Austria and West Germany support liberalization the most. The majority of respondents from Lithuania, Malta and Bulgaria also maintain this position. Countries who support a stronger role of the state in the economy are Belgium, Greece and especially Luxembourg in the old member states, and Latvia, Slovakia and Turkey outside the EU-15 group. According to these results, a small yet decisive shift of interests in the direction of a greater role for the state may arise with the accession of East European countries to the EU.

To summarize the results of our descriptive analysis, no unitary pattern exists regarding the support of EU economic ideals. The citizens from the old EU member states support some dimensions more strongly. Other dimensions have greater support among citizens of the accession countries. Citizens from the accession countries show higher levels of support for individual achievement and competition than do citizens of old EU member states. The roles reverse concerning the opening of the labor market, the role of the state and generalized trust in fellow citizens. Old member states support the idea of the open market and trust fellow citizens to a much greater degree than in the accession countries. Support for the EU concept of a more passive state role is stronger in West European countries, while the majority of citizens in both accession groups indicated support for state intervention in the economy. Turkey adopts an intermediary position for most questions. Despite such ambivalence in the descriptive findings, the next section tries to empirically determine where the individual countries stand in regard to the EU position.

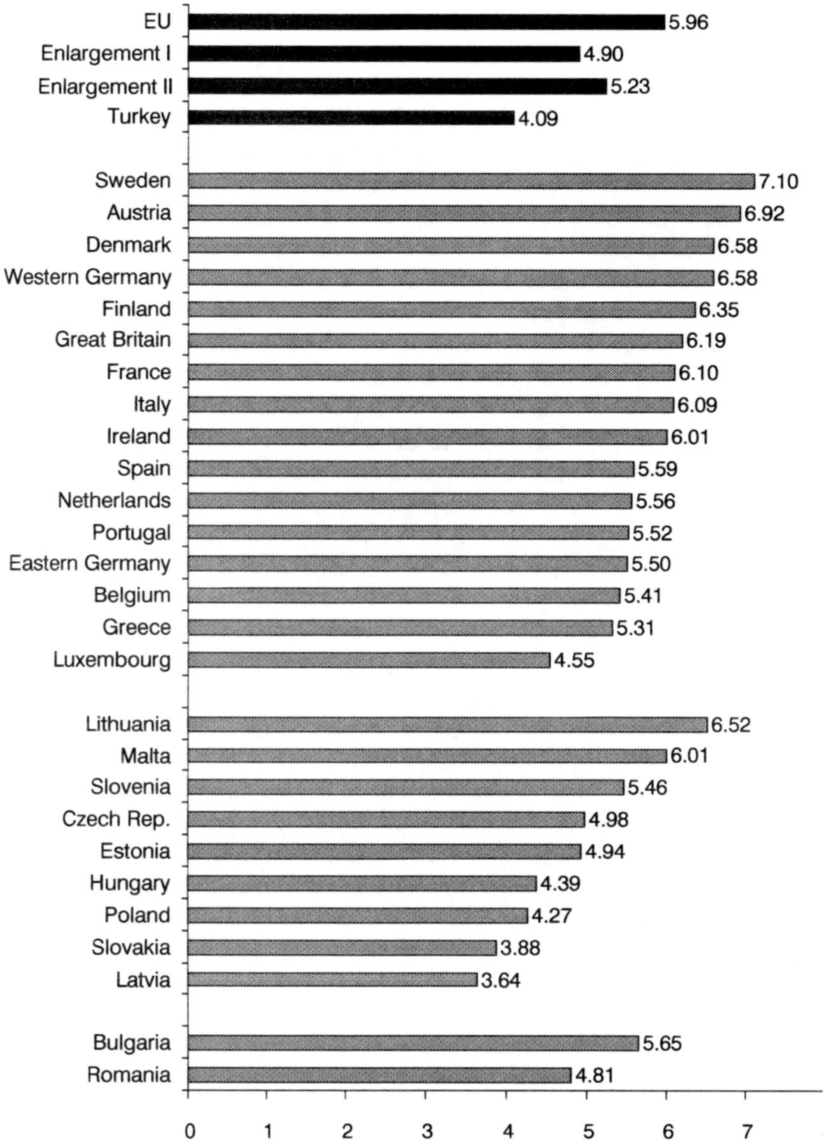

EU	5.96
Enlargement I	4.90
Enlargement II	5.23
Turkey	4.09
Sweden	7.10
Austria	6.92
Denmark	6.58
Western Germany	6.58
Finland	6.35
Great Britain	6.19
France	6.10
Italy	6.09
Ireland	6.01
Spain	5.59
Netherlands	5.56
Portugal	5.52
Eastern Germany	5.50
Belgium	5.41
Greece	5.31
Luxembourg	4.55
Lithuania	6.52
Malta	6.01
Slovenia	5.46
Czech Rep.	4.98
Estonia	4.94
Hungary	4.39
Poland	4.27
Slovakia	3.88
Latvia	3.64
Bulgaria	5.65
Romania	4.81

Figure 4.7 Attitudes towards state intervention in the economy (mean)

Classification of the countries in respect to their economic beliefs

The goal of our analysis is to determine the degree to which citizens of an expanded European community support the EU's blueprint of the economy. We also want to integrate the individual results of the indicators into an overall picture using discriminant analysis. Unlike the other value spheres analyzed in this study, no benchmark country group that could be classified as representative of the EU ideals emerged from the descriptive findings. Rather, there are two country groups that particularly support different aspects of the EU's blueprint. Sweden, Denmark and the Netherlands form one such group that adheres strongly to the EU ideals of "labor market openness" and "generalized trust." The Scandinavian countries are also one of the strongest advocates of "state control of the economy."[14] The citizens of these countries support the EU's "philosophy of openness," which refers to openness of the labor market, openness toward fellow citizens (generalized trust) and liberal conditions for entrepreneurial activities. The second group, Accession II countries Romania and Bulgaria, most strongly advocate the EU position on competition and achievement.

In our chapter on religion (Chapter 2), we distinguished between two groups – one who supported EU ideals and one who did not – with the help of discriminant analysis. Discriminant analysis can also be used for simultaneous consideration of several groups, in this case three. With N groups, the number of discriminant functions is N-1. Due to the fact that we have two benchmark country groups, we calculate two discriminant functions to isolate the benchmark countries from the non-benchmark European countries. Sweden, Denmark and the Netherlands form the first benchmark group, Bulgaria and Romania form the second. The third group is made up of all other members.

Almost all of the indicators analyzed above are used in the discriminant analysis.[15] We use the Educational Goals Index for achievement orientation and the item "most people can be trusted" for generalized trust. We include the two items for competition – competition is good and performance oriented payment – as well as attitudes toward the statements "When jobs are scarce, employers should give priority to citizens over immigrants" and "The state should give more freedom to firms" for gauging attitudes toward the economic order.[16]

The results of the discriminant analysis are summarized in Table 4.1.

We first look at the results for the goodness of fit in the overall analysis. For the first function, the eigenvalue and canonical correlation are relatively good. As groups are clearly distinguished in the first function, it is natural that the values drop in the second function. "Explained variance" also provides an important indicator for the separation of the groups, in that it specifies the percent to which both functions explain the overall discriminant analysis. Function 1 accounts for 75 percent, while function 2 only accounts for 25 percent of the variance. The percentage of correctly classified people (40.6 percent) is relatively slight. Looking more closely at the numbers, however, it becomes evident that both benchmark groups can be rather precisely predicted with both discriminant functions. Misclassifications are most common for non-benchmark countries (group 3). This is, however, not an issue because we classify the people from group 3 to one of the benchmark groups in order to determine the actual support of the EU economic blueprint.

Table 4.1 Economic values: differentiation between benchmark countries and other countries

	Discriminant function "dimension of openness"[a]	Discriminant function "dimension of achievement"[a]
Achievment orientation		
Index: importance of achievement orientation as an educational goal	−0.183	0.789
Generalized trust		
"Most people can be trusted"	0.604	
Competition orientation		
"Competition is good"	0.189	0.588
"A performance orientated salary is fair" (Category of reference: unfair)		0.316
Attitudes towards the openness of the labour market:		
"When jobs are scarce, employers should give priority to national citizens over immigrants" (Category of reference: agree)	0.809	
Role of state		
"State should give more freedom"	0.268	
Eigenvalue	0.287	0.018
Canonical correlation	0.472	0.132
% of explained variance by the discriminance function[b]	75.600	24.400
Group centroids		
Benchmark 1 (SE, DK, NL)	1.336	−0.575
Benchmark 2 (BG, RO)	−0.432	0.738
Group 3 (other countries)	−0.147	0.017

Classification results[c]		Groups (predicted)	
	Benchmark 1	Benchmark 2	Group 3
Benchmark 1 (SE, DK, NL)	80.4 % (1,880)	6.3 % (147)	13.3 % (312)
Benchmark 2 (BG, RO)	6.9 % (98)	75.8 % (1,076)	17.3 % (246)
Group 3 (other countries)	23.1 % (3,954)	44.6 % (7,630)	32.3 % (5,518)
Classified correctly	40.6 %		

a Pooled within-group correlations between discriminating variables and canonical discriminant function.
b Explained variance refers to rotated solution.
c In order to take all countries into account equally, cases were weighted by sample size.

The question now becomes which dimensions are defined by both discriminant functions and which aspects separate our three groups. The resulting pattern is clear. The first function forms the EU ideal for the "openness and closure" dimension, as portrayed by the first benchmark group. The question on the openness of the job market has the most significant influence of all the variables. This function is determined to a smaller degree by generalized trust and also by the passive role of the state. For the second dimension on "achievement and competition," questions about educational goals and the two questions about competition have the strongest influences. This function separates the second benchmark group from group 3, indicated by the group mean values of the discriminant functions. Whereas group 3 is situated relatively close to zero for both functions, Sweden, Denmark and the Netherlands for the first function, and Romania and Bulgaria for the second, show high values. Both benchmark groups exhibit a negative value for the other function, which indicates that the two functions partially contradict one another.[17]

The position of the citizens regarding these two dimensions of the EU economic blueprint is of particular interest to us. On the basis of the estimated discriminant functions, the discriminant analysis classifies every interviewee into one of the three groups. Table 4.2 indicates the average

Table 4.2 Closeness of countries to the EU economic blueprint (benchmark countries)

	Probability of closeness to EU	Probability of closeness to EU in opening dimension	Probability of closeness to EU in achievement dimension
EU-15	**0.35**	**0.39**	**0.26**
Greece	0.42	0.17	0.41
Ireland	0.41	0.33	0.27
Spain	0.41	0.36	0.23
Portugal	0.40	0.22	0.38
Austria	0.40	0.31	0.29
Italy	0.39	0.32	0.30
Eastern Germany	0.38	0.27	0.35
France	0.38	0.31	0.31
Great Britain	0.37	0.37	0.26
Belgium	0.37	0.38	0.25
Western Germany	0.36	0.32	0.31
Luxembourg	0.36	0.34	0.30
Finland	0.36	0.41	0.23
Netherlands	0.25	0.64	0.11
Denmark	0.25	0.65	0.10
Sweden	0.17	0.78	0.05
Enlargement I	**0.39**	**0.14**	**0.47**
Malta	0.45	0.19	0.36
Slovenia	0.40	0.18	0.42
Hungary	0.40	0.12	0.48
Poland	0.39	0.08	0.54
Slovakia	0.39	0.10	0.52
Lithuania	0.38	0.09	0.53
Czech Rep.	0.37	0.13	0.50
Latvia	0.36	0.13	0.51
Estonia	0.36	0.24	0.41
Enlargement II	**0.35**	**0.10**	**0.55**
Romania	0.36	0.13	0.51
Bulgaria	0.34	0.07	0.59
Turkey	**0.39**	**0.20**	**0.41**

probability that an interviewee from a particular country will fall within one of the three groups.

The probability that an interviewee from a particular country cannot be classified as identifying with either of the EU's economic positions is shown in the first column. There is almost no difference between the groups at the aggregate level. Approximately one-third of the population from the old EU member states, both accession groups and Turkey support neither the achievement nor the openness dimension of the EU. These results remain relatively stable at the country level, with Malta and Greece diverging most from the EU economic blueprint. For the EU ideal of openness, the benchmark countries Sweden, the Netherlands and Denmark show the strongest levels of idenfication. Support for the EU position as a whole is at a similar level in all four country groups, but differs substantially when the EU position is broken down into its two component parts. Almost all of the old EU member states show more support for the openness dimension than for achievement, exceptions being Greece, Portugal and East Germany. A majority of citizens in all accession countries and Turkey support the achievement dimension. This result remains constant at the country level despite significant differences within groups. None of the accession countries matched the EU-15's mean value for openness. Vice versa, none of the old EU members matched the accession countries' mean value for achievement.[18] There is a relevant difference in the economic culture of the old EU member states and the accession countries.

Explaining differences in attitudes toward the economy

As demonstrated in the previous section, countries in the wider EU differ in their attitudes toward the economy. In this section, we attempt to explain these differences. In doing so, we refer to the independent variables introduced in the first chapter: modernization, cultural-religious and political-institutional factors.

Modernization is a very complex process, resulting in a one-time historical growth of the economy and in the overall wealth and welfare of the citizens. Daniel Bell (1996, 1979) differentiates between two phases of the modernization process, each associated with different value systems. Bell describes the first phase of modernization as industrialization, in which the dominant sphere of production is industrial goods, industries are the dominant units of production and goods and services are distributed via markets. The degree of production mechanization is high during this stage. Societal modernization leads to a vast improvement in overall societal welfare, accompanied by specific value orientations. These value orientations include achievement, individual responsibility, competition and a rejection of outside or state interventions.

Bell (1979) characterizes the second phase of modernization as post-industrialization; Ronald Inglehart (1997) also refers to this stage and uses the term post-modernization. During post-industrialization, the service sector is increasingly emphasized, technology and science gain more importance, and educational levels climb drastically. Post-industrial societies become welfare societies, in which the one-time historical level of disposable income and consumption reaches the wider public.[19] Specific value orientations are also connected with post-industrial societies. Hedonistic orientations replace values such as competition, thriftiness and a wavering of consumption characteristic of the industrialization phase (Bell 1979). Ronald Inglehart (1997) assumes that the increased possibilities to satisfy material need lead to post-material values that include a desire for self-development and participation. The industrialization values of achievement, competition and economic success are derogated in comparison to these new social values.

The two phases of modernization have varying effects on citizens' value orientations. "Thus, cultural change is not linear, with the coming of post-industrial society it moves in a new direction" (Inglehart and Baker 2000: 22). The societies under analysis differ in their degree of economic modernization. All of the countries are more or less industrialized, but differ in their degree of post-industrialization (see the classification of countries in Inglehart and Norris 2003a: 165ff.). According to the aforementioned theories, this may lead to significant differences in citizens' value orientations toward the economy. We assume that societies not at the post-industrial stage are more likely to support achievement and competition than are further developed societies. We also assume that generalized trust and an emphasis on market openness characterize the more economically developed societies.

Now we turn to cultural-religious factors. We assume that different religions have different economic beliefs that presumably influence their members (Nutzinger 2003, Wuthnow 1994). In his religious sociological studies, Max Weber (1998) attempts to show that the spirit of capitalism has a Protestant origin (1988).

> A specific attitude toward work ethic results from this doctrine. This includes a high priority placed on work and professional performance, a permanent attempt to shape the world. Additionally, it demands systematic self control over one's life style, asceticism regarding non-necessary consumption and continuous reinvestment of attained success.
>
> (Gerhards 1996: 543)

One can assume that compared to other denominations, Protestants are characterized by a greater orientation toward achievement and competition and stronger preferences for market openness and minimal state intervention.[20] Weber distinguishes the Protestant ethic from the Catholic ethic, which does not contain a specific, religiously motivated work ethic. The social sciences lack similarly reliable hypotheses for other religious denominations in Europe.[21]

The influence of Islam on societal attitudes toward the economy has been a controversial topic in the past (Leipold 2003).[22] Helmut Leipold (2003) and Jörg Winterberg (1994) conclude that Islam, at least concerning the central texts of Islam, by all means is comparable with the economic order of social market economy since it incorporates a certain social dimension as well as an orientation toward individual achievement.[23] "Labor was defined as an obligation to all who are able to work" (Wienen 1999: 41). Gainful employment is associated with individual performance on the basis of the interest ban, which can be interpreted as "evidence for a positive attitude toward competition" (Winterberg 1994: 192ff., 205). In contrast, other authors think that Islam has a negative influence on the capitalist economy. Weber describes Islam as a religion that opposes a puritan and ascetical life style (Weber 1985: 376). Leipold (2003) also emphasizes the negative consequences Islam has on economic development – he views the control that Islam claims over all areas of life as excluding the possibility of rationalization in the economic sphere. Empirical findings seem to favor this position: "We find that Christian religions are more positively associated with attitudes conducive to economic growth, while religious Muslims are opposed to the market the most" (Guiso *et al.*: 2003: 228).

There are only a few statements concerning the influence of Orthodox Christianity on economic beliefs.[24] Jan Delhey describes Orthodox Christians "as collectively oriented and subordinated to the state and authorities" (2001: 67). Andreas Buss agrees with this concept and perceives an "absolute rejection of an ethic supporting success," in that "only the unconditional ethical commandment is seen as a positive action" (1989: 48). Strong mythical components of the Orthodox Christian faith minimize such actions (Buss 1989: 44 referring to Weber 1988). Buss concludes by saying that "the active acting, dominant personality, which is the specific occidental ideal of life-style that influences the occidental economic ethic, is not adequate for Orthodox religiosity" (Buss 1989: 95). Our hypothesis assumes that Orthodox Christians, Muslims and, to a somewhat lesser degree, Catholics are less likely to support achievement orientation, open markets, competition and a strong state. We use the data regarding the interviewees' membership in one of the denominations as an indicator for religious influence.

Finally, we assume that a country's political-institutional order influences citizens' values, with two particularly relevant subcategories: socialist legacy and state intervention in the economy. Some of the countries in our analysis were state-planned economies from the end of World War II until 1990, while others were capitalistic market economies. But while the institutional transformation of East European state economies has indeed made substantial progress, observers argue that citizens' attitudes and values do not change as rapidly as do institutions:

> Although the elite push for the "return to Europe" as the best option and the citizens accept this effort for the most part, broad socialist principles

– partially due to the difficult first years of reform – still persist. These principles are in tension with the construction of a capitalistic market economy.

(Delhey 2001: 65)

The main difference between socialist state and capitalist market economies is that socialist state economies do not cede allocation of work, goods and services to enterprises and markets. Rather, the state controls these spheres. We therefore expect that citizens who grew up in a socialist state are more likely to support state intervention in the market and object to competition. The effects of socialist state socialization on achievement orientation and generalized trust are more difficult to evaluate. Socialist societies attempted to motivate their citizens' economic performance through substantial investment in propaganda and provocative symbols like awarding medals of Honor. High levels of surveillance and spying bred distrust among citizens. Socialist societies are also characterized by a lack of intermediary institutions of civil society such as NGOs, which often serve to generate trust in society. We use the number of years a country was under communist control as an indicator of the socialist legacy.

The second aspect of political-institutional order is state intervention in the economy. We assume that the degree of state intervention in the economy influences citizens' attitudes toward the economy, independent from a country's socialist history. More state intervention often leads to regulated competition, which causes incentives for individual performance to drop. Well-developed welfare states also ensure a certain amount of security. Alberto Alesina and George-Marios Angeletos (2003) show that the degree of state intervention in the economy corresponds to particular economic attitudes.[25] We assume that a high level of state intervention reduces orientations toward achievement, competition and approval of market openness. We assume that high levels of state intervention will result in high levels of generalized trust among citizens. A variety of tools exist for measuring state influence. We would ideally use a single indicator for all dimensions (welfare state, state quota, proportion of state ownership etc.), but this was not possible due to the small number of cases (28 countries). We instead use the Index Economic Freedom of the World (EFW), part of the Fraser Institute's Index Size of Government. The EFW summarizes the most important measured values of these dimensions, explained in Chapter 1. We summarize the different hypotheses in Table 4.3.

Tables 4.4 and 4.5 display the standardized regression coefficients of the multiple linear regression models for all relevant variables. We coded all variables so that high positive values signify support for the EU economic blueprint.[26]

The R^2 values, which illustrate the explanatory power of our models, show that the explained variance is rather high for achievement orientation and attitudes toward market openness. Explanations for generalized trust,

Table 4.3 Hypotheses for explaining economic values

	Achievement	Trust	Competition orientation	Open labor market	Passive state role
Modernization					
Industrialization	+	0	+	+	+
Postindustrialization	−	+	−	+	+
Religion					
Protestants	+	+	+	0	+
Roman Catholics	−	+	−	0	−
Orthodox Christians	−	+	−	−	−
Muslims	−	+	−	−	−
Political-institutional environment					
State intervention	+	−	+	+	+
Socialist past	0	−	−	−	−

+ positive correlation expected;
− negative correlation expected;
0 no correlation expected or no hypothesis.

Table 4.4 Explaining achievement and generalized trust: linear regressions

	Achievement orientation		Generalized trust
	Index education goals	"Work always comes first"	
Modernization			
HDI	−0.304	−0.186	0.193
Religion[a]			
Protestants	−0.082	0.075	0.092
Roman Catholics	−0.039	0.125	−0.075
Orthodox Christians	−0.008+	0.068	−0.022
Muslims	−0.082	0.080	−0.007+
Political-institutional environment			
State intervention	−0.009+	−0.054	−0.025
Socialist past	0.116	0.122	0.001+
R^2	0.153	0.084	0.071

The models represent standardized beta-coefficients from the OLS regression analysis.
If not indicated differently, coefficients are significant at the 1% level (* = significant at 5% level, + = not significant).
a Category of reference: people who do not have a religious affiliation.

the role of the state and especially competition orientation are not entirely satisfactory.

Our analysis clearly confirms the postulated and ambivalent influence of modernization. Higher levels of modernization lead to greater trust, increased support for market openness and the rejection of state intervention. Higher levels of modernization have a negative effect on values related to achievement and competition, which supports our theoretical expectations.

Table 4.5 Explaining attitudes towards the economic system: linear regressions

	Competition		Open markets	State intervention
	"Competition is good"	*"Performance orientated salary"*		
Modernization				
HDI	–0.113	–0.042	0.225	0.105
Religion[a]				
Protestants	0.060	0.006+	–0.007+	0.067
Roman Catholics	0.040	–0.009+	–0.191	0.010+
Orthodox Christians	0.022	0.046	–0.043	0.003+
Muslims	–0.021*	0.014+	0.110	–0.043
Political-institutional environment				
State intervention	–0.028	–0.058	–0.085	–0.013+
Socialist past	0.015+	0.083	–0.080	–0.092
R²	0.013	0.018	0.114	0.047

The models represent standardized beta-coefficients from the OLS regression analysis.
If not indicated differently, coefficients are significant at the 1% level (* = significant at 5% level, + = not significant).
a   Category of reference: people who do not have a religious affiliation.

The transition from an industrialized to a post-industrialized society decreases emphasis on achievement and competition and increases generalized trust and market openness.

The findings on the role of religion do not show a clear pattern and do not clearly confirm Guiso *et al.*'s conclusion that "on average religion is associated positively with attitudes that are conducive to free markets and better institutions" (2003: 227). Protestants support the EU economic concepts most strongly and are the only denomination to exhibit a high level of trust and a positive attitude toward a passive, non-interventionist state. Protestantism is not a significant factor in determining citizens' orientation to market openness. Islam fosters market openness, but at the same time Muslims support state intervention in the economy. Catholics and Orthodox Christians maintain similar attitudes related to the economy, characterized by a below average degree of trust and a preference for market closure. Influence on the state role is statistically not significant for either denomination. Finally, the inconsistent influence of religion on the two achievement indicators is noteworthy. All religions are characterized by a below average emphasis on achievement orientation in educational goals. At the same time, all religions show above average support for work orientation. This ambivalence may indicate that our operationalization of the achievement dimension is not ideal. The two achievement indicators appear to emphasize different aspects.

The political-institutional order forms the third group of explanatory factors. Contrary to our expectations, citizens in countries with high rates of state intervention in the economy are more likely to support the idea of market openness. State interventions have a positive impact on competition and achievement. Our hypothesis that state intervention generates a greater degree of trust is the only assumption confirmed by the statistical analysis. The relationship between state intervention and attitudes toward a "passive state role" is not significant. Citizens from former socialist countries show lower levels of support for the concept of a small state role and for market openness. These citizens also maintain above average support for achievement and competition orientations.

Conclusion

The European Union emerged as an economic union. The central pillars of the EU's economic blueprint are competition, market openness and a rather passive state on the one hand, and citizens oriented towards achievement and generalized trust on the other. We attempted to analyze whether and to what degree current and future EU citizens support these beliefs. This chapter showed that significant differences exist between the old member states and the accession countries. Citizens of EU-15 member states support open markets and a passive, non-interventionist role for the state. These countries also exhibit a greater degree of generalized trust. Citizens in accession countries show substantially higher levels of support for achievement orientations and somewhat higher levels of support for competition.

The third section of this chapter, by means of discriminant analysis, shows the overall proximity of the countries to the EU's economic ideal. This made clear that old member states and accession countries support different aspects of the EU economic blueprint. Old member countries, particularly Sweden, Denmark and the Netherlands, emphasize aspects of openness (openness of the labor market, a passive state role and generalized trust). Accession countries support the EU concepts of achievement and competition to a greater degree. Hence, the findings in this chapter are somewhat more ambivalent than those in the other chapters in which we have analyzed other value spheres. In light of our findings, we cannot say that the EU position is more strongly supported by the original members than by new member states and accession candidates. Because these new member states and accession candidates support achievement and competition to a higher degree, one can expect that EU enlargement will lead to a new economic dynamic.

Furthermore, we concede that the contextual variables modernization, religion and political-institutional order do not explain the citizens' economic attitudes very well. The degree of modernization is the best explanatory factor among these variables, and its impact goes in the direction that we theoretically expected. The more modernized a country becomes, the more strongly the citizens endorse market openness and a passive state role. More modernized societies also have greater levels of generalized trust. Higher degrees of modernization also have negative effects on achievement and competition values.

5 Concepts of the welfare state in the European Union

A welfare state attempts to create a social safety net and to attenuate social inequality. The development of the modern welfare state began at the end of the nineteenth century, when legal social security systems were introduced in several European countries. After WWII, an expansion of welfare state measures took place in Western countries. Initially, international comparative research worked with a convergence thesis, which assumed that social security would rise as a country's economy grew (Wilensky 1975). Further research revealed that the degree of welfare state development was independent of economic growth to a certain degree. Several typologies have been developed to describe the differences among welfare states. Gösta Esping-Andersen (1990) developed the most well-known typology, which distinguishes between three welfare state models: the social democratic system (e.g. Sweden), the conservative (e.g. Germany and Italy) and the liberal (e.g. USA).[1]

Edeltraud Roller (2000a) used Esping-Andersen as a starting point and developed her own typology, which describes four welfare state models differentiated by the number of state regulated spheres.[2] The number of regulated spheres increases from model to model. In the *liberal* model, the state only assumes responsibility in extreme cases like sickness, age or inability to work. In the *Christian democratic* model, the state also takes measures to create equal opportunities. In the *social democratic* model, the state becomes responsible for equality of outcomes and full employment. The *socialist* welfare state additionally controls wages and salaries (Roller 2000a). We use Roller's typology in our analysis. First, we reconstruct the EU welfare state blueprint by interpreting central legal texts of the EU. Second, we test the extent to which the member states and accession candidate countries' citizens support this blueprint. Third, we attempt to explain the similarities and differences. The chapter concludes with a summary of our findings.

The EU welfare state blueprint

Due to the fact that the term "welfare state" has different political and scientific meanings, reconstructing the EU's blueprint of an ideal welfare state proves to be rather difficult. The term "European social model" also has different meanings in the social scientific and political realms. François Mitterand and Jacques Delors developed and promoted the concept of "social space" and the "European social model" in the 1980s (Aust *et al.* 2000, Ostner 2000).[3] They argued that Europe's economic integration should be complemented by a social dimension. Most recently, in his comprehensive dissertation, Daniel C. Vaughan-Whitehead (2003: 6) compiled elements that constitute the European social model.[4] We cite the author's graphic depiction.

The Different Elements of the European Social Model
Labor law on workers' rights
Employment
Equal opportunities
Anti-discrimination
Workers' participation, information and consultation
Social partner recognition and involvement
Social dialogue and collective bargaining
Involvement of civil society
Public services and services of general interest
Decent or "fair" wages
Social protection
Social inclusion
Fundamental working and social rights
Regional cohesion
Transnational social policies and tools

The political concept of a European social model is multifaceted and goes far beyond the *social scientific* definition of a welfare state. The idea of a European social model broaches issues in very different social realms, described in other chapters of this study. The following dimensions can be differentiated as a result of classifying the multiplicity of themes:

1   a right to participation, which refers to the relationship of work and capital as well as to problems of internal co-determination,
2   labor law regulations in the workplace (security, health),
3   tolerance (anti-discrimination) and civil society, both of which relate to the organizational form of democracy,
4   public services, such as securing energy supply and transportation,
5   wage policy,
6   full employment,
7   social security and social protection.

The concept of a European social model is not primarily concerned with the social security system, but rather with the workplace and operational working relations.[5] Only the last three dimensions of the European social model potentially belong to the semantic field of the social scientific notion of welfare state. Long-term management of social security and protection (pt. 7) is fundamental to the social scientific understanding of the welfare state. This corresponds to what Roller describes as a liberal or basic model. Ensuring full employment through state regulation in the job market (pt. 6) is very similar to the social democratic model. State intervention in wage policy to rectify social inequality (pt. 5) corresponds to a socialist welfare state model.

In reconstructing the EU's welfare state model, we do *not* orient ourselves to the expansive concept of the European social model. We instead use Roller's typology as our basis and ask which of the various models the EU favors. The constitutional treaty serves as the most important document for these ends.[6] Part I of the constitutional draft discusses the EU's goals and values. Solidarity is defined as a central value in Article I-2 (Conference of Representatitives 2004). "Social market economy aiming at full employment and social progress" is considered a fundamental EU goal (Article I-3). It is not possible, however, to conclude that the EU advocates a social democratic welfare state model simply because it adopts the goal of full employment. The question of whether full employment is established through state regulated measures or through a subordinated state role remains unanswered. Part I of the constitutional draft also promotes social protection and intergenerational solidarity. Unlike the goal of full employment, these general goals are more clearly expressed in later articles. Article 94 from Part II of the constitutional draft is titled "social security and social assistance." We cite this article in its entirety because it includes the most important elements of the EU's welfare state blueprint.

Article II-94: Social security and social assistance
(1) The Union recognizes and respects the entitlement to social security benefits and social services providing protection in cases such as maternity, illness, industrial accidents, dependency or old age, and in the case of loss of employment, in accordance with the rules laid down by Union law and national laws and practices.
(2) Everyone residing and moving legally within the European Union is entitled to social security benefits and social advantages in accordance with Union law and national laws and practices.
(3) In order to combat social exclusion and poverty, the Union recognizes and respects the right to social and housing assistance so as to ensure a decent existence for all those who lack sufficient resources, in accordance with the rules laid down by Union law and national laws and practices.

(Conference of Representatives 2004)

The EU clearly and concretely supports a welfare state protecting its citizens from basic risks associated with unemployment: sickness (including invalids and people in need of long-term care), maternity leave, age.[7] This welfare state model almost perfectly matches Roller's liberal or basic model. More detailed versions of a European welfare state do not exist in a legally binding form.[8] Even this preferred basic welfare state model is formulated in a qualified way in that securing definitive achievements in this field remains a right of individual member states. This means that "a 'European social state' will consequently not emerge" (Leibfried and Pierson 2000: 352).[9]

That European social policy is not very well developed is a generally accepted fact. Fritz Scharpf (1996) analyzed European integration as a process of negative integration. Negative integration is the political creation of a free common market and the removal of trade barriers without politically devising the consequences of such deregulation (which would be positive integration). Using game theory, Scharpf attempts to explain why a positively-integrated European welfare state did not emerge and probably never will. In his view, poorer EU countries are not interested in European-wide social standards. Labor productivity and capital is clearly less substantial in these countries than in the more economically developed EU countries. If poorer countries want to be competitive, factor costs, above all, wages, ancillary wage costs and environmental costs, must be very low. An equalization of wages and social standards would probably lead to higher unemployment rates in these countries. Poorer EU countries are therefore strong advocates for the preservation of country-specific standards and exercise their veto against standardized regulations.[10] This constellation will likely stay in place with the accession of further countries who have even less factor productivity. It is therefore unlikely that a standardized European welfare state will develop in the near future (Vobruba 2001: 102ff.).

The citizens' attitudes toward the welfare state

The following section analyzes the extent to which citizens in member states and accession countries support the EU welfare state blueprint. The EU advocates a basic welfare state model, in which social security is guaranteed for cases of sickness, disability, old age, parental leave and unemployment. Additionally, it promotes a right for housing. The EU expects its citizens to show solidarity for those who are unable to ensure their livelihood because they are sick, handicapped etc. The European Values Study contains a question that precisely measures this kind of support, as follows:

> I will now read to you different groups of people. Tell me on the basis of this list how much value you place on the living requirements for …
> 1) older people in our country, 2) the unemployed in our country and 3) sick and handicapped people in our country.

Possible answers ranged from "not at all," "not so much," "to a certain extent," "a lot" to "very much." One could argue that the question is not a good indicator of attitudes toward the welfare state because it does not refer to the state itself and does not measure the extent to which interviewees assign responsibility to the state for the three groups. The question does, however, give information as to whether one is, in principle, prepared to support the elderly, the unemployed, and the sick and handicapped. We assume that general support for these groups represents a positive disposition of support for a state social policy, an assumption for which we found empirical support. An additional question asked interviewees whether they believe the state or the individual should assume responsibility for providing for these groups. In a correlation analysis, a positive correlation emerges between attitudes toward state responsibility and the three questions concerning the care of the sick, handicapped, elderly and unemployed.[11]

Table 5.1 shows the results for the three approval categories ("very much," "a lot" and "to a certain degree") as well as the countries' means (in parentheses) for the particular questions. A high percentage value and high country mean signify high levels of support for a particular group.

First, we look at the approval for supporting the elderly. The approval rating in all four aggregate groups is around 90 percent, and there is hardly a difference between the old EU member states and the accession countries.[12] Turkey shows an even higher approval rate. There is also general approval at the country level. The old member states of Ireland, Portugal and East Germany show above average support for the elderly. In the accession countries, Malta, then Slovakia, express support for the elderly to the highest degree. A comparatively smaller degree of solidarity is evident in Luxembourg and Latvia. But the approval rate is overall very high. A similar picture emerges for attitudes towards the sick and handicapped in that the significant majority in all four country groups supports the sick and handicapped. The country level differences are similar to our findings for the first question. Ireland, Portugal and Malta make up the leading countries, and Luxembourg and Latvia have the lowest levels of support in their respective groups. The results are somewhat different for attitudes toward the unemployed. The average level of support is around 80 percent, which is indeed very high, but less than for the other groups. Additionally, the differences between the countries are somewhat more pronounced. Turkey shows the most support for the unemployed. Denmark, Luxembourg, the Netherlands, Latvia and Hungary maintain the lowest approval ratings in their respective groups.

We assume that the unemployed receive less support from their fellow citizens than the sick and elderly because they are seen as being responsible for their current status. Elderly, sick and handicapped people are not faulted for being in their situation.[13] This is not necessarily the case for the unemployed; either the system is at fault in that there are not enough jobs provided for those citizens willing to work, or the individual is seen as having a bad work ethic.

Table 5.1 Support of the EU welfare state blueprint (percentage and mean of support of different groups in need)

	Elderly people	Sick and disabled people	Unemployed people
EU-15	91.9 (3.82)	90.8 (3.69)	81.4 (3.31)
Ireland	96.2 (4.33)	97.5 (4.30)	87.5 (3.58)
Portugal	97.7 (4.28)	96.0 (4.05)	86.4 (3.57)
Italy	96.3 (3.97)	96.1 (3.94)	90.6 (3.66)
Greece	96.1 (3.94)	94.9(3.96)	89.8 (3.59)
Eastern Germany	98.6 (4.03)	94.8 (3.70)	91.9 (3.55)
France	90.9 (3.85)	90.0 (3.71)	85.6 (3.53)
Great Britain	93.1 (3.98)	92.3 (3.83)	77.3 (3.18)
Sweden	94.8 (3.92)	94.1 (3.78)	78.8 (3.23)
Spain	95.3 (3.77)	90.1 (3.52)	91.5 (3.55)
Finland	89.4 (3.68)	88.0 (3.56)	85.9 (3.42)
Belgium	90.7 (3.69)	89.1 (3.55)	76.4 (3.14)
Western Germany	95.1 (3.75)	90.1 (3.47)	83.0 (3.16)
Austria	88.7 (3.53)	87.8 (3.49)	75.2 (3.13)
Netherlands	89.2 (3.58)	90.5 (3.48)	72.9 (2.95)
Denmark	79.1 (3.51)	82.8 (3.53)	62.3 (2.82)
Luxembourg	78.2 (3.26)	77.8 (3.19)	66.3 (2.85)
Enlargement I	90.2 (3.72)	89.3 (3.63)	81.3 (3.35)
Malta	93.7 (4.14)	94.1 (4.06)	81.4 (3.38)
Slovakia	94.8 (4.02)	93.8 (3.82)	88.5 (3.57)
Lithuania	94.3 (3.94)	94.0 (3.75)	92.5 (3.71)
Poland	95.2 (3.97)	89.0 (3.73)	87.3 (3.54)
Czech Rep.	85.0 (3.45)	93.2 (3.77)	85.5 (3.40)
Slovenia	91.6 (3.48)	92.5 (3.60)	90.7 (3.53)
Hungary	89.2 (3.74)	83.2 (3.43)	69.0 (3.02)
Estonia	89.6 (3.52)	86.5 (3.38)	80.2 (3.27)
Latvia	77.9 (3.23)	76.6 (3.13)	55.7 (2.69)
Enlargement II	89.6 (3.86)	87.2 (3.71)	83.8 (3.59)
Bulgaria	96.6 (4.04)	93.0 (3.78)	90.9 (3.73)
Romania	82.5 (3.68)	81.1 (3.63)	76.7 (3.44)
Turkey	94.5 (4.21)	97.3 (4.38)	94.9 (4.27)

The countries follow a similar pattern for all three questions in Table 5.1. Correlations between the three items are also significant.[14] We did not therefore carry out a complex discriminant analysis. We instead formed an index by adding up the three indicators. The index values range from 0 "absolutely no support" to 12 "very strong support (see Figure 5.1)."[15]

The majority of citizens in all countries adopt the EU position by demonstrating their support for the elderly, sick and unemployed.[16] On the aggregate level, EU member states and Accession I countries yield very similar results. Citizens in Accession II countries show higher levels of support for the elderly, sick and unemployed, and Turkey supports this EU concept the most. Latvia and Luxembourg are the countries with the lowest levels

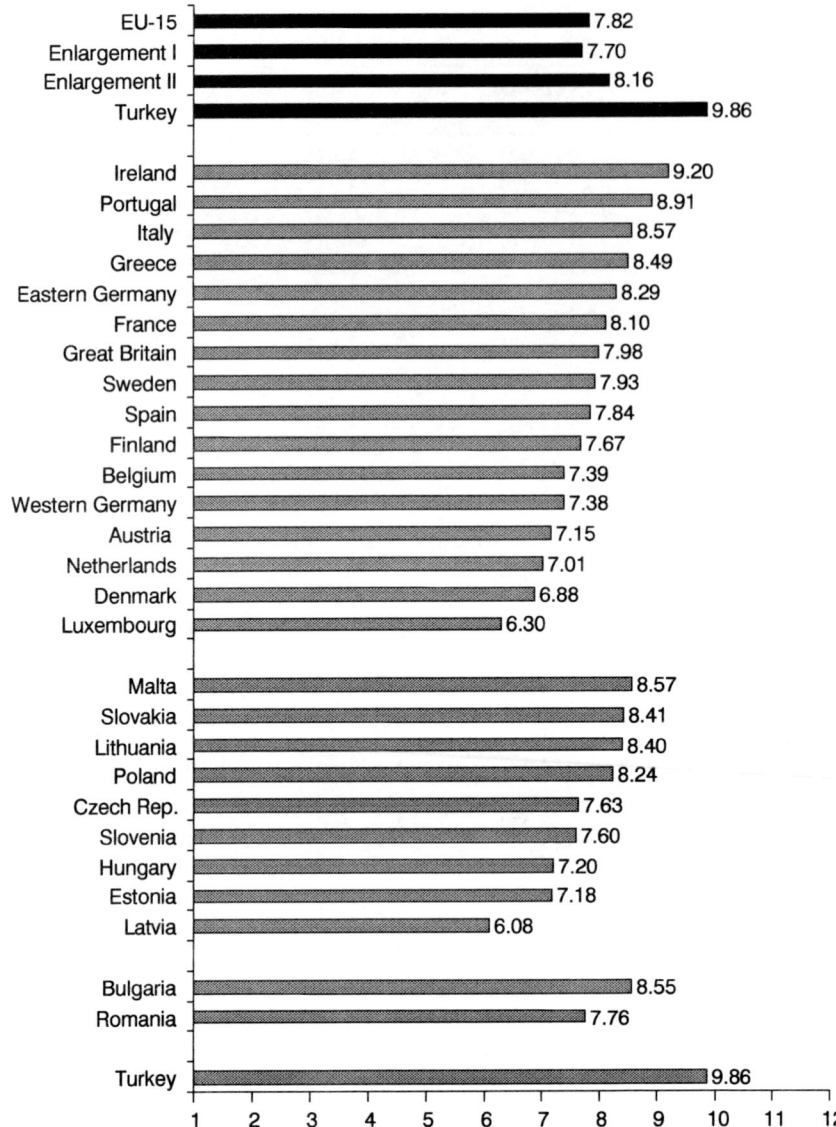

Figure 5.1   Support for elderly, sick, handicapped and unemployed (mean index)

of support, followed by Denmark and the Netherlands. The next section attempts to explain these differences.

As mentioned above, the three indicators are not ideal for measuring the citizens' attitudes toward the welfare state because the questions do not directly refer to the state. The data from the 1996 International Social Survey Programme (ISSP) "Role of Government III" includes such a reference and is therefore a better operationalization of the EU's welfare state blueprint.

Apart from the state's responsibility for the sick, elderly and unemployed, this survey also asks about provision of housing, another integral part of the EU blueprint. The disadvantage to using this data set is that the ISSP survey was not carried out in all member and accession countries. The following question from the ISSP is well suited for measuring the EU blueprint.

> Please indicate the extent to which the state should be responsible for the following items: 1) Providing health care for the sick, 2) Securing a fair standard of living for the elderly, 3) Providing for those not able to support themselves financially with adequate accommodations, 4) Ensuring an adequate standard of living for the unemployed.

The interviewee could choose from the following answers: "The state should ...:" "definitely be responsible," "be responsible," "not be responsible" or "by no means be responsible." Table 5.2 provides the percentage values for the two positive approval alternatives.[17]

The results support the findings from the European Values Study. The approval of the EU welfare state blueprint is extraordinarily high in all countries. This is particularly true for the elderly and sick. Support for providing accommodation for the unemployed is somewhat lower. Holding the state responsible for supporting the unemployed is particularly low in Hungary and in the Czech Republic. Unfortunately, the survey was not carried out in Turkey.

Table 5.2 "The state should take responsibility for ..." (%)

	Provide health care for the sick	Provide a decent standard of living for the old	Provide decent housing for those who can't afford it	Provide a decent standard of living for the unemployed
EU-15	**97.1**	**97.3**	**88.3**	**85.8**
Spain	99.2	98.9	98.0	93.9
Ireland	99.1	99.1	93.9	91.5
Eastern Germany	99.1	98.4	91.1	91.6
Sweden	96.2	97.7	81.8	90.3
Great Britain	98.6	98.1	88.6	78.7
Italy	98.6	98.0	88.1	75.1
Western Germany	96.6	96.0	77.9	80.4
France	88.7	92.4	86.8	80.9
Enlargement I	**98.1**	**98.0**	**84.0**	**71.8**
Slovenia	97.2	96.4	90.8	86.4
Poland	97.9	98.5	90.5	81.2
Latvia	98.7	99.5	85.7	82.6
Hungary	99.3	98.2	76.1	62.8
Czech Rep.	96.8	96.6	79.7	44.7
Enlargement II				
Bulgaria	97.2	97.8	79.9	87.6

We now summarize the descriptive findings. The EU advocates a rather basic welfare state conception in which the state provides support to those not able to care for themselves. This is particularly the case for the elderly, sick, handicapped, unemployed and homeless. The EU blueprint does not extend past this basic model of the welfare state. Our analysis shows that a majority of citizens in all countries support at least this minimal welfare state model. We used ISSP data to measure whether citizens desire a welfare state model beyond the type spelled out by the EU. We again use Roller's typology, but as the data does not allow for a differentiation between the liberal and the Christian democratic model, we differentiated between three variants: a basic model (Roller's "liberal model"), a social democratic model and a socialist model.[18] Based on this distinction we can group interviewees into three categories: 1) Interviewees who want the state to be responsible for at least two of the three groups (the sick, elderly or unemployed) while rejecting a further state role are classified as advocates of the basic liberal model; 2) Interviewees are classified as advocates of the social democratic model if they also define one of the two following tasks as state responsibilities: "reduction of income inequality" or "provision of jobs;" 3) Interviewees are classified as advocates of the socialist model if they also advocate legal controls on wages and stipends.

The results in Table 5.3 show a clear pattern. Citizens' beliefs clearly go beyond the EU blueprint in all countries. In their view the EU-preferred minimal welfare state does not go far enough. The socialist model has the highest approval rate in all three aggregate categories. This holds true for almost all countries except Sweden and West Germany, where the social

Table 5.3 Support of different welfare state models (%)

	No welfare state	Basic model	Social democratic	Socialist model	Not classified
EU-15	0.5	8.9	29.8	56.5	4.4
Sweden	0.7	20.2	40.9	34.5	3.7
Great Britain	0.2	15.1	32.5	46.7	5.6
Western Germany	0.8	13.7	46.8	34.0	4.7
Ireland	0.1	9.7	43.1	43.6	3.6
France	1.9	8.5	23.9	56.0	9.7
Italy	0	6.7	18.0	69.3	6.0
Eastern Germany	0	2.8	13.9	80.7	2.6
Spain	0	1.3	19.6	77.6	1.6
Enlargement I	0.5	4.7	21.8	69.1	3.9
Czech Rep.	2.2	12.1	24.2	54.8	6.8
Hungary	0.1	5.1	30.8	61.0	2.9
Poland	0.4	3.1	17.2	76.7	2.6
Latvia	0	3.0	21.9	71.8	3.3
Slovenia	0.2	1.2	11.6	82.5	4.5
Enlargement II					
Bulgaria	0	6.7	12.1	76.7	4.6

democratic model is preferred. Only a minority supports the EU's basic liberal model. One must consider, however, that the data was collected in 1996. Roller (2000a: 98) shows in her time comparison between 1985 and 1996 that support for a reduced role of the state increases over time. One can assume that this trend has continued up until today. Earlier, an intense debate raged over whether the social security system was feasible. State services were reduced in all countries, even under social democratic governments. We assume that this development has had consequences on citizens' attitudes. The number of claims for state-welfare services has probably also decreased. Even if this portends the development of such a trend, a discrepancy between the EU welfare state blueprint and the citizens' attitudes will continue to exist. While the EU advocates a minimal welfare state model on the European stage, the citizens desire a greater degree of state welfare and intervention in the economy. This disparity between the EU and its citizens has increased and may increase further with EU expansion.

Explaining differences in attitudes toward the welfare state

We have seen that support for the elderly, sick, handicapped and unemployed is very similar in the different European countries. Nevertheless, certain differences do exist, which we will attempt to explain in this section. Our analysis primarily uses the European Values Study, because it is the only survey to include all relevant countries. The three categories from Table 5.1 – attitudes toward the elderly, sick/handicapped and unemployed – form the dependent variables. As independent variables, we use both individual variables and macro contexts.

There are a number of studies that investigate the factors influencing attitudes toward the welfare state, some of which are comparative empirical studies (Blekesaune and Quadagno 2003, Delhey 2001, Hasenfeld and Rafferty 1989, Künzler *et al.* 1999, Mau 2003, Roller 2000a, Svallfors 1997). Most of these studies focus on individual characteristics in order to explain attitudes toward the welfare state, and the individual's constellation of interests plays a significant role. The studies show that those people or groups who profit or who could profit from welfare state measures are more likely to support a welfare state. Vekeskel Z. Hasenfeld and Jane A. Rafferty (1989) demonstrate that such relationship exists, and Stefan Svallfors (1997: 293) shows that underprivileged classes are more likely to support a redistributive, interventionist state. Roller also arrives at similar results (2000a: 106). If one adheres to the argument that interviewees' interests influence their beliefs toward the welfare state, then the following hypothesis can be deduced. First, we assume that older people are more concerned for the elderly (their own age group) than are younger people. The elderly are also more likely to support aid for the sick and unemployed, because they are more likely to become ill as they age. Additionally, the unemployment rate for the job-seeking elderly is higher than that of younger citizens. We also assume that jobless people are more likely to support social protection for the unemployed. In regard to support for the unemployed, we take into consideration whether an interviewee is employed.

Apart from individual interests, the cultural and structural societal contexts of individuals may also influence their attitudes toward a welfare state. Similar to earlier chapters, we distinguish between the three factors of modernization, religion and the role of the state.

In his seminal 1958 study, *The Passing of Traditional Society*, Daniel Lerner argues that the process of modernization is accompanied by the development of empathy.

> High levels of empathy, which only occur in modern societies, form part of the prevailing personal life style, this is one of the most important hypotheses of our study. Modern society entails industrialization and urbanization as well as a participatory society.
>
> (Lerner 1958: 365)

Empathy includes the ability to place oneself in another's shoes and to take on the role of the others, even if they are not family members or close friends. This is different than in traditional societies where empathy is limited to close friends and family members.[19] This hypothesis can be used for the question at hand. Solidarity with the sick, elderly, handicapped and unemployed is an expression of empathy in that it is not limited to relatives and close friends, but refers to *abstract* groups of people requiring help. One can expect from Lerner's hypothesis that the level of support for a greater welfare state increases with the degree of modernization. Again we determine a country's modernization by using the Human Development Index.

We expect that a country's religious traditions influence citizens' attitudes toward the welfare state. All religious denominations support the concept of helping weaker members, albeit to different degrees (Schwinger 2003: 159). We therefore assume that members of religious communities support the sick, handicapped, elderly and unemployed more than people lacking a religious affiliation. Furthermore, we assume that the degree of church integration has an influence on how one views the welfare state. We assume that the more people are integrated into the daily practices of their church, the more strongly they advocate a welfare state. We measure the degree of integration through church attendance.

Different denominations have developed varying attitudes toward the proper form of the welfare state. We assume that these attitudes influence their members accordingly. Referring to Christianity, Kaufmann expresses his view "that there is no uniform Christian influence on the development of the welfare state. Rather, depending on the religious denomination and the relation of church and state, this influence differs" (Kaufmann 1988: 68). Esping-Andersen suggests a relationship between Catholicism and an enlarged, conservative welfare state model (Esping-Andersen 1990: 53 and 122ff.). Catholicism certainly focuses more on corporative structures than on a strong central state (Esping-Andersen 1990: 61).

In Protestant denominations, a greater emphasis on self-responsibility is evident. The Protestant ethic is characterized by "personal responsibility for the improvement of one's own fate" and merges "public welfare with individual initiative" (Manow 2002: 208).[20] Therefore, in comparison to Catholic countries, Philip Manow speaks of a "Protestant restrained welfare state" (Manow 2002: 210). This is particularly the case for Calvinism. Alfred Müller-Armack notes "how little their dogma encourages social sympathy. The Old Testament notion of a wrathful God visibly hardens the mind toward poverty and suffering" (Müller-Armack 1959: 234). Michael Opielka attests to the overall Christian, particularly Catholic, social ethic as "a meaningful and often unperceived development of the West European welfare state" (Opielka 2003a: 180, Kaufmann 1988 and 1989, Kersbergen 1997). Consequently, we expect the support of the elderly, sick and unemployed to be associated with membership in the Catholic or, to a smaller extent, Protestant Church.

Islamic and Orthodox Christian welfare state beliefs are more difficult to reconstruct, but it does seem that these religions emphasize the principle of personal responsibility to a much lesser degree. Additionally, the connection between religion and state is much stronger. Regarding the Orthodox Church, Müller-Armack argues that "the lack of individual entrepreneurship is compensated by the activities of the almighty state" (Müller-Armack 1959: 93). We assume that this deficit of self-initiative and the role of the state in the Orthodox Church lead to substantial support for the welfare state. In Islam the state is interpreted as an instrument for implementing an Islamic societal order, and the demand for socio-political engagement of the state is therefore substantial. With the poor tax ("zakat"), the Islamic faith possesses a tool that several Islamic economists have interpreted as a basis for a well-constructed welfare state (Hildebrandt 1996: 10ff.). Overall, we assume that Protestants and, to a lesser degree, Catholics support the welfare state less strongly than Orthodox Christians and Muslims.

Finally, we turn to the role of the state. We assume that there is a causal relationship between a country's institutions and its citizens' attitudes. The direction of the causality between the two factors is nevertheless a controversial subject. While the welfare state regime and its activities may influence the convictions of its citizens (Edlund 1999, Blekesaune and Quadagno 2003), it may also work the other way around. We know that politicians in a democratic society must adhere to the values and preferences of their citizens. It may therefore be the case that citizens' values influence political decisions and, consequently, the institutional structure of the welfare state. Empirical evidence regarding this relationship is ambivalent. In his eight-country study, Stefan Svallfors (1997) determined a relationship between regime type and citizens' convictions toward state redistribution.

This relationship, however, is not valid for Sweden. In his fourteen-country study, John Gelissen (2000) comes to a different conclusion: "The findings give no support to the claim of a systematic variation between levels of popular support for the welfare state and its institutional set-up" (Gelissen 2000: 285).

In international comparative studies on welfare states, the extent of a country's welfare provisions is often measured by a small number of key indicators, like public social expenditure. Authors who distinguish between welfare state regimes have criticized this approach. Nevertheless, we use the degree of public social expenditure as a variable for measuring a welfare state for three reasons. First, we have concentrated solely on protection against risks in our definition of the European welfare state. We have not considered the complicated aspects of equality. Second, key figures, such as public social expenditure, are still the best predictors for the degree of redistribution effects in the welfare sector (Busch 1998: 276ff.). Third, the numbers are available for the majority of countries in a readily comparable form, which allows us to carry out a comparative analysis. We use the public expenditures for social needs ("public social expenditure") in proportion to the GDP as our indicator (OECD 2002). High values represent a significant state influence.[21]

The results of our regression models are illustrated in Table 5.4. The results of the aforementioned additive support index are located in the last column.

Table 5.4 Explanation of support of elderly, sick, handicapped and unemployed people: linear regressions

	Elderly people	Sick and handicapped people	Unemployed people	Additive index
Level of modernization				
HDI	0.187	0.224	0.082	0.189
Religion[a]				
Protestants	0.050	0.049	−0.022	0.030
Roman Catholics	0.026	0.003 +	−0.009 +	0.008 +
Orthodox Christians	0.095	0.104	0.069	0.104
Muslims	0.092	0.111	0.126	0.128
Integration into church	0.098	0.088	0.075	0.101
State Intervention				
Publ. soc. expendit.	−0.221	−0.281	−0.164	−0.258
Other variables				
Age	0.207	0.104	0.112	0.164
Unemployment			0.085	0.030
R^2	0.089	0.070	0.068	0.092

The models represent standardized beta-coefficients from the OLS regression analysis.
If not indicated differently, coefficients are significant at the 1% level (* = significant at 5% level, + = not significant).
a Category of reference: people who do not have a religious affiliation.

Ten percent of the variance in attitudes toward the elderly and for the additive index are explained through our analysis. The aforementioned factors explain attitudes toward the sick, handicapped and unemployed somewhat less. As expected, a higher degree of modernization leads to greater solidarity with the elderly, sick and unemployed. The Human Development Index is the strongest explanatory factor. The postulated influence of religion is also confirmed by our data. Higher levels of integration into religious communities positively and significantly affect support for the elderly, unemployed and the sick and handicapped. The effect produced by affiliation with different religious denominations is also, by and large, validated. Catholics differ only slightly from people with no religious affiliation, whereas Orthodox Christianity and Islam have a positive influence on attitudes toward the welfare state. The Protestant faith is the only denomination that deviates from the hypothesis. Protestants show higher levels of support than Catholics for the elderly and the sick, but demonstrate even less empathy for the unemployed than people without a religious affiliation. In contrast to our assumption, the existence of a strong welfare state does not lead to greater support of the elderly, sick and handicapped, and unemployed. Rather, support declines as the strength of the welfare state increases. Using an explanation offered by Ronald Inglehart (1997: 256ff.), one may assume that this is due to the effect of diminishing marginal utility. Because the welfare state is successful, the necessity of solidarity is not considered as important and consequently gains less support. This is only a speculation, however, and requires further research to be substantiated.

In regard to the socio-demographic variables, all of our hypotheses were confirmed. Age has a strong influence on citizens' attitudes toward all three groups. This is particularly the case for support of the elderly. Our hypothesis concerning the unemployed is also well proven. If the respondent is unemployed, this clearly increases solidarity with other unemployed people.

Conclusion

A highly developed welfare state is a common structural element in all Western European countries (Alber 1989: 34). The central goal of the welfare state is to protect "against the standard risks of old age, invalidity, sickness, unemployment and, only recently, maternity leave" (Schmid and Niketta 1998: 14). European countries achieve these ends in very different manners. Consequently, different welfare regimes are identifiable.

In this chapter, we first reconstructed the EU welfare state blueprint. There are a number of regulations and initiatives along with a significant amount of rhetoric surrounding the "European social model." The EU actually advocates a very basic model of a welfare state that protects its citizens against basic factors rendering them unemployable: sickness, being handicapped, maternity leave, age and unemployment. No additional concepts of a European welfare state exist in a legally binding form.

In the second part of this chapter, we analyzed citizens' attitudes toward the welfare state. The vast majority of citizens in all countries display solidarity with the elderly, sick and unemployed. This corresponds to the EU welfare state blueprint. Our analysis also revealed that the citizens' welfare state concepts exceed those of the EU. Most citizens desire a more active social state that intervenes in economic affairs. This is particularly valid for the new member states and accession candidates.

Finally, we attempted to explain the differences in citizens' attitudes. It is evident that those who stand to profit most from a welfare state also support it most strongly. Nevertheless, the most influential factors are the degree of modernization and the level of a country's public social expenditure. High levels of modernization have a positive influence on the solidarity of citizens, whereas high levels of public social expenditure have a negative effect, contrary to the conclusions of several earlier studies.

European citizens demand a strong welfare state, and several scholars have also advocated that the European welfare state take on a stronger form (Busch 1998: 292). Past experience has shown, however, that there is no consensus between member states to strengthen the EU's socio-political activities. This disinclination toward strengthening the EU's welfare state activities is likely to increase with eastward expansion. Governments of poorer EU countries have no interest in expanding welfare state standards, even if their citizens express high levels of support. The old EU countries face a similar constellation. The elite in almost every country pushes for a reduction of welfare state activities due to the difficulty of financing these programs, which is contradictory to most of the citizens' wishes. The extent to which this constellation affects the citizens' approval of the European integration process and its legitimacy remains an open question (Kersbergen 1997).

6   Democracy and civil society in a wider Europe

Although today's European Union began as an economic community, it has increasingly evolved into a political union. The Treaties of Amsterdam and Maastricht were particularly important for this development. The EU sees itself as a union of democratic states and characterizes its own institutional order as democratic. The constitutional draft clearly expresses the fundamental significance democracy plays in the EU. In fact, a quotation from Thucydides comes before the preamble, "Our Constitution ... is called democracy because power is in the hands not of a minority but of the greatest number." Article 2 of the draft continues to define EU basic values, saying that democracy belongs among the core values of the EU: "The Union is founded on the values of respect for human dignity, freedom, democracy, equality, the rule of law and respect for human rights, including the rights of persons belonging to minorities." The constitutional draft further specifies the EU's conception toward a particular form of democracy. It sees itself as a union of representative democracies and also endorses elements of a participatory democracy in which the inclusion of civil society is emphasized (Conference of Representatives 2004). In the first section of this chapter, we reconstruct the EU's understanding of democracy in greater detail. We then analyze the extent to which current and future EU citizens hold democratic values. Finally, we attempt to explain the differences in democratic beliefs.

Support of the basic values and principles of democracy, however, is only one side of the coin. International comparative political research has increasingly signaled that a democracy's stability depends on the development of a civil society.[1] Not only must citizens accept and support the democratic structure imposed from above, but also internalize it. David Easton (1979: 190ff.) distinguishes attitudes toward the political regime (democracy) from attitudes toward the political community, which constitute a civil society.

> Using the concept of "political regime," he signifies the key characteristics of institutional order ... These features form the political system's identity as democratic and demarcate it from authoritarian and totalitarian regimes. Furthermore, the political community as a unit, to which the

individual feels he belongs and to which he shows his loyalty, fulfills an important function for the regime's survival.

(Gabriel 1994: 99)

Consequently, the second part of this chapter analyzes civil society. We first reconstruct the EU concepts of civil society and then analyze civic engagement in different countries. Finally, we attempt to explain the discovered differences.

Democracy as representative democracy

EU concepts of democracy

In an etymological sense, democracy means popular government. Robert Dahl, among others, emphasizes that democracy in the sense of popular rule is impossible and therefore remains an ideal. A government of the many is, however, feasible. Dahl characterizes this as a polyarchy, the model for a representative democracy. "Representative systems with widely inclusive adult electorates are a special, twentieth-century historically distinctive type of (non-ideal) democracy" (Dahl 1997: 94). Dahl (1989: 10ff.) defines seven distinguishing criteria that form a polyarchy and representative democracy: 1) Elected representatives make government decisions, 2) Elected representatives are chosen in free, fair and rotational elections, 3) All adults maintain the active right to vote, 4) All adults maintain the passive right to vote, 5) All citizens have the right to express their opinion toward political issues freely, 6) Different sources of information are free and legally accessible, 7) Every citizen has the right to found a party or interest group independent of the state. Using Dahl's criteria the EU can be defined as a polyarchy, or representative democracy. Likewise, it expects its member states to share these convictions. We discuss each criterion in the subsequent paragraphs.

Elected representatives make EU decisions. This includes officials of both the European Parliament and members of the European Council and Council of Ministries. The latter groups are made up of nationally-elected government representatives. Article 46, "The principle of representative democracy" in Title VI, "The democratic life of the Union" of Part I of the constitutional draft, reads as follows:

(1) The functioning of the Union shall be founded on representative democracy. (2) Citizens are directly represented at Union level in the European Parliament. Member States are represented in the European Council by their Heads of State or Government and in the Council by their governments, themselves democratically accountable either to their national Parliaments, or to their citizens.

(Conference of Representatives 2004)

The European Parliament and national governments are chosen in free elections every four or five years (Article I-19–2 of the constitutional draft). At the European level, the constitutional draft grants all citizens the active and passive right to vote (Article 8: EU citizenship). Likewise, national constitutions afford the active and passive right to vote to their citizens. Article II-71 regulates the freedom of expression and information. This article states,

> (1) Everyone has the right to freedom of expression. This right shall include freedom to hold opinions and to receive and impart information and ideas without interference by public authority regardless of frontiers. (2) The freedom and pluralism of the media shall be respected.

Article II-72 of the constitutional draft regulates the freedom to assemble and associate.

> (1) Everyone has the right to freedom of peaceful assembly and to freedom of association at all levels, in particular in political, trade union and civic matters, which implies the right of everyone to form and to join trade unions for the protection of his or her interests. (2) Political parties at the Union level contribute to expressing the political will of the citizens of the Union.

Comparing the EU constitutional regulations to Dahl's criteria, a double legitimacy of representative democracy within the EU becomes apparent. European citizens elect the European Parliament, and national citizens elect their respective national governments either in a direct or parliamentary manner.[2] Member states must observe these EU beliefs because regulations codified in EU law are binding. Complaints concerning violations are handled by the European Court of Justice. The Commission, Council or the European Parliament can also threaten member states with sanctions to enforce compliance with the democratic rules. Under certain conditions, like a grave and persistent violation of fundamental rights, Article 7 of the Amsterdam Treaty grants the Council the right to suspend certain member state privileges. For example, when the FPÖ party gained seats in the Austrian government, the EU applied sanctions.[3] Finally, as a central requirement for admitting accession candidates, the Copenhagen criteria require countries to accept and implement EU regulations (European Commission 2001b). Turkey is currently carrying out various political reforms, such as more rights for the Kurdish minority, in order to satisfy membership demands. Only time will tell whether they will succeed in this goal.

Citizens' attitudes toward democracy

Unfortunately, it is not possible to measure all dimensions of the EU's blueprint on democracy with the available data. Therefore, we focus on measuring the support of democracy at a more abstract level. In doing so, we utilize Dieter Fuchs's proposal (1997, 1999a, 1999b, 2000), which distinguishes three hierarchical levels of support for democracy: basic values, structure and performance (Fuchs 1997: 83ff.). Support for basic democratic values constitutes the topmost level, political culture. Citizens must perceive democracy as the best option among different political systems and reject autocratic systems. The second level, citizens' attitudes toward the political structure of democracy, refers to the selective implementation of democratic culture and delineates the democratic institutional system set forth in national constitutions. Citizens rejecting a particular democratic institutional system may still hold democratic values. For instance, if citizens want the European Parliament to make more laws or want the ability to elect the president of the Commission directly, this counts as a change within the institutional system and is still completely compatible with democratic values. Attitudes toward the political process form the third and lowest level of Fuchs's model. This refers to concrete actions taken by actors within an institutional system in order to achieve their goals. Once again, a critical position does not necessarily contradict democratic values. For example, criticizing the Commission neither signifies a citizen's desire for other institutional systems or anti-democratic feelings. Seeing as how acceptance of the first level of basic democratic values is the only level central for our purposes, we will solely focus on this level in the following analysis.

Four items measure basic attitudes toward democracy and democratic culture. Two of these items measure direct support for democracy. The first reads as follows:

> I'm going to describe various types of political systems and ask what you think about each as a way of governing this country. Please tell me whether you find the following forms of government are very good, pretty good, good, rather bad or very bad.

One of the political systems for which respondents had to give an opinion was democracy ("one should have a democratic political system"). The second item that measures direct support for democracy reads: "I'm going to read off some things that people sometimes say about a democratic political system. Please tell me whether you completely agree, agree, disagree or completely disagree." One of these statements was "Democracy may have problems but it's better than any other form of government." The results from Table 6.1 show almost universal support for the idea of democracy among all citizens. This finding confirms Hans-Dieter Klingemann (1999),

Table 6.1 Support of democratic values (%)

	"The country should have a democratic political system"	"Democracy is better than any other form of government"
EU-15	93.6	93.5
Denmark	98.0	98.6
Greece	97.9	96.6
Sweden	97.4	94.3
Netherlands	96.7	96.4
Italy	96.6	94.3
Austria	96.3	96.9
Western Germany	95.4	97.3
Spain	94.3	93.8
Eastern Germany	92.1	92.8
Luxembourg	92.1	95.0
Portugal	91.9	92.6
Ireland	91.6	93.2
Belgium	90.6	92.0
France	89.2	93.3
Finland	88.3	90.5
Great Britain	86.8	77.7
Enlargement I	88.1	89.3
Malta	93.6	93.9
Czech Rep.	92.9	92.6
Slovenia	89.5	90.1
Latvia	88.2	88.9
Hungary	87.4	83.0
Estonia	86.8	90.3
Lithuania	85.8	90.7
Slovakia	84.1	84.5
Poland	83.6	89.3
Enlargement II	87.9	81.2
Romania	88.7	78.2
Bulgaria	87.0	84.3
Turkey	91.7	87.9

who showed abstract democratic values to be universal values, seeing as they enjoy support in almost every society.

The results of the second dimension for measuring democratic culture – support or rejection of autocratic regimes – are somewhat different. Two items are available for measuring this dimension. Interviewees were asked to respond to the following statements: "Having a strong leader who does not have to bother with parliament and elections" and "Having army rule." The percentage of respondents who considered these statements to be "very good" or "fairly good" are reported in Table 6.2.

The first question appears to measure attitudes towards democracy particularly well, in that a government controlled by the parliament and citizens is a central characteristic and a good measure of Dahl's first criterion. At the aggregate level, it is apparent that few old and Enlargement I state

Table 6.2 Support of authoritarian values (%)

	"The country should have a strong leader who does not have to bother with parliament and elections"	"Having the army rule the country"
EU-15	**24.0**	**4.8**
Greece	8.7	9.7
Denmark	13.9	0.8
Italy	15.6	4.4
Western Germany	15.6	1.9
Austria	16.3	1.8
Sweden	21.1	6.6
Spain	23.1	7.8
Eastern Germany	23.3	1.9
Finland	25.2	5.7
Great Britain	25.8	6.8
Ireland	26.8	4.2
Netherlands	27.2	1.1
Belgium	31.6	4.5
France	34.5	4.0
Portugal	36.5	9.0
Luxembourg	44.8	7.6
Enlargement I	**27.5**	**5.8**
Czech Rep.	16.8	2.1
Estonia	18.6	3.3
Malta	18.9	4.1
Slovakia	19.8	7.4
Hungary	20.4	3.0
Poland	22.2	17.8
Slovenia	23.9	4.6
Lithuania	53.7	4.7
Latvia	57.8	5.4
Enlargement II	**56.5**	**19.8**
Bulgaria	45.0	11.3
Romania	66.7	27.9
Turkey	**66.1**	**24.7**

citizens show acceptance of totalitarian rule. This does not hold true for Bulgaria and Romania, and especially not for Turkey. More than half of Accession II citizens and two-thirds of the Turkish population are receptive to the idea of a strong leader (see Pickel and Jacobs 2001: 6). Answers to the second question yield similar results, albeit to a much lesser degree. With the integration of Bulgaria and Romania into the EU, support for one of the EU's central pillars, the idea of democracy, will dissipate. If Turkey accedes, this support will dissipate further.

Excursus: Attitudes toward different normative models of democracy

We have focused solely on support of core democratic elements. Within this broad concept, there exist multiple models compatible with basic democratic principles. From discussions on democratic theory, Dieter Fuchs derives three models of democracies: a libertarian model, a liberal model and a socialist model.[4] All three models share the aforementioned core democratic elements, but differ in certain additional features. Ensuring individual freedom is central to the *libertarian* model. The state's only role is to protect the rights of the individual. Further laws and state responsibilities are interpreted as an attack on an individual's rights and are therefore opposed. In this regard, the libertarian model propagates a minimal state role. In the *liberal* model outlined by John Rawls, the individual must first be put in the position to take advantage of his or her freedom. It therefore becomes necessary that everyone be protected against basic risks and that basic social rights are ensured. The liberal model advocates a limited welfare state in this regard. If put to the test, however, the principle of freedom outweighs equality. In the *socialist* model, the principle of equality has priority over freedom. Under constitutional law, the state is responsible to safeguard its citizens' well-being and to establish equality. This can only be realized in a complete welfare state that intervenes in the economy and aims to redistribute resources. Additionally, the socialist model includes more direct citizen participation (see Fuchs 1997: 88, 1999b: 125). Table 6.3 (Fuchs 1999b: 125) summarizes the key features of all three models.

In previous chapters, we have seen that the EU prefers a moderate welfare state that guarantees basic needs, but guarantees almost no additional social rights. In regard to economic controls through political means, the EU also maintains a more passive, liberal position. Even though the EU acknowledges the importance of European citizens and has become more receptive to them in the past few years, one cannot speak of widespread participation because citizens do not have direct influence on political decisions. We will analyze this more closely in the next section. Overall, the EU prefers a liberal democratic system, but this may not be the type of democracy that EU citizens prefer. We are, unfortunately, unable to operationalize all of Fuchs's aspects with the

Table 6.3 Dimensions of different democracy models

	Libertarian democracy	Liberal democracy	Socialist democracy
Political realization of social rights	no	yes	yes
Constitutional guarantee of social rights	no	no	yes
Constitutional guarantee of direct citizen participation	no	no	yes

available data, due to the fact that a measurement for civil participation is missing. As Table 6.3 shows, two attributes satisfactorily distinguish the three models from one another. Questions concerning the political realization of social rights (the distinguishing characteristic of the liberal model) and the constitutional safeguarding of social rights (the distinguishing characteristic of the socialist model) allow one to determine interviewees' preferences for a particular model. By using the following questions, we are able to operationalize the three models.

The first attribute relates to the political realization of social rights. Unlike the libertarian model, the liberal model is characterized by the guarantee of "just care with basic social commodities" (Fuchs 1997: 89). An item in the European Values Study measures this value directly:

> In order to be considered "just," what should a society provide? Please tell me for each statement if it is important or unimportant to you: Guaranteeing that basic needs are met for all, in terms of food, housing, clothes, education, and health.

The interviewee answered the question on a 5-point scale ranging from "very important" to "not at all important." First of all, the question is directed at the society and not the state. Second, the scale is a measurement of what people think to be "just." Therefore, this question is best used to separate the libertarian model from the other two more "ambitious" variants of democracy.

The difference between the liberal and socialist model lies in the constitutional guarantee of social rights. The former model does not include this concept, whereas the latter supports it. The following question measures citizens' attitudes toward the constitutional safeguarding of basic needs. Respondents were asked to identify where they stood on a scale of 1 to 10 regarding two positions: "Individuals should take more responsibility for providing for themselves" (10) *or* "the state should take more responsibility to ensure that everyone is provided for" (1). If an interviewee desires the state neither to take responsibility for social security nor provide basic needs, then we place them in the libertarian model. If an interviewee believes that the state should provide basic needs, but also endorse individual responsibility in all respects, we categorize them in the liberal model. Finally, we place all interviewees who support the provision of basic needs as well as the state taking on most responsibilities in the socialist model (see Table 6.4).[5]

Table 6.5 shows the percentage of people from each particular country who support the three models. Few people support the libertarian model in Europe. Only the Czech Republic and Denmark demonstrate support levels above 10 percent. Most interviewees prefer the liberal or socialist model. Citizens of the EU-15 countries in particular support the liberal model; the former GDR is the only country in this group with a majority supporting the socialist model. The picture for the new member states is rather different,

Table 6.4 Measuring three models of democracy

		"Individuals should take more responsibility for themselves (10)" or "The state should take more responsibility in ensuring everyone is provided for (1)"	
		Values 6–10	Values 1–5
"In order to be 'just', what should a society provide? Guarantee that basic needs are met for all" (1 = very important; 5 = not at all important	Value 3–5	Preference for libertarian model (6.2%)	not classified (6.1%)
	Value 1–2	Preference for liberal model (51.1%)	Preference for socialist model (36.6%)

Table 6.5 Support of different models of democracy (%)[1]

	Libertarian democracy	Liberal democracy	Socialist democracy
EU-15	6.7	56.7	30.8
France	6.9	*68.9*	21.1
Western Germany	6.3	*68.7*	21.1
Austria	9.7	*65.0*	20.4
Great Britain	5.2	*63.8*	25.3
Sweden	9.6	*63.6*	22.9
Ireland	3.8	*62.9*	27.5
Netherlands	6.0	*60.1*	29.9
Luxembourg	6.9	*59.7*	23.5
Finland	4.3	*59.6*	32.1
Portugal	5.5	*56.7*	31.9
Belgium	5.1	*53.7*	36.9
Denmark	21.5	*50.9*	17.6
Greece	1.8	*48.8*	44.8
Italy	5.7	*44.3*	42.2
Spain	5.7	*43.2*	41.4
Eastern Germany	3.9	42.7	*47.1*
Enlargement I	5.9	41.1	*46.9*
Malta	3.3	*54.3*	41.0
Poland	5.1	*49.5*	40.3
Lithuania	4.2	*48.9*	39.6
Czech Rep.	16.0	*44.5*	32.5
Hungary	0.9	40.8	*52.7*
Slovakia	2.0	37.7	*55.0*
Latvia	2.2	33.8	*57.7*
Estonia	8.3	31.6	*49.0*
Slovenia	3.0	26.3	*65.8*
Enlargement II	4.9	*50.6*	36.8
Romania	2.5	*52.3*	36.9
Bulgaria	7.7	*48.7*	36.6
Turkey	4.1	*47.8*	41.5

1 Italicized numbers indicate the majority in the particular country. Within each group, countries were sorted according to their support of the liberal model.

because in five countries, a plurality prefers a socialist democratic model. Also in the remaining accession countries sizeable minorities support the socialist democratic model.

In conclusion, the EU sees itself as a liberal democracy that advocates the provision of basic needs for its citizens but does not go so far as to include state responsibility. Consequently, enforceable social rights are not part of the constitutional draft. Pluralities in all EU-15 member states and in three accession countries support this liberal model. The new EU members prefer a socialist democratic model, in which the state takes on responsibility for social security. Therefore, we assume that demands concerning this policy will grow with EU enlargement.

Explaining democratic values

The emergence and stability of democracies has been a major field of research in comparative political science. With the so-called third wave of democratic transformation after the dissolution of the Soviet Union, this field has once more experienced a revival (Berglund *et al.* 1998, Huntington 1991). In this research, citizens' democratic values take a backseat to the origin and stability of democratic institutions. Some of the explanations offered in this field, however, can also be used to explain democratic values.

In his 1959 essay "Some Social Requisites of Democracy," Seymour M. Lipset asserts that a relationship between socio-economic modernization and democratization exists. This relationship has been empirically verified in several studies (Vanhanen 1997, Lipset 2000). Four causal relations lie behind this correlation (Rössel 2000). First, economic growth leads to the emergence of a middle class, which prevents social polarization. Second, economic growth leads to more consumption among all classes, which has a tempering effect on labor unions. Third, this leads to the assumption that the elite becomes less skeptical toward democracy. Finally, modernization goes hand-in-hand with an improved educational system. A higher level of education leads to more tolerance and to the rejection of ideologies that attempt to reduce freedom. In regard to this last factor, Lipset explicitly refers to democratic values and claims that a causal relation between modernization and democratic values exists. Other authors (Dalton 1988, Inglehart 1997, Welzel 2000 and 2002) have further expanded upon this thesis, saying that modernization leads to increased economic and cognitive resources, which, in turn, results in an increase of citizens' participatory abilities and claims. This civic participation increases pressure to build democratic institutions. Thus, modernization is not a sufficient condition for democratization, but it does bring societies into what Samuel Huntington calls a "transition zone," where democratization is first made possible.

From a historical perspective, democracies first developed in Protestant countries, and then later in Catholic, Orthodox Christian and Muslim countries. Two hypotheses can explain this historical difference. First, in comparison to other religions, Protestantism emphasizes the concept of individualism, an element conducive to forming democratic attitudes. Second, the link between church and state, which would complicate the development of democratic institutions, is not as strong in the Protestant faith (Lipset 2000: 399). The negative relationship between Catholicism and democracy, however, becomes invalid for the period following World War II.

The number of democracies in Orthodox Christian and in Muslim countries is substantially below average (Lipset 2000). Only one-quarter of the 47 countries with a Muslim majority are democracies today (Norris and Inglehart 2002: 238). Samuel Huntington (1996) assumes that the Muslim faith contains elements that are incompatible with democratic ideals. Empirically, this thesis is extremely controversial. By using data from the World Values Survey, Pippa Norris and Ronald Inglehart (2002) as well as Yilmaz Esmer (2002) tested whether Muslim citizens' views on democratic values differ from their Christian counterparts. Both studies show that citizens' democratic value orientations in Muslim countries do not significantly differ from those of citizens in Christian countries (see also Tessler 2002). Using our data, we will test Huntington's thesis of whether Muslims and Orthodox Christians support democratic ideals less than Catholics and Protestants.

Finally, we assume that a population's experience with their democratic institutions will affect attitudes toward democracy. The longer people live in a democracy, the more they come to trust the democratic institutional system and the more they support the ideas implemented by the system. "The chance of acquiring the typical value orientation toward democracy may vary with time and depend on the consistency of the democratic structures" (Gabriel 1994: 103). This socialization hypothesis of democratic attitudes has been empirically tested several times (Müller and Seligson 1994). In another example, Dieter Fuchs (1999a) explains differences in democratic attitudes between East and West Germany by referring to this socialization hypothesis. Consequently, in our analysis, we utilize a variable measuring the number of continuous years as a democracy since 1920 (Inglehart 1997: 357ff.).

Tables 6.6 and 6.7 include the results from our multiple regression models. The dependent variables are the four aforementioned attitudes toward democratic values.[6] We also formed an additive index from the two variables measuring support of democracy and support of an authoritarian regime.[7] The regression models do not provide a suitable explanation of the differences in attitudes. This is particularly the case for support of democratic values. The explanation of attitudes toward authoritarian regimes is somewhat better. Both modernization factors confirm our expectations, in that the degree of modernization and the interviewee's level of education have a clear positive effect on support for democracy and rejection of an authoritarian regime. On the other hand, experience with democracy, measured by the number of continuous years under democratic rule, does not play the positive role we hypothesized. This corresponds to other findings, which state, "Assumption that the acceptance of democratic principles is strongest in countries with

Table 6.6 Explaining support of democratic values: linear regressions

	"The country should have a democratic political system"	"Democracy is better than any other form of Government"	Additive index "support of Democracy"
Modernization level			
HDI	0.272	0.268	0.268
Education	0.166	0.154	0.178
Religion[a]			
Protestants	0.036	0.024	0.039
Roman Catholics	0.041	0.048	0.049
Orthodox Christians	0.117	0.067	0.109
Muslims	0.147	0.118	0.143
Years under democratic rule	−0.045	−0.044	−0.033
R^2	**0.065**	**0.059**	**0.078**

The models represent standardized beta-coefficients from the OLS regression analysis.
If not indicated differently, coefficients are significant at the 1% level, * = significant at 5% level, + = not significant.
a   Category of reference: people who do not have a religious affiliation.

Table 6.7 Explaining support of authoritarian values

	"Having a strong leader"	"Having the army rule the country"	Additive index "support of authoritarian regime"
Modernization level			
HDI	0.427	0.267	0.435
Education	0.150	0.115	0.160
Religion[a]			
Protestants	0.006+	−0.010+	−0.001+
Roman Catholics	−0.030	−0.059	−0.048
Orthodox Christians	0.005+	−0.069	−0.022
Muslims	−0.027	−0.071	−0.058
Years under democratic rule	−0.242	−0.101	−0.225
R^2	**0.101**	**0.075**	**0.126**

The models represent standardized beta-coefficients from the OLS regression analysis.
If not indicated differently, coefficients are significant at the 1% level, * = significant at 5% level, + = not significant.
a   Category of reference: people who do not have a religious affiliation.

a long democratic tradition is not confirmed" (Gabriel 1994: 104). We can conclude that less support for democracy is found in traditional democratic countries. Moreover, these countries more strongly advocate authoritarian regimes.

The influence of religion and religious affiliation is also ambivalent. On the one hand, members of religious communities support democracy more strongly than people with no religious affiliation. At the same time, however, the more religious support authoritarian regimes more strongly, with Protestants being the only exception to this finding. Muslims differ from the other denominations in that their support is particularly strong for both forms of government. Before summarizing our analysis, we investigate the second field of democratic values – attitudes toward civil society.

The citizens' Europe: civil society

The concept of civil society has experienced a revival in academic and political debate over the last 20 years. Analysts partially attribute the collapse of socialist states to civil societal activities, which brought about a peaceful societal transformation through protest. Other scholars focus on established Western democracies, hoping that groups in civil society can solve structural problems. Civil societal engagement is seen as a solution to political disenchantment and as a vehicle to social integration in ever-increasingly individualized societies (Gosewinkel *et al.* 2003).

We focus on the *political* function of civil society in democracies (Gabriel *et al.* 2002). The thesis that a developed civil society is a necessary prerequisite for a vital democracy has been a central topic of democratic theory since Alexis de Tocqueville. Robert D. Putnam's work (1993, 2000) especially enriched the debate. Putnam considers civil society to consist of a network of voluntary organizations in society, such as self help groups, work unions, neighborhood associations, farmers' cooperatives, churches etc. Putnam associates his civil society concept with social capital development theory. Membership and participation in voluntary organizations lead to cooperative learning, development of mutual trust, and experience in producing collective goods. Putnam characterizes these capabilities as social capital. The social capital produced by participation in civil society thus has various positive political consequences (Paxton 2002). Not only does cooperation between people from different social backgrounds bridge social cleavages and strengthen the democratically important value of tolerance, but citizens engaged in civil society groups also critically observe democracy and elected officials.[8] As a result, the political elite feels controlled by citizens and proves to be more responsive to their demands. In this manner, a core element of democracy is strengthened in that a strong connection between political decisions and the citizens' will is formed.[9] It is a controversial topic as to whether all of Putnam's hope associated with civil society holds true (see the contributions in Pharr and Putnam 2000).

Increased discussion concerning the concept of civil society did not go unnoticed by the EU (Kaelble 2003). The EU has discovered that the citizens and actors in civil society are important elements for democracies. The EU has thus developed corresponding beliefs toward the role of civil society in the democratic decision-making process.[10] In the following section, we will reconstruct this role more precisely. We then test whether and to what degree the development of civil society differs among member states and accession countries. Finally, we attempt to explain these differences.

How the EU perceives the role of civil society

The EU blueprint of representative democracy has been supplemented with elements of participatory democracy over the last couple of years. In a commitment to cultivate dialogue with citizens, organizations and the civil society, the Commission will engage in expansive hearings. Section 4, Article 47 of the constitutional draft provides evidence of this phenomenon (Conference of Representatives 2004). The article states:

> 1. The institutions shall, by appropriate means, give citizens and representative associations the opportunity to make known and publicly exchange their views in all areas of Union action. 2. The institutions shall maintain an open, transparent and regular dialogue with representative associations and civil society. 3. The Commission shall carry out broad consultations with parties concerned in order to ensure that the Union's actions are coherent and transparent. 4. Not less than one million citizens who are nationals of a significant number of member states may take the initiative of inviting the Commission, within the framework of its powers, to submit any appropriate proposal on matters where citizens consider that a legal act of the Union is required for the purpose of implementing the Constitution. European laws shall determine the provisions for the procedures and conditions required for such a citizens' initiative, including the minimum number of member states from which such citizens must come.

Even though this formulation sounds very vague in regard to the role of civil society in the democratic decision-making process, it certainly provides constitutional anchoring. There are three other EU documents that define the role of civil society more specifically. These include the 2001 "European Governance" White Book, the "Report from the Commission on European Governance" as well as the 2002 "General principles and minimum standards for consultation of interested parties by the Commission" (EU Commission 2001a, 2002, 2003). All three documents highlight the importance of integrating civil societal actors. The EU hopes to improve support for its institutions by strengthening these actors.

The July 2001 White Book argues that the EU has lost contact with its citizens and that citizens feel alienated by Brussels. The Irish rejection of the Nice Treaty demonstrates this viewpoint. Citizens see the EU as incapable of dealing with important issues like unemployment, a problem the EU seems unable to get under control. An additional problem is that citizens do not sufficiently understand the way in which the institutions function. This lack of knowledge causes people to turn their back on the EU. EU "governance" reform should improve this situation, and the EU will also make proposals to improve EU communication and information policies. By offering channels for feedback, criticism and protest, citizens might feel more involved in the discussion concerning Europe. Moreover, the White Book recommends that the role of the European Economic and Social Committee should be strengthened and receive an advisory role in formulating proposals. The authors also demand "a greater culture of consultation and dialogue."

After the publication of the "European Governance" White Book, the Commission produced a December 2002 report, which presented a summary of achievements. In this report, the Commission describes how it has improved its information policy, particularly regarding the internet. For example, a website including an overview of civil society organizations was created.

Lastly, the Commission released a 2002 report entitled "General principles and minimum standards for consultation of interested parties by the Commission." The Commission emphasized that EU institutions maintain legislative power, but also clarified that civil societal actors should play an important advisory role. Furthermore, they established minimum standards and procedural criteria that must be followed when interacting with civil societal actors (publication requirements, adherence to time periods, acknowledgement of receipt etc.).

We now summarize the findings of the EU's blueprint for civil society. The EU sees itself as a representative democracy with a double legitimacy at the national and supranational level. Participatory elements have augmented this belief over the past few years. Although actors in civil society do not directly take part in the decision-making process, their strength has increased. Reasons for strengthening civil society bear resemblance to Robert Putnam's belief that civil society is an important factor for the stability and quality of a democracy. A strong civil society reduces the likelihood of alienating citizens from EU institutions, in that it makes citizens feel included in the decision-making process (European Commission 2001a: 3ff.). EU representatives are, now to a much greater degree, held accountable and forced to involve civil societal actors. Consequently, representatives are likely to incorporate the interests of citizens and civil society. Such responsiveness is a feature of a good democracy and also strengthens the citizens' identification with democratic institutions.

Strength of the civil society in EU member and accession countries

In this section, we analyze the degree to which civil society has developed in the different countries. The European Values Study allows us to determine three key figures for measuring the strength of civil society.

First there is membership in voluntary associations: The European Values Study posed the following question:

> Please look carefully at the following list of voluntary organizations and activities and say, which, if any, you belong to? Social welfare services for elderly, handicapped or deprived people; Religious or church

organizations; Education, arts, music or cultural activities; Labor unions; Political parties or groups; Local community action; Third world development or human rights; Conservation, environmental, animal rights groups; Professional associations; Youth work; Sports or recreation; Women's groups; Peace movement; Voluntary organizations concerned with health; Other groups; Belong to none.

The spectrum of groups is very comprehensive, in that it includes traditional interest organizations like labor unions, new social movements and different welfare-oriented groups. By naming the additional category of "other groups," the question remains open. However, the question does not determine whether interviewees are members of several organizations within any given category. We formed two variables for the analysis of this question. The first measures the number of categories of groups to which an interviewee belongs. The second variable measures whether an interviewee is a member of at least one organization (see Table 6.8).

Membership in civil society groups is highest in the EU-15 countries. The Enlargement I countries exhibit lower levels in comparison. The civil society sector is even less developed in Bulgaria and Romania, while civil society in Turkey is the least developed. There is significant variation within the first two country groups at the national level. The Scandinavian countries Finland, Sweden and Denmark along with the Netherlands demonstrate the greatest citizen participation in civil society groups, whereas the Southern European countries Spain and Portugal show the least activity. In Accession I countries, the Czech Republic, Slovenia and Slovakia significantly exceed the group average.[11]

Next we look at activity in voluntary associations. Membership in an organization or group says little about the interviewee's participation in the group's activities. One can argue that the effect Putnam and the EU desire for civil societies will only materialize when people actively participate in the groups. Fortunately, the European Values Study poses the question whether the interviewee is *active* in the group in which he or she is a member. We have constructed two variables from this question. One variable adds up the number of groups in which an interviewee is active. The second variable measures whether an interviewee is an active member of at least one organization. We discuss the empirical results after briefly presenting a third measure of civil societal engagement.

Finally we turn to social capital. We constructed an index of social capital, following Pippa Norris' suggestions (2002: 149). Social capital is composed of two dimensions. The first is structural, consisting of membership and activities in civil societal organizations. The second is cultural, consisting of trust in other citizens. According to Putnam's concept, the structural element of membership in voluntary associations generates the cultural element. We use the question regarding active membership in a voluntary organization to measure the first dimension. We use the following question to measure the

Table 6.8 Membership in civil society organizations

	Membership in at least one organization (%)	Mean of memberships in organizations
EU-15	57.7	**1.34**
Sweden	95.7	3.22
Netherlands	92.4	3.09
Denmark	84.4	1.91
Finland	80.1	1.86
Austria	66.8	1.50
Belgium	65.2	1.57
Luxembourg	58.2	1.39
Ireland	57.1	1.20
Greece	56.4	1.25
Western Germany	50.9	0.86
Italy	42.1	0.78
Eastern Germany	42.0	0.62
France	39.4	0.63
Great Britain	33.6	0.60
Spain	30.9	0.53
Portugal	27.6	0.40
Enlargement I	**39.8**	**0.64**
Slovakia	65.0	1.13
Czech Rep.	60.2	1.04
Slovenia	51.7	0.98
Malta	42.2	0.63
Estonia	33.5	0.51
Latvia	31.4	0.41
Hungary	30.8	0.45
Poland	25.0	0.40
Lithuania	18.6	0.26
Enlargement II	**22.0**	**0.34**
Bulgaria	22.9	0.36
Romania	21.1	0.31
Turkey	7.8	0.12

second dimension: "Generally speaking, would you say that most people can be trusted or that you need to be very careful in dealing with people?" (Answer alternatives being: "most people can be trusted" and "can't be too careful.") We combine these two variables into an additive index with values ranging from 1 (little social capital) to 3 (high degree of social capital).

On the aggregate level, the pattern from Table 6.8 is repeated in Table 6.9. Citizens in the EU-15 member states are distinctly more active in civil society groups and possess a higher level of social capital than citizens from the other three groups. Once more, Turkey reported the lowest values for both dimensions. Significant variations also exist in the first two country groups at the national level. Sweden is the model country for a highly developed civil society, while Spain and Portugal maintain much lower levels in these dimensions. In Accession I countries, the Czech Republic and Slovakia exhibit

Table 6.9 Doing voluntary work in civil society organizations and social capital

	Voluntary work in at least one organization (%)	Mean of voluntary work in organizations	Social capital
EU-15	32.3	0.56	1.70
Sweden	56.1	1.15	2.22
Netherlands	49.2	0.93	2.09
Denmark	37.2	0.57	2.03
Finland	38.0	0.64	1.96
Great Britain*	42.3	0.83	1.71
Ireland	32.6	0.61	1.69
Belgium	35.4	0.69	1.65
Greece	39.8	0.96	1.64
Austria	30.4	0.48	1.63
Eastern Germany	16.4	0.19	1.60
Italy	26.1	0.46	1.58
Spain	17.6	0.27	1.57
Luxembourg	30.2	0.63	1.55
Western Germany	22.0	0.28	1.54
France	27.1	0.38	1.48
Portugal	16.4	0.23	1.29
Enlargement I	25.3	0.40	1.46
Slovakia	51.4	0.81	1.68
Czech Rep.	33.2	0.50	1.58
Slovenia	28.5	0.54	1.50
Malta	28.6	0.52	1.49
Estonia	18.0	0.29	1.41
Lithuania	15.8	0.20	1.41
Latvia	22.4	0.29	1.40
Hungary	15.4	0.26	1.38
Poland	13.9	0.21	1.32
Enlargement II	17.3	0.24	1.36
Bulgaria	18.8	0.27	1.46
Romania	15.7	0.21	1.26
Turkey	6.4	0.10	1.13

*   There is no information for "activities in other voluntary organizations" available for Great Britain. Therefore the values for Great Britain are probably slightly underestimated.

above average values, which reach the average values of old EU countries. Overall, it is evident that the EU's blueprint for civil society receives the highest support from the old EU countries. Every EU expansion will dilute support for the EU civil society, as civil societal engagement in subsequent accession countries is lower on average.

An attempt to explain the strengths of civil society in the different countries

This is not the first attempt to explain membership and engagement in civil societal groups. Rather, we follow other authors' hypotheses and operationalizations. The works of Pippa Norris (2002) and James E. Curtis *et al.* (1992, 2001) are particularly helpful, due to the fact that they work with similar data sets (i.e. World Values Survey) and investigate country differences (most recently Paxton 2002). While Norris focuses primarily on the consequences of a strong civil society, Curtis *et al.* attempt to provide an explanation for its causes. The authors reconstruct hypotheses already existing on this topic, some of which are similar to variables explaining democratic values.

Some authors assume that a relationship exists between the level of modernization and the strength of civil society (Smith and Shen 2002). There are two reasons for this expected relationship. First, modernization leads to greater professional specialization and to differentiation among status positions. Interest organizations often emerge as trade or other associations in which people maintain similar social positions. These groups then try to implement their members' interests into the political process (Smith 1972). Seymour M. Lipset (1994: 2) assumes that this chain of causality, in which a middle class with several interest groups emerges due to economic development, explains the processes of democratization. Second, modernization is connected to a rise in welfare and free time. Along with higher education, these resources make people more flexible, thus making membership in associations easier. "Higher average levels of formal education in a nation tend to make people of that nation more ready and able to participate in associations as individuals on average ..., leading to greater associational prevalence in the aggregate" (Smith and Shen 2002: 101). In his research, David H. Smith (1972, Smith and Shen 2002) shows that a strong relationship does in fact exist between economic modernization and the development of civil society. We measure the degree of societal modernization with the Human Development Index. We expect a positive relationship between the degree of modernization and the development of the civil society sector. Additionally, we incorporate the interviewees' level of education into our analysis.

The USA represents the classical model of a developed civil society, which Alexis de Tocqueville attributes to its religious structure. The first groups of settlers were the Puritans, a Protestant sect that fled from religious persecution by the Anglican Church. These Puritan settlements consisted of decentralized, small units with an anti-hierarchical structure, emphasizing individual responsibility and self organization (de Tocqueville 2000, Lipset 1996). Unlike the denominations of Catholicism, Orthodox Christianity or Islam, the Protestant Church seems to be more egalitarian, participatory and anti-hierarchical. This gives their members a good opportunity to participate in church activities and to practise cooperation with others. These effects may transfer to the way these members engage in other civil societal groups.

Several authors have tried to test the thesis that Protestantism supports civil society engagement, unlike Orthodox Christianity, Islam, or Catholicism (Lipset 1994, Verba *et al.* 1995, Inglehart and Baker 2000, Curtis *et al.* 2001).

We adopt the ideas of these studies and test whether Protestants engage in civil society more than members of other religious denominations.

Finally, some scholars assert that the political-institutional environment influences the strength of civil society. The incentive for engaging in voluntary organizations is greater in democratic systems because restrictions for such engagement are lower than in dictatorships or totalitarian systems. Democracies link political decisions to citizens' preferences, which motivates citizens to join organizations and associations so that their interests and preferences are better heard. As compared to dictatorships and totalitarian systems, democracies have distinctly fewer restrictions to founding or to participating in voluntary organizations. Freedom of expression, assembly and demonstration are ensured rights in democracies. Membership in associations is also often fiscally supported. Consequently, we assume that the civil societal sector is more developed in societies that have a long history of democracy than in countries who have only had a short period of time as a democracy (Inglehart 1997, Inglehart and Baker 2000, Lipset 1994, Curtis *et al.* 2001). We measure this variable with the number of years a country has maintained democratic rule without disruption.

Marc M. Howard (2002) introduces another difference. He also shows that the civil societal sector in democracies is distinctly more developed than in authoritarian regimes. But in a comparative study between post-authoritarian (i.e. South Africa, South Korea, Chile and Argentina) and post-communist regimes, he illustrates that civil societal engagement in post-communist societies is clearly less developed than in post-authoritarian regimes. Howard offers three explanations for this difference. 1) Although communist regimes attempted to suppress the autonomous civil societal sector, this does not distinguish them from authoritarian governments. Communist regimes also constructed a state-controlled sector for association, in which citizen membership was partly obligatory.[12] This negative experience with a state-ordered civil society seems to have had a particular effect on citizens, reducing their readiness to organize in an association. 2) Communist regimes' massive control over public life led to the formation of a societal sphere, namely private networks of friends, in which one could express oneself freely. These networks have survived the transformation to democracy and a market economy and continue to play a very important function. As a result, the need to integrate in civil societal organization is rather small. 3) Lastly, many citizens in former communist societies are very disappointed with the results of the transformation process. They are satisfied with neither the economic nor political developments. The consequence is a blocking of civil society engagement. Bernhard Weßels (2003) demonstrates that membership in civil societal organizations in post-communist countries has drastically declined between 1990 and 2000. A large portion of this change is due to a downturn in the number of trade unions.

In order to test Howard's thesis, we include the variable "years a country was under communist control" in the regression analysis (Inglehart 1997).

Table 6.10 reflects the results of our causal analysis.[13] Some authors consider excluding union membership from the analysis because membership in unions is sometimes involuntary (Smith 1975: 239, Curtis *et al.* 2001: 789). We therefore conducted a separate analysis for which we excluded union membership, but this does not change the structure of the results.

As the R^2 values show, membership in civil society organizations and social capital can be explained very well, while the active engagement in these groups cannot. This might be due to the fact that the variation of this variable is rather small. Which factors explain membership in civil societal organizations? All models confirm the expected relationship between the degree of modernization and the level of civil societal involvement. The more modernized a society, the more people take part in voluntary organizations and the higher the levels of social capital. This is true for both modernization indicators, in which education has a rather strong influence. It is also apparent that democracies provide a propitious environment for the development of civil society. The longer a country is under democratic control, the more developed its civil society becomes (for similar results see Paxton 2002). The thesis that Protestants exhibit a higher level of civil societal engagement is also confirmed. The impact of other religions on civil society involvement is ambivalent and often not significant. Our analysis does not confirm Howard's findings (2002) that a socialist experience reduces engagement in voluntary organizations, regardless of the length of democratic control.[14]

Table 6.10 Explaining membership and activity in civil society organizations: linear regressions

	Membership in organizations	Activity in organizations	Social capital
Modernization level			
HDI	0.110	0.040	0.118
Education	0.197	0.150	0.215
Religion[a]			
Protestants	0.116	0.054	0.117
Roman Catholics	−0.007+	0.028	−0.011+
Orthodox Christians	0.018	0.042	−0.015*
Muslims	0.021	−0.007+	−0.028
Political-institutional environment			
Years under democratic rule	0.252	0.095	0.100
Years under socialist rule	0.055	−0.002+	0.012+
R^2	0.159	0.045	0.118

The models represent standardized beta-coefficients from the OLS regression analysis.
If not indicated differently, coefficients are significant at the 1% level, * = significant at 5% level, + = not significant.
a   Category of reference: people who do not have a religious affiliation.

Classification of different countries in regard to their democratic attitudes

In the previous sections, we looked at democracy and civil society separately. In this section, we analyze the two dimensions together. A simultaneous consideration of all variables allows us to determine the overall support of the EU blueprint. Discriminant analysis allows us to determine which of the variables separate the countries the most. We are then able to calculate the extent to which each interviewee and each country supports the EU blueprint.

The first task is to define reference groups, made up of so-called benchmark countries, for each dimension that embodies the EU blueprint to the highest degree. Denmark, West Germany and Austria form the reference group for EU democratic values.[15] The Netherlands and particularly Sweden act as benchmark countries for the civil society dimension. Table 6.11 depicts the results of a discriminant analysis.[16] The measures of fit for the analysis show that 60.3 percent of all interviewees were classified correctly. The majority of misclassifications can be traced back to Group 3 (non-benchmark countries). Due to the fact that the interviewees in Group 3 are not benchmark countries, this does not present a significant problem. Similarly, misclassifications between Groups 1 and 2 are also not particularly problematic, in that both dimensions are closely related.[17] Despite this relationship, both dimensions are surprisingly well-reflected in the data. Only two variables of the civil society dimension ("social capital" and "average activity") load on the democracy dimension. Social capital shows a positive effect on both aspects. Average membership rates in organizations discriminate best between countries. Other variables also exhibit very high values of explained variance. Due to its small variance, the variable "activity in organization" is the only one that does not separate countries well.

Our goal is to analyze the proximity of the countries to the EU blueprint. Table 6.12 provides results regarding national proximity to the EU blueprint on the country level. The first column illustrates the probability that an interviewee will support democratic values. The second column presents data for above average support of civil society. High values in the final column give the probability that an interviewee supports neither dimension, which would indicate that he or she is relatively far removed from the EU position.[18]

First, we look at the aggregate level, which reveals a by-now familiar pattern. Support for the EU position is greatest in the old member states and subsequently decreases with each accession group. Whereas only 40 percent of the old EU citizens are categorized as "distanced" from the EU position, this number rises to 52 percent in new member countries and to 60 percent in Accession II countries. Two-thirds of all interviewees from Turkey show low levels of support for democracy and civil society. Some national differences exist within the aggregate groups. The Czech Republic and Malta are the

Table 6.11 Civil society involvement and democratic values: differentiation between benchmark countries and the remaining countries

	Discriminance function	
	"Civil society"[a]	*"Support of democracy"*[a]
Civil society		
Membership in organization	0.929	
Social capital	0.495	0.141
Activity in organization	0.355	−0.225
Democracy		
"Democracy is better than any other form of government"		0.731
"Having a strong leader" (disagreement)		0.633
"Having the army rule the country" (disagreement)		0.555
"The country should have a democratic political system"		0.533
Eigenvalue	0.279	0.040
Canonical correlation	0.467	0.196
% of explained variance[b]	80.500	19.500
Group centroids		
Benchmark 1 (DK, A, W-G)	0.246	0.618
Benchmark 2 (SE, NL)	1.577	0.228
Group 3 (remaining countries)	−0.209	−0.119

Classification results[c]	Groups (predicted)		
	Benchmark 1	Benchmark 2	Group 3
Benchmark 1 (DK, A, W-G)	60.6 % (1,584)	14.2 % (372)	25.2 % (659)
Benchmark 2 (SE, NL)	28.1 % (522)	55.5 % (1,032)	16.5 % (306)
Group 3 (remaining countries)	31.3 % (5,337)	7.9 % (1,350)	60.8 % (10,390)
Classified correctly	60.3 %		

a   Pooled within-group correlations between discriminating variables and canonical discriminant function.
b   Variance refers to rotated solution.
c   In order to take all countries into account equally, cases were weighted by sample size.

only Accession I countries close to the EU-15 average for the democracy dimension, whereas Bulgaria and Romania exhibit values below the average for Accession I countries. Turkey is the farthest from the EU blueprint in both dimensions. The Scandinavian countries and the Netherlands exhibit particularly strong support for the EU position.

Summary

The EU feels an obligation to provide the basic principles of a representative democracy and also expects this from its member states. More than 80 percent of European citizens support democracy and consider it the best form of government; however, an affinity to authoritarian regimes is apparent in a couple of countries. This is particularly the case in Turkey and Romania, and

Table 6.12 Closeness of countries to the EU blueprint (benchmark countries)

	Probability of closeness to EU-position "democracy"	Probability of closeness to EU-position "civil society"	Probability of distance EU-positions in both dimensions
EU-15	**0.35**	**0.26**	**0.39**
Sweden	0.27	0.53	0.19
Netherlands	0.28	0.52	0.20
Denmark	0.43	0.32	0.25
Finland	0.31	0.35	0.34
Austria	0.39	0.26	0.35
Belgium	0.34	0.27	0.39
Western Germany	0.43	0.17	0.40
Greece	0.39	0.20	0.41
Luxembourg	0.32	0.27	0.42
Ireland	0.35	0.23	0.42
Eastern Germany	0.38	0.16	0.46
Italy	0.37	0.17	0.46
France	0.36	0.15	0.49
Spain	0.35	0.16	0.49
Portugal	0.29	0.15	0.56
Enlargement I	**0.31**	**0.17**	**0.52**
Czech Rep.	0.36	0.20	0.44
Malta	0.37	0.15	0.48
Slovenia	0.32	0.20	0.49
Slovakia	0.29	0.20	0.51
Estonia	0.31	0.15	0.54
Hungary	0.31	0.14	0.54
Poland	0.28	0.14	0.58
Lithuania	0.28	0.13	0.59
Latvia	0.25	0.15	0.60
Enlargement II	**0.26**	**0.14**	**0.60**
Bulgaria	0.31	0.15	0.55
Romania	0.22	0.14	0.65
Turkey	0.22	0.12	0.66

also with the majority in Latvia and Lithuania, who feel more assured with a strong leader able to govern without a parliament and elections.

The second dimension of the EU blueprint is the strength of civil society. The EU propagates greater involvement of civil societal actors in the decision making process. This has particularly been the case over the past couple of years. Various studies have shown that a developed civil society, which includes significant citizen participation in associations and generalized trust in others, positively affects democracy (Putnam *et al.* 1993). We have seen that civil society is strongest in the old EU member states, while this support decreases with every accession round. A discriminant analysis including all variables of both dimensions confirms and strengthens these assertions.

We also attempted to explain attitudes toward democracy and civil society. The degree of a society's modernization has a clear and positive influence on both dimensions. In this regard, the modernization process might lead to an alignment with and to a stronger support of democracy in accession countries. The EU wants to encourage this sort of modernization (Delhey 2003a). Cultural factors also influence democracy and civil society. On the one hand, members of all religious communities support democracy somewhat more than people with no religious affiliation. On the other hand, with the exception of Protestants, they also support authoritarian regimes to a greater degree. Moreover, the Orthodox Christian and especially Islamic tradition have a negative influence on the development of social capital. We assume that these religious traditions change at a much slower rate than modernization factors.

Overall, the expansion of the EU will not only make attitudes toward the political realm more heterogeneous but will also lead to less support of the EU position. Therefore, it appears that Oskar Gabriel is correct in stating that present, distinctive national characteristics

> [will] influence the rapidity and direction of the future socio-economic and political integration process. ... Even after the establishment of a common European market, the process of European integration will discover its boundaries when it attempts to address the cultural characteristics of its member states.
>
> (Gabriel 1994: 131)

7 Summary and future prospects

The number of member states in the European Union is growing substantially in a short amount of time. Ten new countries acceded into the "Club of 15" on May 1 2004, with Bulgaria and Romania following in 2007. Furthermore, the European Council decided to enter into accession talks with Turkey following a contentious recommendation from the Commission in December 2004. Croatia and Macedonia have also become accession candidates. The economic performance of most new EU member states pales in comparison to old member states and has sparked an academic debate regarding the EU's ability to economically and politically integrate these countries.

Economic differences are not the only issues pertinent to the integration of new members; cultural differences also have a significant impact. The stability of the EU's institutional structure is dependent on citizens' beliefs about an ideal society. The expanded EU will prove unstable in the long run if its institutions are not compatible with the value orientations of its citizens. All EU member states, accession countries and candidates are democracies in which decision makers cannot afford to neglect the values and preferences of their constituents. If decision makers ignore these values and preferences, the citizens will not re-elect them. This structurally anchored connection between decision makers and citizens' value orientations forces political elites to be responsive to the wishes of the citizens. One fitting example comes from the rejection of the constitutional draft in France. In a referendum in May 2005, French citizens rejected the constitutional draft created by the heads of governments in EU member states. In subsequent debates concerning the referendum, political observers repeatedly stressed that the citizens' vote reflected not only an opinion on the EU Constitution, but also on domestic problems in France. This hypothesis is supported by a special Eurobarometer survey that focuses directly on the rejection of the Constitution, carried out shortly after the referendum in France. Table 7.1 shows the motives of those who voted against the Constitution, as taken from the Eurobarometer Report (European Commission 2005: 17).

Economic values, such as those analyzed in Chapter 4, form the main reasons why the French rejected the Constitution. French citizens believe the process of European integration leads to disadvantages for themselves

Table 7.1 Reasons put forth by French people who voted against the European Constitution

Why did you vote "No" for the referendum?	*Percentage (multiple answers possible)*
It will have negative effects on the employment situation in France/relocation of French enterprises/loss of jobs	31
The economic situation in France is too weak/there is too much unemployment in France	26
Economically speaking, the draft is too liberal	19
Opposes the president of the Republic/the national government/certain political parties	18
Not enough social Europe	16
Too complex	12
Does not want Turkey in the European Union	6
Loss of national sovereignty	5
Lack of information	5
I am against Europe / European integration	4
I do not see what is positive in this text	4
The draft goes too far/advances too quickly	3
Opposition to further enlargement	3
Not democratic enough	3
Too technocratic/juridical/too much regulation	2
I am against the Bolkestein directive	2
I do not want a European political union/a European federal State/the *United States* of Europe	2
The draft does not go far enough	1
Other answers	21
Don't know/No answer	3

and for their national job market. As evidenced in Chapter 4, citizens throughout the EU, not only in France, oppose opening the European job market. The French used the constitutional referendum to express this underlying value orientation. The referendum in France is therefore a good example with which to demonstrate that citizens' values are important and can fundamentally influence the political process.

Summary of the results

Our analysis in this book was structured by three research questions. First we described the EU blueprint of an ideal society. We then measured how far each country was from this EU norm for each value sphere and then tried to account for these differences. We now summarize our findings according to these three questions.

A definition of the cultural identity of the EU is necessary to determine whether EU accession countries culturally fit into the EU. We reconstructed the EU's value order and blueprint of an ideal society using EU legislation. We used EU legislation because the citizen-elected member state governments have ratified the law, which shows a certain level of acceptance. We also used other official, less binding EU documents like the constitutional draft to create the EU cultural identity blueprint. When reconstructing the EU's value order, we distinguished between five different spheres of values – religion, family, economy, the welfare state and politics – and determined the EU's conceptions for each sphere. A brief summary of the EU blueprint for each sphere is given below.

Religion: The EU sees itself as a secular society and is consequently not based on any particular religion like Christianity. The EU protects the freedom of religion for individuals and for religious communities, but also defines boundaries for religious communities through the principles of tolerance and non-discrimination. Moreover, the EU expects its member states to separate religion from political and societal spheres.

Family and gender roles: EU family policy is particularly concerned with the equality of men and women in the workplace and supports an egalitarian relationship between men and women. This includes employment of women and a partial socialization of children outside the family. This manner of up-bringing is only feasible if an infrastructure for raising children outside the family is put in place. The traditional domestic division of labor must also be addressed and questioned.

Economy: The EU's primary economic goal is to improve the welfare of all citizens in its member states. To realize this goal, the EU hopes to implement a particular economic system based on competitiveness, market openness and a rather passive state role. Citizens should also be prepared to participate in the economy through an orientation toward achievement and generalized trust.

Welfare state: Despite much rhetoric regarding a European social model, the EU advocates a minimalist welfare state. This model aims to protect citizens against basic risks that can arise through unemployment due to sickness, disability, parental leave or age. Further concepts of a European welfare state do not exist in legally binding form.

Form of government: The EU sees itself as a group of democratic states and characterizes its own institutional order as democratic. The EU mainly understands democracy in a representative form and supplements this understanding with elements of participatory democracy, particularly the inclusion of civil society.

These ideal societal values of the European Union are not exclusively European, however. Yasemin Soysal (2003) has shown that European values are also typical in other regions of the world. Even though some values have a Western origin, they have since become universal. Freedom of religion, religious tolerance, democracy, gender equality and the emancipation of women, economic growth and the ideal of a market economy are values that appear in both EU documents as well as UN legislation, for example.

After determining the blueprint of an ideal society, we tested whether citizens in member states and accession countries support the EU concepts and whether significant country differences exist. We answered both questions for every value field, and our findings are summarized in the graphs in Figures 7.1 to 7.4; they show the discriminant function values for every value sphere.[1]

The economic values discussed in Chapter 4 are separated for achievement and openness. In those spheres where no discriminant analysis was conducted (family/gender and welfare state), we use results from our factor analysis to measure concurrence with the EU position.[2] Both discriminant functions as well as factor values assign a mean value of 0 and a variance of 1, so the data is roughly comparable. All of the values are relative measures – a value of 0 indicates average support for the EU position. Positive values represent above average support, whereas negative values show below average support.

A clear pattern arises at the aggregate level in Figures 7.1 to 7.3. In the spheres of religion, family/gender, democracy, civil society and the market openness/state aspect of the economy, the fifteen "core countries" show the highest levels of support for the EU blueprint, while the ten accession states support it somewhat less. Support diminishes in Bulgaria and particularly

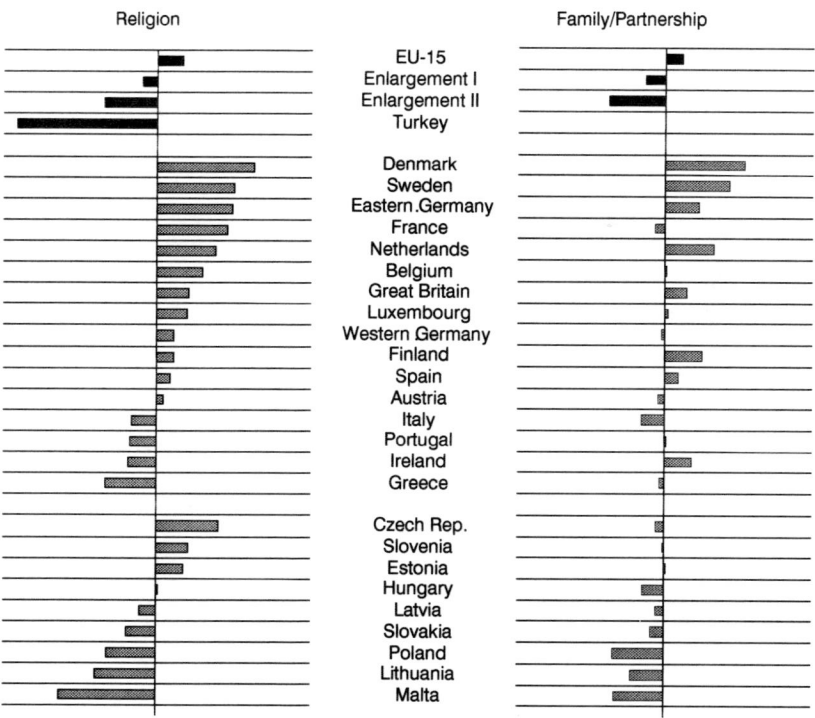

Figure 7.1 Religious values and family/gender values

Romania, and Turkey exhibits the least support. Therefore, as the EU expands, support for its blueprint will decrease.

A different pattern emerges concerning the achievement orientation aspect of the EU's economic blueprint and for welfare state concepts. For welfare state concepts, overall variance between countries is very small. The EU advocates a basic model of the welfare state, which practically all citizens in all countries support. Most citizens demand more than just the basic model by supporting social democratic or socialist variants of the welfare state model. Turkey shows the strongest support for the welfare state, followed by Accession II countries. Support in EU-15 countries is below average.

Values regarding the achievement dimension of the economic blueprint are the only ones that deviate from the overall pattern of our findings. EU-15 citizens show a below average achievement motivation and therefore show

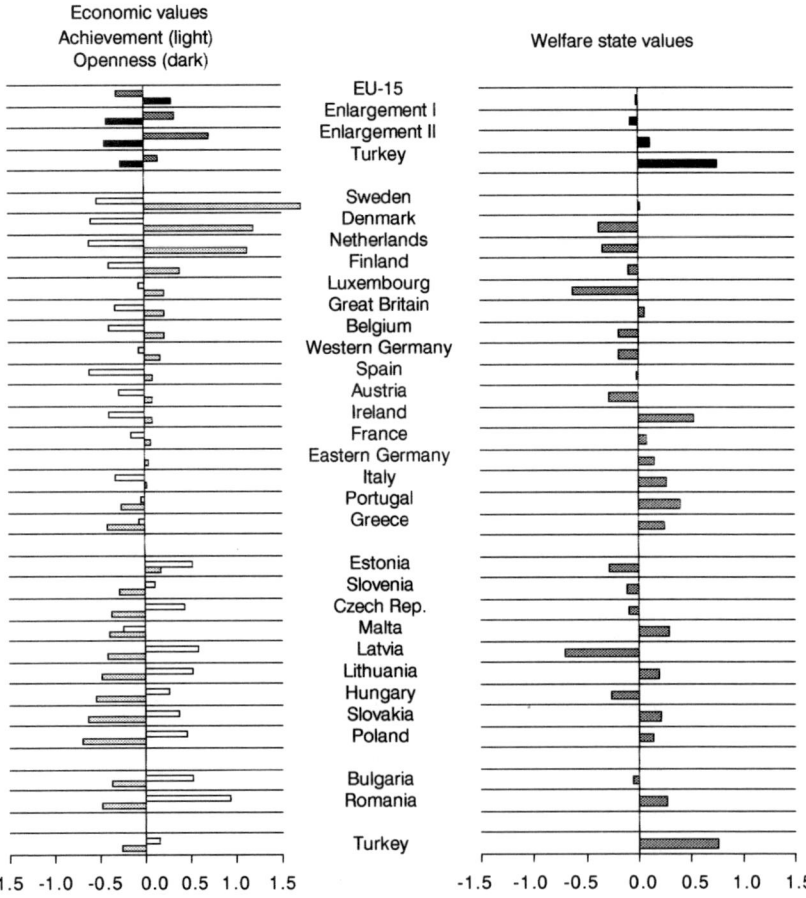

Figure 7.2 Economic values and welfare state values

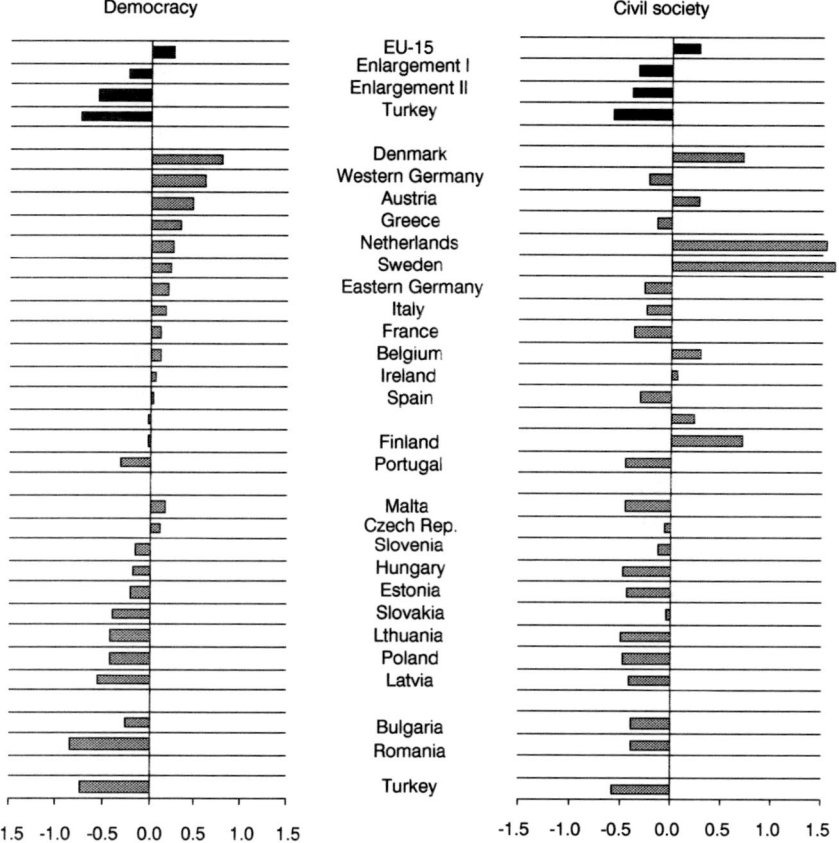

Figure 7.3   Democratic values and civil society

less support for EU ideals than citizens from Turkey, Accession I and especially Accession II countries. As the EU expands, support for its blueprint in this dimension will increase.

We can now sum up the similarities and differences between the countries for all value spheres. There are two possibilities available to develop such a measure. One could create a ranking system for all countries for each of the six value spheres (counting democracy and civil society separately) and thereby determine a mean value that measures the countries' proximity to the EU blueprint. The main weakness of this method is that the variances between countries are given equal weight, even if the factual differences are not significant. A better method is therefore to consider the discriminant function values and factor values respectively. This measurement differentiates between large and small variances. We calculated the mean values for all six spheres, all of which received equal weight in our calculation.[3] Figure 7.4 provides the values for the aggregate groups and for every country.

Figure 7.4 shows a by now familiar pattern. The group of the EU-15 countries supports the EU concepts in their entirety. Accession countries support the EU's ideals to a lesser degree, which is particularly true for Accession II countries and Turkey. At the national level, these results stay true with some overlap between groups. The Netherlands and Scandinavian countries show the strongest levels of support for the EU blueprint. Southern European countries like Spain, Italy, Greece and Portugal show below average values. Out of the new EU countries, only the Czech Republic and, with some reservations, Slovenia support the EU blueprint to the same extent as do the EU-15. These two countries were the leaders during the accession process for the Enlargement I group. Latvia, Malta, Lithuania and Poland exhibit the lowest values in this group. Relatively significant differences exist between the Accession II countries. Bulgaria is on a similar level to the Southern EU-15 countries, but Romania along with Turkey supports EU concepts the least. The "mismatch" between the EU blueprint and the citizens' value orientations is greatest in these countries. Whether the EU

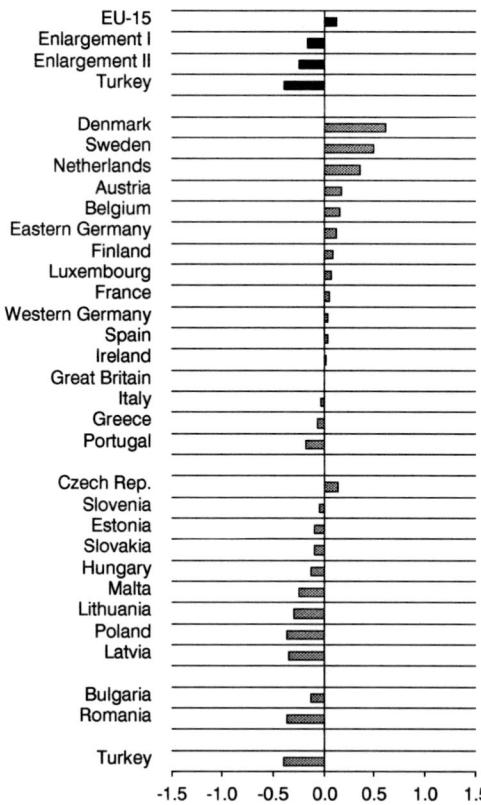

Figure 7.4   Closeness of countries to EU blueprint (all value spheres)

overstretches itself culturally depends largely on the amount of time it takes for these citizens to assimilate the values of other core members.

Our final step was to determine possible causes for the cultural similarities and differences. In doing so, we considered the different EU and accession countries as templates for various social conditions existing in society that may influence value beliefs. Depending on the value sphere, we employed different explanatory factors, but predominantly used the three variables modernization, religion and political institutions. Both the degree of economic modernization and the level of education influence citizens' value orientations. We attempted to formulate hypotheses as to how modernization and education may influence a particular sphere of values and to explain the causal relationship between a country's degree of modernization and the citizens' value orientations. The various religious denominations in the EU and in the accession countries have individual perspectives regarding societal ideals. We reconstructed these religious concepts for each value sphere and tested whether these concepts affect the value orientations of their adherents. We also assumed that a country's political-institutional order influences its citizens' values. We attempted to specify the degree to which certain characteristics of political regimes may influence citizens' value orientations.

In classifying the countries with these three macro categories, we have not done justice to the particular historical developments of individual countries. Comparative social scientists stress the importance of historical, path-dependent developments of individual countries. These scholars criticize approaches that treat countries as a complex of variables. We agree with this critique, but believe that both methodologies are compatible. Systematic analyses such as ours can develop a rough sketch of the differences between countries and cultures but cannot replace a historical approach complete with microanalyses of particular conditions. This study did not take developmental, historical paths of individual societies into account. Consequently, the explanatory power of our findings is limited. Despite this shortcoming, we are able to explain the value orientations of citizens relatively well through the three chosen macro factors. Table 7.2 provides the findings for each value sphere.[4]

A high level of modernization, as measured by the HDI and the interviewee's level of education, increases support for the EU blueprint in almost every sphere. Religious membership also influences citizens' value orientations. In this respect, Protestantism increases support for the EU blueprint, whereas other denominations often show a negative or ambivalent influence. The individual's degree of integration into religious institutions is often more influential than nominal membership in an individual denomination.

We can also look at value differences for the aggregate of all six value spheres (see Table 7.3). The vagueness of the dependent variable "general support of EU value conception" prevents us from deriving concrete hypotheses like we did for individual value spheres. We are also unable to consider the

Table 7.2 Explanations of the six analyzed value spheres: linear regressions

	Religion	Family	Economy Achievement	Economy Openness	Welfare	Democracy	Civil society
Modernization							
HDI	0.217	0.131	-0.281	0.267	0.163	0.384	0.046
Education	0.129	0.272	0.101	0.216	-0.009+	0.181	0.165
Religion[a]							
Protestants	-0.108	0.025	-0.007+	0.105	0.040	0.046	0.134
Roman Catholics	-0.214	-0.106	0.020*	-0.117	0.020*	-0.010+	-0.091
Orthodox Christians	-0.187	-0.064	0.020*	-0.037	0.094	0.015*	-0.022
Muslims	-0.235	0.067	-0.043	0.096	0.108	0.021	0.007+
Integration into church	-0.437	-0.079	-0.030	0.008+	0.123	-0.011+	0.104
Political-institutional environment							
GEM		0.124					
State intervention							
Index size of government		-0.037	-0.073				
Public social expenditure			0.126	-0.234			
Years under socialist rule				-0.078			0.099
Years of democratic rule						-0.115	0.360
R²	0.506	0.171	0.140	0.187	0.067	0.118	0.190

The models represent standardized beta-coefficients from the OLS regression analysis.
If not indicated differently, coefficients are significant at the 1% level, * = significant at 5% level, + = not significant.
a   Category of reference: people who do not have a religious affiliation.

effect of political regimes on citizens' values because this variable takes on different meanings depending on the value sphere. Examples include the institutional separation between church and state in the case of religion and political support for a dual income model in the case of the family sphere. Consequently, we can only test modernization and religious backgrounds toward the comprehensive EU blueprint.

Although we use relatively few explanatory variables for this model, it has significant explanatory power, accounting for 28 percent of the variance. The explanatory power of this variable exceeds the causal analyses of particular attitudes presented above, which surely relates back to the vagueness of the dependent variable. Different understandings of survey questions among respondents may lead to measurement errors, but when viewed at the aggregate level, these shortcomings appear to balance out.

The results in Table 7.3 confirm and strengthen the findings for the individual value spheres. Modernization indicators influence levels of support for EU values most strongly. As economic modernization and levels of education rise in a country, then its citizens are more likely to support EU concepts. Religious tradition is also influential. Whereas membership in the Protestant faith slightly increases the respondent's support for the EU blueprint, membership in the other three denominations and high levels of integration into the church or mosque increase the chance that the respondent will reject the EU blueprint.

The results of our analysis do not confirm Samuel Huntington's thesis that there is a cultural divide of Protestants and Catholics versus Orthodox Christians and Muslims. The lower degree of support for the EU blueprint in Turkey and in the predominantly Orthodox Christian Accession II countries is not related to religious orientation. Rather, the countries' degree of modernization and the level of the citizens' integration into their religious institutions determine support for the EU blueprint. The degree

Table 7.3 Explanation of generalized support of the EU blueprint: linear regressions

	"Support of the EU-script"
Modernization	
HDI	0.321
Education	0.298
Religion[a]	
Protestants	0.082
Roman Catholics	−0.147
Orthodox Christians	−0.089
Muslims	−0.021
Integration into church	−0.093
R^2	0.282

The models represent standardized beta-coefficients from the OLS regression analysis. Coefficients are significant at the 1% level.
a Category of reference: people who do not have a religious affiliation.

of modernization in these countries is particularly low and integration into religious institutions is high, which leads to below average levels of support for EU values.[5] Our findings strengthen the heavily criticized and "obsolete" modernization theory (Knöbl 2001). This *theoretical* critique is unfounded if the criticized theory continues to have explanatory power and cannot be replaced by other better theories. Our results suggest this is the case, and we see little reason to dispense with modernization theory. The next section focuses on the meaning of our findings, with a special emphasis on the possible admission of Turkey into the EU.

Political implications of the findings

Further EU expansion is a politically controversial topic. EU member states debate particularly as to whether Turkey should be admitted. Turkey had associated member status in the former EEC in 1963 and has since then requested full membership. The 2004 decision to open accession talks with Turkey sparked heated political debate in several member states that focused not on economic differences, but rather perceived *cultural* differences. Critics assert that current EU member states are fundamentally different from Turkey due to separate religious, historical and intellectual traditions. Furthermore, they contend that these differences justify that Turkey should not belong in a common union with Europe. Some supporters for Turkey's admittance doubt the fundamental nature of such cultural differences and believe that Turkey's membership in the EU would force Turkey to assimilate so-called Western values. Other supporters emphasize the possibility that cultural heterogeneity may enrich the EU (Leggewie 2004).

Our empirical analysis may help to objectify this debate. This book has shown that the EU's societal ideals are strongly supported by citizens of old and new member states. Citizens of Accession II countries, particularly Romania, support these values to a lesser degree. Our analysis shows that Turkey significantly deviates from the EU's concepts in several value spheres, which may lead one to assert that Turkey does not fit into the EU. This cultural difference takes on new importance when the size of Turkey's population is accounted for. Turkey has a current population of over 70 million and would become the most populated country in the EU in a few decades due to its high birth rate.

Citizens' value orientations are malleable, and we could only provide snapshots of countries' cultures in our analysis. Germany's development after World War II is particularly a good example of how citizens' value orientations can conform to a top-down, externally-imposed democratic order. Before returning to the "Turkey question," it is worth observing Germany's development more closely. Germany lacked a strong democratic tradition before 1949, and had in fact only experienced a brief democratic regime during the interwar period. The implementation of democracy in 1949 was not an endogenous, democratic development, but a result of foreign occupation after the fall of National Socialism and defeat in WWII. During the occupation period from 1945 to 1949, the Allies implemented a market economy and representative democracy in the Western occupation zones.

Gabriel A. Almond and Sidney Verba (1963) reconstructed democratic attitudes of five countries during the 1950s, including Germany. The authors proposed a typology of three political cultures and attempted to classify the countries empirically.[6] Germany's political culture at the beginning of the 1950s was classified as "subject." Subsequent studies have shown that the political culture of Western Germany changed in a relatively short period of time and that support quickly increased for the democratic value order implemented by the occupying forces. David P. Conradt (1980) compiled data from a 1951 survey conducted by the Allensbach Institute for Public Opinion (Allensbacher Institut für Demoskopie) that asked respondents what was the best time period for Germany over the last century. The possible answers were: "the FRG" (present), "the Third Reich" (1933–45), "the Weimar Republic" (1919–33), "the era of the Kaiser" (1871–1918) or "other time periods." Despite wartime experiences and well-known atrocities carried out during the National Socialist regime, 42 percent of the respondents chose "the Third Reich." This changed drastically in favor of the FRG within eight years. Support for the FRG continuously increased over time, and support for undemocratic periods like the Third Reich and the era of the Kaiser, decreased (see Table 7.4).

This survey question was poorly formulated and is not a good measure of the citizens' political values orientation; it measures preference for regime type rather than democratic attitudes. Time series data, like that compiled by Heiner Meulemann (1996), is somewhat better equipped to operationalize the value dimensions of interest for us (see Table 7.5).

The changes in democratic values between 1950 and 1972 are particularly impressive. Since the beginning of the 1950s, the Institute for Public Opinion has asked about levels of support for single versus multiple party systems. The question is stated as follows: "Do you believe that it is better for a country to have one party so that the greatest platform rules? Or, do you believe a multi-party system is better, where different opinions may be freely expressed?" As Table 7.5 shows, support for a multi-party system, a central element of representative democracy, rose dramatically within several years.

Table 7.4 "What era was best to live in Germany?" (%)

	1951	1959	1963	1970
Federal Republic of Germany	2	42	62	81
Third Reich	42	18	10	5
Weimar Republic	7	4	5	2
Era of the Kaiser	45	28	16	5
Other periods	4	8	7	7

Table 7.5 Value change in Germany (%)

	1950	51	52	54	55	56	57	60	63	67	72	73	80	82
Politics														
"Different parties are better"	53	61	67	70	74	76	76	79			88			
"Need to have parliament"						69	72				82			
Religion														
Attending religious services (Roman Catholics)			51						55	48	35		31	
Attending religious services (Protestants)			13						15	10	7		6	
Educational goals														
Obedience			25				25				14			8
Independence			28				32				45			52

This trend continued from the end of the 1950s until the middle of the 1970s, reaching its apex at 90 percent. Opinions began to stabilize thereafter.

Support for parliamentary institutions, another core element of a representative democracy, developed in the same direction. The following question was posed for the first time in 1956 in a representative survey: "If one adopts a purely pragmatic stance, does Bonn actually need a parliament?" As Table 7.5 shows, the share of people who believed in the necessity of parliament increased from 69 to 82 percent.

Our analysis indicates that a higher degree of integration into a church or other religious communities negatively impacts support for the EU blueprint. Integration into a religious institution is measured by attendance rates. Robert Hettlage compiled the available data for a time series on this question, separating results for Protestants and Catholics (Hettlage 1990: 276). Although these faiths have different values (see Chapter 2), the results in Table 7.5 portray a similar trend. From 1963 to 1980 the proportion of Catholics who regularly attended church declined from 55 to 31 percent, and Protestant attendance rates decreased from 15 to 6 percent. Within 17 years a dramatic change occurred in both denominations.

Table 7.5 also contains information on parents' educational goals for their children. In a survey carried out over several years by the German public opinion research group Emnid, the following question was asked: "Which characteristics should be included in a child's education: obedience and subordination, orderliness and diligence or self-reliance and free will?" Helmut Klages (1984: 17) analyzed this survey, and we used the results from his analysis in our table. Within 50 years, the concept of education fundamentally changed from a focus on obedience to a focus on self-reliance.

The results show that the history of West Germany is a history of value change, in which EU-favored values became increasingly important. There is little doubt that modernization caused this change in values. The 1950s and 1960s were marked by great prosperity that led to an extraordinary increase in people's average income and standard of living. Real wages between "1949 and 1973 rose four-fold in the FRG and, therefore, the rather modest rise in real income and wages during the era of prosperity in the 19th century pales in comparison" (Ambrosius and Kaelble 1992: 17ff.). The substantial increase in real income and wages also fundamentally changed individual consumption patterns (Ambrosius and Kaelble 1992: 20). The standard of living substantially improved, allowing for the purchase of consumer durables (cars, radios, TVs, consumer goods for children). The length of the working week significantly decreased, which created opportunities for travel and leisure (Bundesamt für Statistik 2000: 337). In addition to economic modernization, the level of education also improved in this period. German universities had 247,000 students in 1960, and this number almost doubled to 422,000 in 1970. By 1980 there were over 1 million, and 1,579,000 in 1990 (Bundesamt für Statistik 2000: 68). According to modernization theorists, the increased ability to satisfy material needs along with the rise in educational levels led to value changes. Our causal analysis also supports this thesis. Citizens' value orientations are determined in large part by the level of societal modernization.

What lessons can be taken from German post-war history and applied to EU expansion today? One may conclude that present value differences in EU accession countries might not matter in the future if new member states and accession countries go through a period of modernization similar to that of the old members and if the time period for the modernization process is not too short. The values of citizens in accession candidate countries will change if the following occurs: accession countries continue to modernize, their agricultural sector becomes decreasingly important, the middle class continues to grow and education levels and the standard of living continue to rise. Cultural differences between member states and accession countries will presumably fade away if these developments take place. Membership in the EU may accelerate modernization, as was the case for Greece, Portugal, Spain and Ireland (Bornschier 2000, Bornschier *et al.* 2004, Delhey 2003a, 2003b). These countries were significantly less modernized at the time of EU accession, but membership has been conducive to modernization. The following example illustrates that such a change can have an impact on the values of the citizens.

The World Values Survey asked whether respondents considered homosexuality to be acceptable. This was done with a 10-point scale ranging from "never justifiable" to "always justifiable." Looking at the distribution of the extreme positions over time, it becomes evident that homosexuality is increasingly viewed as justifiable. In 1981, 52.6 percent of Spaniards answered that homosexuality was not justifiable. This number decreased to

39.9 percent in 1990, 22.4 percent in 1995–97 and finally to 16.7 percent in 1999–2000. Within 20 years, the acceptance rate for homosexuality in Spain fundamentally changed. Furthermore, the Spanish government introduced a legislative draft allowing homosexual marriages in 2004 despite protests by the Catholic Church. Parliament has since approved this law, and now same-sex marriages have the same rights and responsibilities as heterosexual ones. Homosexual couples are also allowed to adopt children. Such legislation would not have been possible without a change in citizens' values. This change was precipitated by modernization in Spain, which was induced by EU membership.

Similar developments could take place in the accession countries and in Turkey if these countries modernize economically. This depends on a number of factors that are hard to predict. The question of whether EU expansion in general, and Turkish membership in particular, demands too much of the EU is an equation with many unknown variables. Decisions on EU expansion must consequently be reached by politicians, not social scientists. The social sciences can, however, provide politicians with useful information with which to make such decisions.

Notes

1 Research question and conceptual framework

1 The term "eastward enlargement" is not completely accurate, in that two of the accession countries, Malta and Cyprus, are in Southern Europe.

2 The Deutsche Bank convergence indicator includes the following variables: Per-capita GDP, the percentile rate of GDP growth in comparison to the previous year, percentile proportion of investments in terms of GDP, unemployment rate, percentile proportion of the agrarian sector in terms of the GDP, percentile proportion of the industrial sector in terms of the GDP, increase of the consumer price in comparison to the previous year, percentile proportion of household balance in terms of GDP, percentile proportion of the public debt in terms of the GDP, percentile rate of the trade balance in terms of the GDP, percentile rate of foreign direct investment in terms of GDP, the percentile rate of exports that results with EU countries.

3 The methodological and theoretical procedures follow the excellent analysis of the *political* culture of Western, Central and Eastern European countries by Dieter Fuchs and Hans-Dieter Klingemann (2002).

4 The list of literature concerning the theme of "values" is long. We base ourselves on the very thorough reconstruction from Jan van Deth and Elinor Scarbrough (1995).

5 John Meyer has shown that institutional blueprints are very often not implemented. He refers to this as "structural de-coupling" (Meyer *et al.* 1997).

6 For example, if one would like to eat pea soup for lunch and it is not on the menu at a restaurant, then one's desire to eat pea soup will not be fulfilled due to the restriction. Conversely, ordering pea soup, if it is an option at a restaurant, will only occur if the individual wants it to occur. A second example that is more apposite to the question at hand is as follows. Some citizens in a society speak out against the freedom of worker movement guaranteed by the EU, because, among other reasons, this could endanger their own jobs. This preference would be more likely if a political party existed that championed this point of view. The citizens would have to elect this party in order to transfer their preferences to the political decision-making arena. If such a party does not exist, then the citizens' preferences will not materialize.

7 In their experiments with apes, Sarah Brosnan and Frans B. M. de Waal (2003) show that even apes apparently follow a norm of fairness in their actions. They at least seem to repudiate unjust payment.

8 Bryan Caplan points out, "whether voters' beliefs are rational or irrational, electoral competition pressures politicians to do what voters want. ... It is costly for politicians to have biased estimates of voters' *reactions* to their decisions, but cheap to have biased estimates of policies' *actual effects*" (Caplan 2003: 219).

Therefore, even if the elites are actually pro-European, they must still align their policies with the citizens' wishes.

9 Information regarding the European Values Study and the World Values Survey is available at the following URLs: http://www.europeanvalues.nl and http://wvs.isr.umich.edu.

10 The preparation for an international comparative data set demands a high level of coordination and, therefore, a significant amount of time. The complete EVS data set was finished in April 2003, two years after the completion of the data collection, and released in June of the same year for research purposes.

2   Religion in a wider Europe

1 Although the theme of religion and politics has not generally been a central theme for political scientists, this has changed in the past couple of years. Two new edited editions are devoted to this topic (Minkenberg and Willems 2003, Brocker et al. 2003).

2 Several other authors assume that European culture emanates from a Christian tradition, even though they do not define precise boundaries, "The cultural roots of the European community cannot ignore religious connections" (Robbers 1995: 175). "This common belonging to Christianity is a foundation of the European identity. This is what separates Europe from other continents" (Rémond 1998: 22, see also Maurus 1998, Schilling 1999). The actual contents of this Christian legacy are only in the most seldom cases explained.

3 In December 2003, the CDU faction in the Bundestag brought forth a proposal for a resolution in the Parliament that the government should lobby for a reference to God at the meeting of the European Council. The proposal was rejected.

4 A current popular explanation assumes that a lack of market mechanisms (state support for particular religious affiliations, lacking plurality) leads to a lack of demand in the religious sphere (Finke and Stark 1992, Stark 2000, Chaves and Cann 1992). Nevertheless, Pollack and Pickel could empirically refute this assumption for Europe (2000), and Voas *et al.* (2002) raise methodological objections.

5 As Olaf Müller, Gert Pickel and Detlef Pollack (2003) have shown, state socialism has led to a reduction of membership in churches throughout Central European countries. At the same time, the authors show that large differences exist between the religious affiliations. The Catholic Church has proven able to stabilize their membership rate much more successfully than the Protestant Church.

6 The question of how often one attends church contains eight categories in all, ranging from "never, practically never" (1) to "more than once a week" (8).

7 The regularity of attending church in previous socialist societies was exposed to large variations in the past 15 years (Pollack 2003). Shortly before and after the transformation of these societies from socialistic to democratic regimes, the church experienced approval and recognition from the citizens. This is particularly related to the political opposition role adopted by the church in a few socialist countries during the socialist period. Afterwards citizens' support for the church declined so that one can speak of normalization for the time period that the Values Study's data was collected (1999/2000).

8 In their analysis of Christian countries, Pollack and Pickel (2003) show that the regularity of church attendance depends on the proportion of Catholics. Catholics are traditionally more strongly connected to their church in comparison to Protestants and the Orthodox Christians.

9 The correlation between both variables amounts to 0.70 (Pearson's correlation, p-value: 0.01).
10 The correlations between the three question range between 0.52 and 0.69 (Eta).
11 In regards to the question of social issues, the difference in responses between Enlargement I and Enlargement II countries and between Enlargement I and old EU members is not statistically significant.
12 The European Values Study asks two additional questions that measure the separation of religion and politics, which we did not use in our analysis. In these two questions, citizens were asked whether religious leaders should influence government decisions and how people vote in elections. Both a correlation analysis and a factor analysis show that these questions clearly measure other dimensions than the two questions we chose.
13 The correlation between both questions accounts for 0.62 (Pearson's correlation, p-value: 0.01).
14 Due to the fact that the question was asked in a different manner in Hungary, the results for Hungary are probably overrated.
15 A good overview of the surveys that investigate religious attitudes in Turkey is available in an article by Emin Köktas (2002). The evidence differs from our results in some respects, which has to do with the different manner in which the questions were formulated. Kayhan Mutlu (1996) investigated the religious attitudes of students from a university in Ankara and demonstrated that religiosity has risen from 1978 to 1991. He argues that these religious attitudes are completely compatible with democratic beliefs.
16 In order to give a better overview, the variables were recoded so that high values signify a strong religious orientation.
17 We assume that the groups are of equal size.
18 If one calculates a discriminant analysis on the country level with these four groups, then the countries are almost 90 percent correctly classified.
19 In fact, the Czech Republic's values are comparable to those of the benchmark countries. If one adds the Czech Republic to the benchmark countries in the discriminant analysis, then the classification is only improved by 1 percent. Need and Evans explain the strong secularization in the Czech Republic by referring to the conflict between Catholicism and nationalism present since the early fifteenth century (Need and Evans 2001).
20 We recoded all dependent variables so that high values signify a strong separation between religion and the secular world as well as a high tolerance rate toward other religions.
21 Since the variables were measured on different scales, the "range" of both scales was adjusted.
22 High values represent a greater degree of church attendance.
23 See the articles "politics and religion" and "church and state" published in the encyclopedia *Religion in Geschichte und Gegenwart* edited by Hans Dieter Betz *et al.* (2003). See also the articles "church and state" and "politics and Christianity" in *Theologische Realenzyklopädie* edited by Gerhard Müller *et al.* (1976).
24 The assumption that Christianity is in favor of a separation of religion and state, whereas Islam is not, is extremely contentious. Dietrich Jung attempts to prove the assertion that political and religious spheres in Islam form an inherent unit as historically false (Jung 2002).
25 These economic conditions are of course determined by the ownership of the means of production and the class structure, which will be left aside here.
26 The situation in Sweden changed in 2000; however, at the time of the survey, Sweden still had a state church.
27 Zulehner and Denz (1994) come to a similar conclusion.

3 Family values, gender roles and support for the emancipation of women

1 This is a necessity, however, and is not a sufficient provision for real gender equality in the workplace. Kristin Bergmann (1999) provides evidence of enormous differences between EU member states despite the legal adaptation to this provision.

2 The equality and family concepts of the EU were part of the negotiations with the accession countries of Central and Eastern Europe (Bretherton 2001) and were carried out with a 31-chapter checklist. The content of each chapter emphasized various points concerning the legal and structural assimilation of the accession countries to the EU (agriculture, environment, statistics etc.). The equal treatment of men and women is negotiated in Chapter 13 (Employment and Social Policy) and, consequently, forms one required criterion necessary to accede to the EU. This holds true even if some authors do not interpret the implementation of "gender mainstreaming" principles as sufficient (Bretherton 2001).

3 The manner in which different countries achieve this may vary greatly.

4 The neutral choice of "neither agree nor disagree" existed only for Austria and Ireland. The aggregate calculations for EU countries consequently do not include these countries.

5 The question is identical with our first indicator. Nevertheless, it makes sense to include this question in the index, since we are analyzing a different data set and using a broader theoretical concept.

6 The formation of an additive scale is problematic, since the individual variables have a different range. It remains unclear how Inglehart and Norris (2003a) solved this problem. They only indicate that all five variables were included in the index, which was standardized on a 100-point scale.

7 Christian Welzel (2000) offers a good overview of literature regarding this theoretical argument of modernization.

8 Another commonly used measurement for the level of modernization is per-capita GDP. We also carried out a regression analysis with this variable instead of the HDI. The results remained constant.

9 The definitions are derived from the entries of the key words "family," "woman" and "man" in the excellent encyclopedia *Religion in the Present and Past* edited by Hans Dieter Betz *et al.* (2003) and from the entries in the encyclopedia *Theologische Realenzyklopädie* edited by Gerhard Müller *et al.* (1976).

10 Franz-Xaver Kaufman *et al.*'s excellent volume provides a good overview of ten country reports.

11 Several authors note an additional relationship between religion and a particular welfare state model (Kaufmann 1988, Martin 1978). Countries with a Catholic tradition have developed the most advanced welfare state, which corresponds closely to the "family support model." On the other hand, Protestant countries have developed welfare states supporting the other two family models. This relationship is not valid for Central and East European countries.

12 The first dimension is determined by the strength to which welfare state institutions support the concept of a nuclear family. Indicators to measure this dimension are the extent to which family credits for young children and tax relief for families with small children exist. The second dimension measures welfare state institutions' degree of support for employment of both men and women. Indicators for this dimension are, for example, the amount of day nurseries, paid maternity leave and public assistance for the elderly. Encouraging a nuclear family will more likely lead to supporting a bourgeois family model, whereas encouraging dual-income families will more likely lead to a rejection of this model.

13 Gorän Therborn (2000: 122 ff.) describes the emancipation process of women in the different European countries by interpreting the country's statutory provisions. According to this, Bulgaria and Romania, for example, belong to those countries where women's right to self-determination occurred very early. Our descriptive analysis shows however that this only maintains a slight effect on citizens' attitudes. Changes in the law do not necessarily change the citizens' attitudes. This is particularly true when a demand from above is issued, as was the case in socialist societies.

14 The countries were classified in the following manner:

   a Portugal, Luxembourg, Greece, Malta and Turkey were not considered due to the reasons mentioned above.

   b "Dual earner mode:" Sweden, Finland, Denmark and all of the former socialist countries.

   c "Family support model:" Belgium, France, Germany, Italy, Austria, Ireland and Spain.

   d "Market-oriented:" Great Britain and the Netherlands.

15 The Beta-values in the regression model are quite similar independent of whether one uses the Gender Empowerment Measure or Korpi's classification as an independent variable.

16 The influence of education is substantially larger in comparison to the HDI. This could be due to the fact that education is measured at the individual level, whereas the HDI is measured at the country level.

17 The substantially smaller influence on the second dependent variable traces back to the fact that Turkey could not be considered in this regression due to missing data.

4 Economic concepts of an expanded EU

1 See the essays in the books edited by Hans-Hermann Höhmann (1999, 2001, 2002).

2 In 1999, the consumer price index for the per-capita GDP of the ten candidate countries in the first accession group amounted to only 44.2 percent of the value of EU-15 countries. If one also considers Bulgaria and Romania, then the value decreases to 38.5 percent (Heidenreich 2003).

3 In this regard, Giering (2001) and Friedrich (2002) point out that the tasks listed in Article 3 consist of very different levels of responsibilities.

4 This is justified as follows: "In the single market, the European Union has a legal system for effectively penalizing anti-competitive behavior. However, such measures have no effect on a global scale. Consequently, measures to ensure competition may increase competition within the single market, but weaken the competitiveness of European firms vis-à-vis their international competitors. An international system for regulating competition has yet to emerge" (Turek 1997: 49).

5 In the framework of the GATT negotiations, attempts have been made to liberalize world trade. These negotiations have not yet reached the level achieved by the EU (Müller-Graff 2000).

6 "The provisions in articles 28 and 29 shall not preclude prohibitions or restrictions on imports, exports or goods in transit justified on grounds of public morality, public policy or public security: the protection of health and life of humans, animals or plants, the protection of national treasures possessing artistic, historic or archaeological value, or the protection of industrial and commercial property" (Thiel 1996: 128).

7 State support is allowed if they "have a structural impact, be final in character and benefit the entire branch of industry" (Turek 1997: 48, also see Art. 92–4 ECT).

8 Max Weber coined this argument: "One whose lifestyle does not suit the requirements for success in a capitalistic society, will not succeed or, at least, not get very far" (Weber 1988: 56).

9 When necessary, we recoded the following indicators so that high values correspond to the EU position.

10 The correlation between the two indicators, which amounts to 0.117 (Spearman's Rho) is not very high. The correlation with the educational goal of "hard work" is, however, clearly better (Spearman's Rho: 0.209).

11 Estonia is the only former socialist country that the 2003 Index of Economic Freedom classifies as a free market economy. This indicates that a relationship exists between values and economic behavior (Pejovich 2003).

12 Unfortunately, the data set does not include all of the countries analyzed here. Therefore, we forgo an extended presentation of the data.

13 The European Social Survey contains only six out of ten countries which joined the EU in 2004, in addition Bulgaria, Romania and Turkey are missing in the ESS.

14 The results practically do not change, even if one leaves out the Netherlands due to their central stance regarding this ideal.

15 The second achievement indicator ("Work should always come first") will not be considered, since no comparable data is available for Austria.

16 Since the answer alternative "neither" for the question regarding openness of the job market cannot be interpreted, it was not considered in the analysis.

17 This contradiction does not hold true for the competition aspect. Rather, it is a factor for the performance aspect, as shown by the coefficient in Table 4.1 (the performance aspect is negative, whereas one of the competition indicators is positive for function 1).

18 Only Greece and Portugal maintain country values for both dimensions almost equivalent to those of the accession states.

19 The development of the Federal Republic of Germany illustrates this development to a post-industrial society very well. The real wages increased fourfold from 1949 to 1973 in the FRG. The modest increase of real income and wages during the phase of prosperity during the nineteenth century pales in comparison to this relatively short time period (Ambrosius and Kaelble 1992: 17ff.).

20 Samuel Eisenstadt (1970) subordinates the influences of Protestantism on economic attitudes to the development of modern capitalism (see also Greenfeld (2001), Delacroix and Nielsen (2001)).

21 Most new studies on religion and the economy are concerned with the influence of religion on economic growth (e.g. Barro and McCleary 2003).

22 Most authors view the interest ban, as the "centerpiece of the Islamic economy," but this is only a secondary concern in our analysis (Hildebrandt 1996: 12, Wienen 1999).

23 The pricey handouts or so-called *zakat* are often considered another central precept. "This interpretation that the poor should be supported by the rich is grounded in the principle of the social state in Islamic society. This is found in concepts of several Islamic economic ideologies, which include moral-charitable elements as well as strive toward a legal social partnership" (Hildebrandt 1996: 10ff.).

24 This also holds true for empirical research. Guiso *et al.* (2003) analyze Catholics, Protestants, Jews, Muslims, Hindus and Buddhists. Orthodox Christians fall under the category "other affiliations," but is not further specified.

25 The authors assume a reciprocal influence between structure and culture. In our case, we only analyze the influence in one direction, namely the influence of the structure on the citizens' values.

26 A logit regression model would statistically be more appropriate because some questions were asked with two possible answers. We conducted a logit regression, but the results were not substantially different. We indicate only the coefficients from the linear regression model on the grounds that it provides a better comparison.

5 Concepts of the welfare state in the European Union

1 A number of publications concerning this typology exist: Leibfried and Pierson (1995), Lessenich and Ostner (1998), Manow (2002), Obinger and Wagschal (2001), Schmidt (1998), Schmid (1996), Vobruba (2001), Vogel (1999).

2 Esping-Andersen distinguishes between three analytical dimensions that help to determine the three welfare state systems: de-commodification, stratification and the relationship of the market to the state. Roller's typology mainly deals with the first dimension and describes the degree to which security of a citizen's existence is independent from income.

3 The major outcome of this development is the 1994 Commission "White Papers on Social Policy."

4 For more information on European social policies, see Keller (2001), Kleinmann (2002), Kowalsky (1999), Leibfried (1996), Leibfried and Pierson (2000), the contributions in Schmähl and Rische (1997) and Schulte (2001).

5 Work protection measurements are substantially developed at the EU level (Vobruba 2001: 103).

6 Part III, Article II of the constitutional draft contains an abundance of socio-political related regulations. These relate to the 1961 European Social Charter and the 1989 Community Charter of Fundamental Social Rights of Workers. These aforementioned charters are not considered in the following analysis.

7 Article 95, Part II specifies health protection more clearly: "Everyone has the right of access to preventive health care and the right to benefit from medical treatment under the conditions established by national laws and practices. A high level of human health protection shall be ensured in the definition and implementation of all Union policies and activities."

8 An abundance of social policy programs and initiatives exist for fighting poverty, indirect ramifications of the currency union and the common market. "Indirect" European social policies and EU "soft law" (Leibfried and Pierson 2000, Schulte 2001) are not considered here. Great Britain, who blocked the attempt to adopt stronger, more stringent socio-political tasks with its veto, is a prominent example in this case.

9 Because the constitutional draft envisages further unanimity concerning provisions of the European Council in the field of social policy, no significant changes will come about in the foreseeable future.

10 It is a proven empirical fact that the level of welfare-state regulations highly depends on a society's wealth, at least in inner-European comparisons. The correlation coefficient between GDP per capita and the social contribution as a percentage of GDP maintains a value around 0.8 (Busch 1998: 276ff.). This is at the very least an indicator that the aforementioned convergence theory (Wilensky 1975) is not completely false, despite all of its critics.

11 The correlation coefficients are not particularly high (although all are significant (p-value: 0.01). The relationship between state responsibility and care for the elderly amounts to 0.045, for sick and handicapped people 0.055 and for the unemployed 0.129. The lower values from the first two correlations are partially

due to the extremely lopsided distribution of support for the elderly, sick and handicapped.

12 Nevertheless, the mean differences are in almost all cases (the exceptions are the EU members and Accession II countries) at a 5 percent level of significance.

13 Even if certain sicknesses are caused, to a certain extent, by a particular lifestyle, it can still be assumed that every person tries to remain healthy.

14 Pearson's correlation amounts to between 0.57 and 0.67.

15 We recoded the scale so that it begins at 0, with high values indicating a high level of support. The mean value amounts to 7.9 and the standard deviation is 2.5. The scale exhibits a Cronbach's Alpha of 0.82.

16 Another question from the European Values Study provides further support for this result. Interviewees were asked whether satisfying the basic needs of all people is a prerequisite of a just society. This question also exhibits an average approval of over 90 percent in almost all countries. Since a state reference is lacking, we do not analyze this variable further.

17 The sequential order of the countries arises from their average approval rating of all four categories.

18 The concept "socialist model" is not very accurate because socialist concepts go far beyond controls over wages and stipends. Most importantly, this does not include the collectivization of means of production.

19 On the one hand, empathy is a consequence of the modernization process. Increased economic growth, division of labor, economic interdependence and urbanization increase contact with strangers and create the structural requisites that are necessary for empathy to develop (Simmel 1992). On the other hand, empathy is a necessary requirement in order to interact with strangers at all.

20 Philip Manow also indicates that one must distinguish between Lutherans and reformed Protestant faiths. The latter distinguishes itself by "under-emphasizing communal self help, strictly separating church and state, advocating spiritual asceticism and opposing strong state programs" (Manow 2002: 208).

21 The OECD data on public social expenditure is not available for Bulgaria, Estonia, Hungary, Lithuania, Latvia, Malta, Romania and Slovenia. In order to control our analyses, we used a second measurement, namely the degree of state influence on the economy as measured by the "Index Economic Freedom of the World: Size of Government" (Gwartney and Lawson 2003). The data for this index is available for all countries and correlates with the public social expenditure indicator. The results do not change substantially. The influence of modernization is somewhat reduced.

6 Democracy and civil society in a wider Europe

1 Gabriel Almond and Sidney Verba (1963) expressed their opinion on this issue by calling the ideal mix of political attitudes "civic culture."

2 The commonly discussed lack of democracy within the EU relates to the fact that EU citizens do not elect the European Council, a gathering of national government leaders, nor do they elect the Council of Ministers, made up of government ministers from each European Union member state. Rather, these positions are filled indirectly by national elections. EU citizens must comply with the Council and Commission's decisions, even though they did not directly elect these officials (for a systematic summary on this topic see Benz 1998, Scharpf 1998).

3 On January 31 2000, the Portuguese Prime Minister, acting as the head of the EU Council, made the following statement on behalf of the 14 member states: "The governments of 14 member states will neither accept nor promote official bilateral contacts on the political level with the Austrian government as long as

the FPÖ participates. No support will be given to Austrian candidates who apply for posts in international organizations. Austrian embassies will only function on a technical level in EU capitals." The Commission and Parliament supported this decision (for a legal analysis, see Schweitzer 2000).

4 In some articles, Fuchs also deals with a republican model (Fuchs 1997, 2000).

5 835 interviewees (2.6 percent) show a divergent response pattern. In addition, those who did not answer one of the questions were excluded. Together, 6.1 percent of the population cannot be classified in any of the models.

6 All variables were recoded so that high values signify a high level of support of democracy.

7 For the first case, Cronbach's Alpha yields 0.68, in the latter case, it is 0.49.

8 Consequently, Putnam (2002: 22) distinguishes between two different types of civil societal groups ("Bridging versus bonding associations"). Only the first type produces positive effects for democracy. Pamela Paxton (2002: 259) comes to similar conclusions.

9 Pamela Paxton (2002) demonstrates that the level of civil society in a country has a positive effect on democracy. At the same time, however, the opposite relationship holds true, in which democracies foster the development of civil society.

10 We will not analyze what actual influence actors in civil society have on the EU. A number of analyses already exist (Roose 2003). For a good overview on this topic see Christian Lahusen and Claudia Jauß (2001).

11 This result coincides with Bernhard Weßels' (2003: 178) empirical findings for 12 post-communist societies.

12 A 90 percent organizational participatory rate for trade unions was not uncommon.

13 For the sake of space, we do not give the results for the two variables "membership in at least one organization" and "participation in at least one organization." The results of logit regression models resemble the other findings presented here.

14 In a second regression model, we replaced the variables "years of continuous democracy" and "years under socialist rule" with two dummy variables, which measure socialist and authoritarian legacies (Greece, Portugal, Spain and Turkey). Both variables have a negative influence on civil society. Indeed, the effect caused by the authoritarian regime is greater than that of ex-socialist countries. This partially supports Howard's thesis that both authoritarian and socialist pasts have a negative influence on civil society. Nevertheless, this finding also contradicts his assumption that the effect is greater for former socialist countries.

15 For three variables, Greece also possesses above average support for the democracy dimension. Nevertheless, they are not considered a benchmark country due to the high value given to the indicator "having army rule."

16 Great Britain could not be considered, since the data for active participation in organizations was missing.

17 It is evident that the mean values of both benchmark groups maintain positive values for both functions, while the rest of the countries (Group 3) exhibit negative values.

18 Here, the comparison is relative to other interviewees. Therefore, distance from the EU does not indicate absolute rejection of the EU position, but rather in relation to other interviewees.

7 Summary and future prospects

1 The family sphere variable is missing for Turkey, and the democracy and civil society variable is missing for Great Britain. Therefore, these countries are not considered in these respective fields. Using the data at hand, Turkey trails the rest of the countries in the family sphere, while Great Britain appears to lie somewhere in the middle for democracy/civil society.

2 In the aforementioned chapters, we explained in greater detail why a discriminant analysis makes little sense. The factor for the family sphere explains 63 percent of the total variance, while the factor for the welfare state sphere explains 74 percent.

3 We consider all cases where data exists for at least five of the six spheres. The advantage of this approach is that the Turkish interviewees can be considered, even though data for one sphere is not available.

4 As mentioned above, no data is available for the family sphere in Turkey and the civil society/democratic sphere in Great Britain. These are not considered in the regression model. In the family sphere, this has relevant effects, since the majority of Muslims in our controlled sample live in Turkey.

5 Additionally, it can be assumed that modernization leads to secularization in the long run. This holds true, at least for Europe, and is yet another indirect positive effect of modernization.

6 The three different types of political culture are "parochial," "subject" and "participant." The fourth form favored by these authors was a mixture of the aforementioned types, which they named "civic culture."

Bibliography

Alber, J. (1989) *Der Sozialstaat in der Bundesrepublik: 1950–1983*, Frankfurt/M.: Campus.

Alber, J. (2004) 'Gehört die Türkei zu Europa? Ein Sozialporträt der Türkei im Licht vergleichender Daten der Umfrageforschung', *Leviathan*, 32, 4: 464–94.

Alesina, A. and Angeletos, G.-M. (2003) *Fairness and Redistribution*. Online. Available HTTP: http://post.economics.harvard.edu/faculty/alesina/papers/fairness.pdf (accessed 29 September 2004).

Almond, G.A. and Verba, S. (1963) *The Civic Culture. Political Attitudes and Democracy in Five Nations*, Princeton, NJ: Princeton University Press.

Almond, G.A., Powell, G.B., Strom, K. and Dalton, R.J. (2003) *Comparative Politics Today*, New York: Longman.

Ambrosius, G. and Kaelble, H. (1992) 'Einleitung. Gesellschaftliche und wirtschaftliche Folgen des Booms der 1950er und 1960er Jahre', in H. Kaelble (ed.) *Der Boom 1948–1973. Gesellschaftliche und wirtschaftliche Folgen in der Bundesrepublik Deutschland und in Europa*, Opladen: Westdeutscher Verlag.

Antes, P. (ed.) (2002) *Christentum und europäische Kultur. Eine Geschichte und ihre Gegenwart*, Freiburg: Herder.

Ashford, S. and Timms, N. (1992) *What Europe Thinks: A Study of Western European Values*, Aldershot: Dartmouth.

Aust, A., Leitner, S. and Lessenich, S. (2000) 'Einleitung: Sozialmodell Europa. Eine konzeptionelle Annäherung', in Zentrum für Europa- und Nordamerika-Studien (ed.) *Sozialmodell Europa. Konturen eines Phänomens. Jahrbuch für Europa- und Nordamerika-Studien, Folge 4/2000*, Opladen: Leske + Budrich.

Aust, A., Leitner, S. and Lessenich, S. (2002) 'Konjunktur und Krise des Europäischen Sozialmodells. Ein Beitrag zur politischen Präexplantationsdiagnostik', *Politische Vierteljahresschrift*, 43, 2: 272–301.

Bach, M. (2000a) 'Die Europäisierung der nationalen Gesellschaft? Problemstellungen und Perspektiven einer Soziologie der europäischen Integration', in M. Bach (ed.) *Die Europäisierung nationaler Gesellschaften. Sonderheft 40 der Kölner Zeitschrift für Soziologie und Sozialpsychologie*, Wiesbaden: Westdeutscher Verlag.

Bach, M. (ed.) (2000b) *Die Europäisierung nationaler Gesellschaften. Sonderheft 40 der Kölner Zeitschrift für Soziologie und Sozialpsychologie*, Wiesbaden: Westdeutscher Verlag.

Backhaus, K., Erichson, B., Plinke, W. and Weber, R. (1994) *Multivariate Analysemethoden. Eine anwendungsorientierte Einführung* (7th edn), Berlin: Springer.

Bahle, T. (2003) 'Staat, Kirche und Familienpolitik in westeuropäischen Ländern. Ein historisch-soziologischer Vergleich', in M. Minkenberg and U. Willems (eds) *Politik und Religion. Sonderheft 33 der Politischen Vierteljahresschrift*, Wiesbaden: Westdeutscher Verlag.

Banks, A.S. and Muller, T.C. (eds) (1998) *Political Handbook of the World*, Binghamton: CSA Publications.

Barbier, M. (1995) *La laïcité*, Paris: L'Harmattan.

Barro, R.J. and McCleary, R.M. (2003) 'Religion and Economic Growth Across Countries', *American Sociological Review*, 68: 760–81.

Beck, U. (1997) *Was ist Globalisierung? Irrtümer des Globalismus – Antworten auf Globalisierung*, Frankfurt/M.: Suhrkamp.

Beisheim, M., Dreher, S., Walter, G., Zangl, B. and Zürn, M. (1999) *Im Zeitalter der Globalisierung? Thesen und Daten zur gesellschaftlichen und politischen Denationalisierung*, Baden-Baden: Nomos.

Bell, D. (1979) *Die Zukunft der westlichen Welt. Kultur und Technologie im Widerstreit*, Frankfurt/M.: Fischer.

Bell, D. (1996) *Die nachindustrielle Gesellschaft*, Frankfurt/M.: Campus.

Benz, A. (1998) 'Ansatzpunkte für ein europäisches Demokratiekonzept', in B. Kohler-Koch (ed.) *Regieren in entgrenzten Räumen. Sonderheft 29 der Politischen Vierteljahresschrift*, Opladen: Westdeutscher Verlag.

Berger, J. (1996) 'Was bedeutet die Modernisierungstheorie wirklich und was wird ihr bloß unterstellt?', *Leviathan*, 24: 45–62.

Berger, P.L. (1991) *The Capitalist Revolution. Fifty Propositions about Prosperity, Equality, and Liberty*, New York: Basic Books.

Berglund, S., Hellén, T. and Aarebrot, F.H. (eds) (1998) *The Handbook of Political Change in Eastern Europe*, Cheltenham: Edward Elgar.

Bergmann, K. (1999) *Die Gleichstellung von Frauen und Männern in der europäischen Arbeitswelt. Eine rechtsvergleichende, empirisch-politikwissenschaftliche Untersuchung*, Opladen: Westdeutscher Verlag.

Bertelsmann Stiftung/Forschungsgruppe Europa (1998) *Kosten, Nutzen und Chancen der Osterweiterung für die Europäische Union*, Gütersloh: Bertelsmann Stiftung.

Berthold, N. and Hilpert, J. (1996) 'Wettbewerbspolitik, Industriepolitik und Handelspolitik in der Europäischen Union', in R. Ohr (ed.) *Europäische Integration*, Stuttgart: Kohlhammer.

Betz, H.D., Browning, D.S., Jüngel, E. and Janowski, B. (eds) (2003) *Religion in Geschichte und Gegenwart* (4th edn), Tübingen: Mohr (Siebeck).

Blekesaune, M. and Quadagno, J. (2003) 'Public Attitudes toward Welfare State Policies: A Comparative Analysis of 24 Nations', *European Sociological Review*, 19, 5: 415–27.

Blossfeld, H.-P. and Drobnic, S. (2001) 'Theoretical Perspectives on Couples' Careers', in H.-P. Blossfeld and S. Drobnic (eds) *Careers of Couples in Contemporary Societies: From Male Breadwinner to Dual Earner Families*, Oxford: Oxford University Press.

Bornschier, V. (2000) 'Ist die Europäische Union wirtschaftlich von Vorteil und eine Quelle beschleunigter Konvergenz? Explorative Vergleiche mit 33 Ländern im Zeitraum von 1980 bis 1998', in M. Bach (ed.) *Die Europäisierung nationaler Gesellschaften. Sonderheft 40 der Kölner Zeitschrift für Soziologie und Sozialpsychologie*, Wiesbaden: Westdeutscher Verlag.

Bornschier, V., Herkenrath, M. and Ziltener, P. (2004) 'Political and Economic Logic of Western European Integration. A Study of Convergence Comparing Member and Non-member States 1980–98', *European Societies*, 6: 71–96.

Bosco, A. (1998) 'Die europäische Dimension des sozialen Schutzes und die Aussichten für die Zukunft', in A. Bosco and M. Hutsebaut (eds) *Sozialer Schutz in Europa. Veränderungen und Herausforderungen*, Marburg: Schüren Presseverlag.

Brague, R. (1996) 'Orient und Okzident. Modelle "römische" Christenheit', in O. Kallscheuer (ed.) *Das Europa der Religionen. Ein Kontinent zwischen Säkularisierung und Fundamentalismus*, Frankfurt/M.: Fischer.

Bretherton, C. (2001) 'Gender Mainstreaming and EU Enlargement: Swimming Against the Tide?', *Journal of European Public Policy*, 8: 60–81.

Britannica Book of the Year (2002) *World Data, Religious Affiliation*, Chicago: Encyclopaedia Britannica, Inc.

Brocker, M., Behr, H. and Hildebrandt, M. (eds) (2003) *Religion – Staat – Politik. Zur Rolle der Religion in der nationalen und internationalen Politik*, Wiesbaden: Westdeutscher Verlag.

Brosnan, S.F. and de Waal, F.B.M. (2003) 'Monkeys Reject Unequal Pay', *Nature*, 425: 297–9.

Bundesamt für Statistik (2000) *Datenreport 1999. Zahlen und Fakten über die Bundesrepublik Deutschland*, Bonn: Bundeszentrale für politische Bildung.

Burgsdorf, W. (2004) 'Die europäische Antwort. Wir sind der Türkei verpflichtet', *Frankfurter Allgemeine Zeitung*, 6.1.2004: 31.

Burkart, G. and Kohli, M. (1992) *Liebe, Ehe, Elternschaft. Die Zukunft der Familie*, Munich: Piper.

Burstein, P. (1998) 'Bringing the Public Back in: Should Sociologists Consider the Impact of Public Opinion', *Social Forces*, 77: 27–66.

Burstein, P. (2003) 'The Impact of Public Opinion on Public Policy. A Review and an Agenda', *Political Research Quarterly*, 56: 29–40.

Busch, K. (1998) 'Das Korridormodell – ein Konzept zur Weiterentwicklung der EU-Sozialpolitik', in J. Schmid and R. Niketta (eds), *Wohlfahrtsstaat. Krise und Reform im Vergleich*, Marburg: Metropolis. Online. Available HTTP: http://www.etui-rehs.org/media/files/discussion_papers/1998/dp_1998_02_02 (accessed 19 September 2006).

Buss, A. (1989) *Die Wirtschaftsethik des russisch-orthodoxen Christentums*, Heidelberg: Winter.

Campenhausen, A. Freiherr von (2002) 'Christentum und Recht', in P. Antes (ed.) *Christentum und europäische Kultur. Eine Geschichte und ihre Gegenwart*, Freiburg: Herder.

Caplan, B. (2002) 'Systematically Biased Beliefs About Economics. Robust Evidence of Judgemental Anomalies from the Survey of Americans and Economists on the Economy', *The Economic Journal*, 112: 433–58.

Caplan, B. (2003) 'The Logic of Collective Belief', *Rationality and Society*, 15: 218–42.

Carson, M. (2004) *From Common Market to Social Europe? Paradigm Shifts and Institutional Change in European Union Policy on Food, Asbestos and Chemicals, and Gender Equality*, Stockholm: Stockholm University.

Casanova, J. (2001) 'Secularization', in N.J. Smelser and P.B. Baltes (eds) *International Encyclopaedia of the Social and Behavioral Sciences*, Amsterdam: Elsevier.

Chaves, M. and Cann, D.E. (1992) 'Regulation, Pluralism and Religious Market Structure. Explaining Religions' Vitality', *Rationality and Society*, 4: 272–90.

Coleman, J.S. (1990) *Foundations of Social Theory*, Cambridge, MA: Harvard University Press.

Commission of the European Community (2003) *Continuing enlargement – Strategy paper and Report for the European Commission on the progress towards accession by Bulgaria, Romania and Turkey*. Brussels 05.11.2003. Online. Available http://eur-lex.europa.eu/LexUriServ/site/en/com/2003/com2003_0676en01.pdf.

Conference of Representatives of the Governments of the Member States (2004) 'Treaty Establishing a Constitution for Europe'. Online. Available HTTP: http://europa.eu.int/constitution/futurum/constitution/table/index_en.htm (accessed 19 September 2006).

Conradt, D.P. (1980) 'Changing German Political Culture', in G.A. Almond and S. Verba (ed.) *The Civic Culture Revisited*, London: Sage.

Council of the European Union (2000) *European Social Agenda* (OJ C 157), Online. Available HTTP: http://ue.eu.int/uedocs/cmsdata/librairie/PDF/SocialAgenda_EN.pdf (accessed 3 April 2007).

Curtis, J.E., Baer, D.E. and Grabb, E.G. (2001) 'Nations of Joiners: Explaining Voluntary Association Membership in Democratic Societies', *American Sociological Review*, 66: 783–805.

Curtis, J.E., Grabb, E.G. and Baer, D.E. (1992) 'Voluntary Association Membership in Fifteen Countries. A Cross-National Comparative Note', *American Sociological Review*, 57: 139–52.

Dahl, R.A. (1989) *Democracy and its Critics*, New Haven, CT: Yale University Press.

Dahl, R.A. (1997) 'A Brief Intellectual Biography', in H. Daalder (ed.) *Comparative European Politics*, London and Washington, DC: Pinter.

Dalton, R.J. (1988) *Citizen Politics in Western Democracies. Public Opinion and Political Parties in the United States, Great Britain, West Germany, and France*, Chatham: Chatham House Publishers.

Delacroix, J. and Nielsen, F. (2001) 'The Beloved Myth: Protestantism and the Rise of Industrial Capitalism in Nineteenth-Century Europe', *Social Forces*, 80: 509–53.

Delhey, J. (2001) *Osteuropa zwischen Marx und Markt. Soziale Ungleichheit und soziales Bewußtsein nach dem Kommunismus*, Hamburg: Krämer.

Delhey, J. (2003a) 'Konvergenz und Divergenz der EU-Gesellschaften: Das Beispiel Modernisierung', in R. Caesar, K. Lammers and H.E. Scharrer (eds) *Konvergenz und Divergenz in der Europäischen Union – Empirische Befunde und wirtschaftspolitische Implikationen*, Baden-Baden: Nomos.

Delhey, J. (2003b) 'Europäische Integration, Modernisierung und Konvergenz. Zum Einfluss der EU auf die Konvergenz der Mitgliedsländer', *Berliner Journal für Soziologie*, 13: 565–84.

Delhey, J. (2004) 'Nationales und transnationales Vertrauen in der Europäischen Union', *Leviathan*, 32, 1: 15–45.

Deth, J.W. van and Scarbrough, E. (1995) 'The Concept of Values', in J.W. van Deth and E. Scarbrough (eds) *The Impact of Values*, Oxford: Oxford University Press.

Deutsche Bank Research (2003) *EU-Monitor. Beiträge zur europäischen Union Nr. 11*, December 2003, Frankfurt.

DiMaggio, P. (1994) 'Culture and Economy', in N. Smelser and R. Swedberg (eds) *The Handbook of Economic Sociology*, Princeton, NJ: Princeton University Press.

Dogan, M. and Pelassy, D. (1990) *How to Compare Nations. Strategies in Comparative Politics*, Chatham: Chatham House Publications.

Donges, J.B., Engels, W., Hamm, W., Issing, O., Möschel, W., Neumann, M.J.M., Sievert, O. and Willgerodt, H. (1997) *Vertrauen in die Marktwirtschaft. Eine Zusammenfassung von Studien des Kronberger Kreises aus den Jahren 1990–1992 zu den zukunftsweisenden Wegvorgaben*, Landsberg am Lech: Olzog.

Dorner, K. (2000) 'Kultur und Wachstum. Eine institutionenökonomische und wachstumstheoretische Analyse kultureller Einflüsse auf das Wachstum von Volkswirtschaften', unpublished dissertation, Ulm.

Drobnic, S. and Blossfeld, H.-P. (2001) 'Careers of Couples and Trends in Inequality', in H.-P. Blossfeld and S. Drobnic (eds) *Careers of Couples in Contemporary Societies: From Male Breadwinner to Dual Earner Families*, Oxford: Oxford University Press.

Dülmen, R. van (1990) *Kultur und Alltag in der Frühen Neuzeit. Volume 1: Das Haus und seine Menschen*, Munich: C.H. Beck.

Durkheim, E. (1897/1983) *Der Selbstmord*, Frankfurt/M.: Suhrkamp.

Easton, D. (1979) *A Systems Analysis of Political Life*, Chicago, IL: University of Chicago Press.

Edlund, J. (1999) 'Trust in Government and Welfare Regimes: Attitudes to Redistribution and Financial Cheating in the USA and Norway', *European Journal of Political Research*, 35: 341–70.

Ehmer, J., Hareven, T. and Wall, R. (eds) (1997) *Historische Familienforschung. Ergebnisse und Kontroversen*, Frankfurt/M.: Campus.

Eisenstadt, S.N. (1970) 'Protestantische Ethik und der Geist des Kapitalismus', *Kölner Zeitschrift für Soziologie und Sozialpsychologie*, 22: 48–58.

Eisenstadt, S.N. (1987) *European Civilization in a Comparative Perspective. A Study in the Relations between Culture and Social Structure*, London: Norwegian University Press.

Eisenstadt, S.N. (ed.) (1992) *Kulturen der Achsenzeit. Volume 2: Ihre institutionelle und kulturelle Dynamik*, Frankfurt/M.: Suhrkamp.

Eisenstadt, S.N. (2000) *Die Vielfalt der Moderne*, Frankfurt/M.: Suhrkamp.

El-Saadawi, N. (1991) *Tschador. Frauen im Islam*, Bremen: Con.

Elwert, G. (1987) 'Ausdehnung der Käuflichkeit und Einbettung der Wirtschaft. Markt und Moralökonomie', in K. Heinemann (ed.) *Soziologie wirtschaftlichen Handelns. Sonderheft 28 der Kölner Zeitschrift für Soziologie und Sozialpsychologie*, Opladen: Westdeutscher Verlag.

Engels, F. (1973) 'Herrn Eugen Dührings Umwälzung der Wissenschaft', in K. Marx and F. Engels (eds) *Werke*, Volume 20, Berlin: Dietz Verlag.

Esmer, Y. (2002) 'Is there an Islamic Civilization?' *Comparative Sociology*, 1: 265–98.

Esping-Andersen, G. (1990) *The Three Worlds of Welfare Capitalism*, Princeton, NJ: Princeton University Press.

Esping-Andersen, G. (1999) *Social Foundations of Postindustrial Economies*, Oxford: Oxford University Press.

Esser, H. (1994) 'Werte und die "Konstitution" der Gesellschaft', in E. Horst, J. Rinderspacher and J. Schupp (eds) *Erwartungen an die Zukunft. Zeithorizonte und Wertewandel in der sozialwissenschaftlichen Diskussion*, Frankfurt/M.: Campus.

Europäische Gemeinschaften (2000) 'Gleichstellung von Männern und Frauen. Die neue Rahmenstrategie für die Gleichstellung von Frauen und Männern', *Magazin zum mittelfristigen Aktionsprogramm der Gemeinschaft für die Chancengleichheit von Frauen und Männern (1996–2000)*, Magazin Nr. 9, Luxembourg: Amt für amtliche Veröffentlichungen der Europäischen Gemeinschaften.

Europäische Kommission (1994) *Europäische Sozialpolitik: ein zukunftsweisender Weg für die Union. Weißbuch (KOM (94) 333)*, Luxembourg: Amt für amtliche Veröffentlichungen der EG.

Europäische Kommission (2000a) *Die Wettbewerbspolitik in Europa und der Bürger*, Luxembourg: Amt für öffentliche Veröffentlichungen der Europäischen Gemeinschaften.

Europäische Kommission (2000b) *Sozialpolitische Agenda. Mitteilung der Kommission an den Rat, das Europäische Parlament, den Wirtschafts- und Sozialausschuß und den Ausschuß der Regionen*, Luxembourg: Amt für amtliche Veröffentlichungen der Europäischen Gemeinschaften.

Europäische Kommission (2002) *Die Erweiterung der Europäischen Union. Eine historische Gelegenheit*, Brussels: Generaldirektion Erweiterung, Interinstitutionelle Beziehungen und Informationsabteilung.

Europäische Union – Europäische Gemeinschaft (1998) *Die Vertragstexte von Maastricht mit den deutschen Begleitgesetzen. Herausgegeben von Thomas Läufer*, Bonn: Europa Union Verlag.

European Commission (1994) *European Social Policy – A way forward for the Union*. White Paper (COM (94) 333), Luxembourg. Online. Available HTTP: http://aei. pitt.edu/1118/01/social_policy_white_paper_COM_94_333_A.pdf (accessed 3 April 2007).

European Commission (2001a) *European Governance. A White Paper*. COM (2001) 428 final Online. Available HTTP: http://europa.eu/eur-lex/en/com/cnc/2001/com20010428en01.pdf (accessed 2 April 2007).

European Commission (2001b) Enlargement of the European Union. An Historic Opportunity. Online. Available HTTP: http://ee.europa.eu/spain/pdf/ampliacion_ue_2001_en.pdf (accessed 5 April 2007).

European Commission (2002) *Towards a reinforced culture of consultation and dialogue – General principles and minimum standards for consultation of interested parties by the Commission Communication from the Commission*, COM(2002) 704 final. Brussels, 11.12.2002 Online. Available HTTP: http://eur-lex.europa.eu/LexUriServ/site/en/com/2002/com2002_0704en01.pdf (accessed 2 April 2007).

European Commission (2003) *Rapport from the Commission on European Governance*. Online. Available HTTP: http://ec.europa.eu/governance/docs/comm_rapport_en.pdf (accessed 2 April 2007).

European Commission (2005) *The European Constitution. Post-referendum survey in France*. Online. Available HTTP: http://ec.europa.eu/public_opinion/flash/fl171+en.pdf (accessed 4 April 2007).

European Convention (2003) *Draft treaty establishing a Constitution for Europe*, Brussels. Online. Available HTTP: http://european-convention.eu.int/docs/Treaty/cv00850.en03.pdf (accessed 2 April 2007).

European Council (2000) *Presidency Conclusions*, Lisbon. Online. Available HTTP: http://www.europarl.eu.int/summits/lis1_en.htm (accessed 19 January 2007).

Fehr, E. and Gächter, S. (2002) 'Altruistic Punishment in Humans', *Nature*, 415: 137–40.

Fehr, E. and Rockenbach, B. (2003) 'Detrimental Effects of Sanctions on Human Altruism', *Nature*, 422: 137–40.

Ferree, M.M., Gamson, W.A., Gerhards, J. and Rucht, D. (2002) *Shaping Abortion Discourse: Democracy and The Public Sphere in Germany and the United States*, New York: Cambridge University Press.

Finke, R. and Stark, R. (1992) *The Churching of America: 1776–1990. Winners and Losers in Our Religious Economy*, New Brunswick, NJ: Rutgers University Press.

Fligstein, N. and Stone Sweet, A. (2002) 'Constructing Polities and Markets. An Institutionalist Account of European Integration', *American Journal of Sociology*, 107: 1206–43.

Flora, P. (2000) 'Externe Grenzbildung und interne Strukturierung. Europa und seine Nationen. Eine Rokkan'sche Forschungsperspektive', *Berliner Journal für Soziologie*, 2: 151–65.

Flora, P. and Alber, J. (1981) 'Modernisation, Democratisation and the Development of Welfare States', in P. Flora and A.J. Heidenheimer (eds) *Development of Welfare States in Europe and America*, New Brunswick, NJ: Transaction.

Flora, P., Alber, J. and Kohl, J. (1977) 'Zur Entwicklung der westeuropäischen Wohlfahrtsstaaten', *Politische Vierteljahresschrift*, 18: 705–72.

Franzen, W., Haarland, H.P. and Niessen, H.-J. (2002) *Osteuropa auf dem Weg in die Europäische Union*, Frankfurt/M.: Campus.

Friedrich, H.B. (2002) *Grundzüge einer europäischen Wirtschafts- und Finanzverfassung*. Working Paper 5/2002, Munich: Centrum für angewandte Politikforschung.

Fritzler, M. and Unser, G. (1998) *Die Europäische Union*, Bonn: Bundeszentrale für Politische Bildung.

Fuchs, D. (1997) 'Welche Demokratie wollen die Deutschen? Einstellungen zur Demokratie im vereinigten Deutschland', in O.W. Gabriel (ed.) *Politische Orientierungen und Verhaltensweisen im vereinigten Deutschland*, Opladen: Leske + Budrich.

Fuchs, D. (1999a) 'Soziale Integration und politische Institutionen in modernen Gesellschaften', in J. Friedrichs and W. Jagodzinski (eds) *Soziale Integration. Sonderheft 39 der Kölner Zeitschrift für Soziologie und Sozialpsychologie*, Opladen: Westdeutscher Verlag.

Fuchs, D. (1999b) 'The Democratic Culture of Unified Germany', in P. Norris (ed.) *Critical Citizens. Global Support for Democratic Government*, Oxford: Oxford University Press.

Fuchs, D. (2000) 'Die demokratische Gemeinschaft in den USA und in Deutschland', in J. Gerhards (ed.) *Die Vermessung kultureller Unterschiede. USA und Deutschland im Vergleich*, Opladen: Westdeutscher Verlag.

Fuchs, D. (2002) 'Das Konzept der politischen Kultur: Die Fortsetzung einer Kontroverse in konstruktiver Absicht', in D. Fuchs, E. Roller and B. Wessels (eds) *Bürger und Demokratie in Ost und West. Studien zur politischen Kultur und zum politischen Prozeß. Festschrift für Hans-Dieter Klingemann*, Wiesbaden: Westdeutscher Verlag.

Fuchs, D. and Klingemann, H.-D. (2002) 'Eastward Enlargement of the European Union and the Identity of Europe', *West European Politics*, 25, 2: 19–54.

Fuchs, D. and Roller, E. (1998) 'Cultural Conditions of Transition to Liberal Democracies in Central and Eastern Europe', in S.H. Barnes and J. Simon (eds)

The Postcommunist Citizen, Budapest: Erasmus Foundation and Hungarian Academy of Sciences.

Fukuyama, F. (1995) *Trust. The Social Virtues and the Creation of Prosperity*, New York: Free Press.

Gabriel, O.W. (1994) 'Politische Einstellungen und politische Kultur', in O.W. Gabriel and F. Brettschneider (eds) *Die EU-Staaten im Vergleich: Strukturen, Prozesse, Politikinhalte* (2nd edn), Opladen: Westdeutscher Verlag.

Gabriel, O.W., Kunz, V., Roßteutscher, S. and van Deth, J.W. (2002) *Sozialkapital und Demokratie: Zivilgesellschaftliche Ressourcen im Vergleich*, Vienna: WUV-Universitätsverlag.

Galling, K. (ed.) (1962) *Die Religion in Geschichte und Gegenwart. Handwörterbuch für Theologie und Religionswissenschaft* (3rd edn), Tübingen: Mohr.

Gebhardt, J. (1996) 'Gibt es eine atlantische politische Kultur? Die historisch-politischen Grundlagen der atlantischen politischen Kultur', in W. Kremp (ed.) *Gibt es eine atlantische politische Kultur?*, Trier: Wissenschaftlicher Verlag WTV.

Gelissen, J. (2000) 'Popular Support for Institutionalised Solidarity. A Comparison between European Welfare States', *International Journal of Social Welfare*, 9: 285–300.

Gerhards, J. (1996) 'Religion und der Geist des Kapitalismus. Einstellungen zur Berufsarbeit und zur Wirtschaftsordnung in den USA und Spanien im Vergleich', *Berliner Journal für Soziologie*, 6: 541–9.

Gerhards, J. (2000a) 'Auf dem Weg zu einer theoriegesteuerten empirischen Kultursoziologie', in E. Barlösius, J. Gerhards, R. Hitzler and S. Neckel (eds) *Empirische Kultursoziologie*, Hagen: Studienbrief der Fernuniversität Hagen.

Gerhards, J. (ed.) (2000b) *Die Vermessung kultureller Unterschiede. USA und Deutschland im Vergleich*, Wiesbaden: Westdeutscher Verlag.

Gerhards, J. (2004a) 'Europäische Werte – Passt die Türkei kulturell zur EU?', *Aus Politik und Zeitgeschichte*, B38: 14–20.

Gerhards, J. (2004b) 'Passt die Türkei kulturell in die Europäische Union?', *Frankfurter Allgemeine Sonntagszeitung*, 15.2.2004: 13.

Gerhards, J. and Hölscher, M. (2003) 'Kulturelle Unterschiede zwischen Mitglieds- und Beitrittsländern der EU. Das Beispiel Familien- und Gleichberechtigungsvorstellungen', *Zeitschrift für Soziologie*, 32: 206–25.

Gerhards, J. and Rössel, J. (1999) 'Zur Transnationalisierung der Gesellschaft der Bundesrepublik. Entwicklungen, Ursachen und mögliche Folgen für die europäische Integration', *Zeitschrift für Soziologie*, 28: 325–44.

Gerhards, J. and Rössel, J. (2000) 'Familienkulturen im internationalen Vergleich. Normative Vorstellungen von Ehe, Sexualität und Kindererziehung in den Vereinigten Staaten und in West- und Ostdeutschland', in J. Gerhards (ed.) *Die Vermessung kultureller Unterschiede. Deutschland und USA im Vergleich*, Opladen: Westdeutscher Verlag.

Giering, C. (2001) *Arbeitsteilung in Europa. Modell für ein nachvollziehbares Zuständigkeitsprofil*, Working Paper 12/2001, Munich: Centrum für angewandte Politikforschung.

Girvetz, H.K. (1972) 'Welfare State', in D.L. Sills (ed.) *International Encyclopedia of the Social Sciences*, Volume 16, New York: Macmillan Company & Free Press.

Glazer, N. (2000) 'Disaggregating Culture', in L.E. Harrison and S.P. Huntington (eds) *Culture Matters. How Values Shape Human Progress*, New York: Basic Books.

Gomilschak, M., Haller, M. and Höllinger, F. (2000) 'Weibliche Erwerbstätigkeit und Einstellungen zur Rolle von Frauen', *Österreichische Zeitschrift für Soziologie*, 25: 65–77.

Gosewinkel, D., Rucht, D., van den Daele, W. and Kocka, J. (2003) 'Einleitung: Zivilgesellschaft – national und transnational', in D. Gosewinkel, D. Rucht, W. van den Daele and J. Kocka (eds) *Zivilgesellschaft – national und transnational, WZB-Jahrbuch 2003*, Berlin: Sigma.

Götting, U. (1998) *Transformation der Wohlfahrtsstaaten in Mittel- und Osteuropa. Eine Zwischenbilanz*, Opladen: Leske + Budrich.

Granovetter, M. and Swedberg, R. (eds) (2001) *The Sociology of Economic Life*, Cambridge, MA: Westview Press.

Greenfeld, L. (2001) *The Spirit of Capitalism. Nationalism and Economic Growth*, Cambridge, MA: Harvard University Press.

Grimm, D. (1995) *Braucht Europa eine Verfassung?*, Munich: Carl Friedrich von Siemens Stiftung.

Guiso, L., Sapienza, P. and Zingales, L. (2003) 'People's Opium? Religion and Economic Attitudes', *Journal of Monetary Economics*, 50: 225–82.

Gwartney, J. and Lawson, R. (with N. Emerick) (2003) *Economic Freedom of the World. 2003 Annual Report*, Vancouver: Fraser Institute. Online. Available HTTP: http://www.freetheworld.com/release_2003.html (accessed 29 September 2004).

Haas, E. (1958) *The Uniting of Europe*, Stanford, CA: Stanford University Press.

Habermas, J. (1981) *Theorie des kommunikativen Handelns*, 2 volumes, Frankfurt/ M.: Suhrkamp.

Habermas, J. (1996) 'Braucht Europa eine Verfassung? Eine Bemerkung zu Dieter Grimm', in J. Habermas *Die Einbeziehung des Anderen*, Frankfurt/M.: Suhrkamp.

Haller, M. and Hoellinger, F. (1994) 'Female Employment and the Change of Gender Roles: The Conflictual Relationship between Participation and Attitudes in International Comparison', *International Sociology*, 9: 87–112.

Halman, L. (2001) *The European Values Study: A Third Wave. Source Book of the 1999/2000 European Values Study Surveys*, Tilburg: WORC.

Halman, L. and Petterson, T. (2003) 'Religion und Politik in der zeitgenössischen Gesellschaft: Differenzierung oder Entdifferenzierung? Eine komparative Analyse von EVS/WVS-Umfragedaten aus 38 Ländern', in M. Minkenberg and U. Willems (eds) *Politik und Religion. Sonderheft 33 der Politischen Vierteljahresschrift*, Wiesbaden: Westdeutscher Verlag.

Hantrais, L. and M.-T. Letablier (1996) *Families and Family Policies in Europe*, London: Longman.

Harding, S., Phillips, D. and Fogarty, M. (1986) *Contrasting Values in Western Europe. Unity, Diversity and Change*, Basingstoke: Macmillan.

Harrison, L.E. (2000) 'Promoting Progressive Cultural Change', in L.E. Harrison and S.P. Huntington (eds) *Culture Matters. How Values Shape Human Progress*, New York: Basic Books.

Hasenfeld, Y.Z. and Rafferty, J.A. (1989) 'The Determinants of Public Attitudes Toward the Welfare State', *Social Forces*, 67: 1027–48.

Hechter, M. (1993) 'Values Research in the Social and Behavioral Sciences', in M. Hechter, L. Nadel and R.E. Michod (eds) *The Origin of Values*, New York: de Gruyter.

Heidenreich, M. (2003) 'Territoriale Ungleichheiten in der erweiterten EU', *Kölner Zeitschrift für Soziologie und Sozialpsychologie*, 55: 1–28.

Heider, F. (1958) *The Psychology of Interpersonal Relations*, New York: Wiley.

Henrich, J., Boyd, R., Bowles, S., Camerer, C., Fehr, E., Gintis, H. and McElreath, R. (2001) 'In Search of Homo Economicus. Behavioral Experiments in 15 Small-Scale Societies', *American Economic Review*, 91: 73–8.

Hervieu-Léger, D. (1999) 'Religiöse Ausdrucksformen der Moderne. Die Phänomene des Glaubens in den europäischen Gesellschaften', in H. Kaelble and J. Schriewer (eds) *Diskurse und Entwicklungspfade. Der Gesellschaftsvergleich in den Geschichts- und Sozialwissenschaften*, Frankfurt/M.: Campus.

Hettlage, R. (ed.) (1990) *Die Bundesrepublik. Eine historische Bilanz*, Munich: Verlag C.H. Beck.

Hildebrandt, W.P. (1996) 'Die islamische Wirtschaftsideologie. Eine Untersuchung unter besonderer Berücksichtigung des Falls Pakistan', *Diskussionspapier 51 des Fachbereichs Wirtschaftswissenschaften, Fachgebiet Volkswirtschaft des Vorderen Orients, an der Freien Universität Berlin*, Berlin: Das arabische Buch.

Hödl, E. and Weida, A. (2001) *Europäische Wirtschaftsordnung. Funktionsbedingungen und Herausforderungen eines europäischen Modells*, Frankfurt/M.: Peter Lang.

Höhmann, H.-H. (ed.) (1999) *Eine unterschätzte Dimension? Zur Rolle wirtschaftskultureller Faktoren in der osteuropäischen Transformation*, Bremen: Edition Temmen.

Höhmann, H.-H. (ed.) (2001) *Kultur als Bestimmungsfaktor der Transformation im Osten Europas. Konzeptionelle Entwicklungen – Empirische Befunde*, Bremen: Edition Temmen.

Höhmann, H.-H. (ed.) (2002) *Wirtschaft und Kultur im Transformationsprozeß. Wirkungen, Interdependenzen, Konflikte*, Bremen: Edition Temmen.

Höhmann, H.-H., Kautonen, T., Lagemann, B. and Welter, F. (2002) 'Entrepreneurial Strategies and Trust: a Position Paper', in H.-H. Höhmann and F. Welter (eds) *Entrepreneurial Strategies and Trust. Structure and Evolution of Entrepreneurial Behavioural Patterns in East and West European Environments – Concepts and Considerations. Arbeitspapiere und Materialien der Forschungsstelle Osteuropa Bremen*, Nr. 37, Bremen: Forschungsstelle Osteuropa.

Höllinger, F. (1991) 'Frauenerwerbstätigkeit und Wandel der Geschlechtsrollen im internationalen Vergleich', *Kölner Zeitschrift für Soziologie und Sozialpsychologie*, 43: 753–71.

Hölscher, M. (2006) *Wirtschaftskulturen in der erweiterten EU. Die Einstellungen der Bürgerinnen und Bürger im europäischen Vergleich*, Wiesbaden: Verlag für Sozialwissenschaften.

Höpflinger, F. (1997) 'Haushalts- und Familienstrukturen im intereuropäischen Vergleich', in S. Hradil and S. Immerfall (eds) *Die westeuropäischen Gesellschaften im Vergleich*, Opladen: Leske + Budrich.

Howard, M.M. (2002) 'The Weakness of Postcommunist Civil Society', *Journal of Democracy*, 13: 157–69.

Human Development Report Office/United Nations Development Programme (UNDP) (2000) *Human Development Report*, New York and Oxford: Oxford University Press.

Huntington, S.P. (1991) *The Third Wave: Democratization in the Late Twentieth Century*, Norman, OK: University of Oklahoma Press.

Huntington, S.P. (1996) *Der Kampf der Kulturen. The Clash of Civilizations. Die Neugestaltung der Weltpolitik im 21. Jahrhundert*, Munich: Europaverlag.

Huntington, S.P. (2000) 'Forward. Cultures Count', in L.E. Harrison and S.P. Huntington (eds) *Culture Matters. How Values Shape Human Progress*, New York: Basic Books.

Immerfall, S. (1997) 'Soziale Integration in den westeuropäischen Gesellschaften. Werte, Mitgliedschaften und Netzwerke', in S. Hradil and S. Immerfall (eds) *Die westeuropäischen Gesellschaften im Vergleich*, Opladen: Leske + Budrich.

Immerfall, S. (1998) 'Schwindendes Sozialkapital – Gefahr für den Wohlfahrtsstaat?', in J. Schmid and R. Niketta (eds) *Wohlfahrtsstaat. Krise und Reform im Vergleich*, Marburg: Metropolis Verlag.

Inglehart, R. (1971) 'The Silent Revolution in Europe', *American Political Science Review*, 65: 991–1017.

Inglehart, R. (1988) 'The Renaissance of Political Culture', *American Political Science Review*, 82: 485–532.

Inglehart, R. (1997) *Modernization and Postmodernization. Cultural, Economic and Political Change in 43 Societies*, Princeton, NJ: Princeton University Press.

Inglehart, R. (2000) 'Culture and Democracy', in L.E. Harrison and S.P. Huntington (eds) *Culture Matters. How Values Shape Human Progress*, New York: Basic Books.

Inglehart, R. (2001) 'Sociological Theories of Modernization', in N.J. Smelser and P.B. Baltes (eds) *International Encyclopedia of the Social and Behavioral Sciences*, Amsterdam: Elsevier.

Inglehart, R. and Baker, W.E. (2000) 'Modernization, Cultural Change, and the Persistence of Traditional Values', *American Sociological Review*, 65: 19–51.

Inglehart, R. and Norris, P. (2003a) *Rising Tide. Gender Equality and Cultural Change around the World*, New York: Cambridge University Press.

Inglehart, R. and Norris, P. (2003b) 'The True Clash of Civilizations', *Foreign Policy*, March/April 2003: 67–74.

Inglehart, R., Norris, P. and Welzel, C. (2002) 'Gender Equality and Democracy', *Comparative Sociology*, 1: 321–45.

Jachtenfuchs, M. (2002) *Die Konstruktion Europas. Verfassungsideen und institutionelle Entwicklung*, Baden-Baden: Nomos.

Jacobs, J., Müller, O. and Pickel, G. (2003) 'Persistence of the Democracies in Central and Eastern Europe: Consolidation, Stability, and People's Power of Resisting', in D. Pollack, J. Jacobs, O. Müller and G. Pickel (eds) *Political Culture in Post-Communist Europe. Attitudes in New Democracies*, Aldershot: Ashgate.

Jagodzinski, W. and Dobbelaere, K. (1993) 'Der Wandel kirchlicher Religiosität in Westeuropa', in J. Bergmann, A. Hahn and T. Luckmann (eds) *Religion und Kultur. Sonderheft 33 der Kölner Zeitschrift für Soziologie und Sozialpsychologie*, Opladen: Westdeutscher Verlag.

Jagodzinski, W. and Dobbelaere, K. (1995) 'Secularization and Church Religiosity', in J.W. van Deth and E. Scarbrough (eds) *The Impact of Values. Beliefs in Government. Vol. 4*, Oxford: Oxford University Press.

Joas, H. (1997) *Die Entstehung der Werte*, Frankfurt/M.: Suhrkamp.

Johnstone, D. (2003) *Comparative Social Policy in Europe*, Frankfurt/M.: Peter Lang.

Jung, D. (2002) 'Religion und Politik in der islamischen Welt', *Aus Politik und Zeitgeschichte*, B 42-3: 31–8.

Jung, D. (2003) 'Religion und Politik in der Türkei: Säkularistische Theokratie oder kemalistisches Panoptikon?', in M. Brocker, H. Behr and M. Hildebrandt (eds) *Religion – Staat – Politik. Zur Rolle der Religion in der nationalen und internationalen Politik*, Wiesbaden: Westdeutscher Verlag.

Kaase, M. (1983) 'Sinn oder Unsinn des Konzepts "Politische Kultur" für die Vergleichende Politikforschung oder auch: Der Versuch einen Pudding an die Wand zu nageln', in M. Kaase and H.-D. Klingemann (eds) *Wahlen und politisches System. Analysen aus Anlaß der Bundestagswahl 1980*, Opladen: Westdeutscher Verlag.

Kaelble, H. (1986) *Auf dem Weg zu einer europäischen Gesellschaft. Eine Sozialgeschichte Westeuropas 1880–1980*, Munich: C.H. Beck.

Kaelble, H. (1997) 'Europäische Vielfalt und der Weg zu einer europäischen Gesellschaft', in S. Hradil and S. Immerfall (eds) *Die westeuropäischen Gesellschaften im Vergleich*, Opladen: Leske + Budrich.

Kaelble, H. (2003) 'Gibt es eine europäische Zivilgesellschaft?', in D. Gosewinkel, D. Rucht, W. van den Daele and J. Kocka (eds) *Zivilgesellschaft – national und transnational. WZB-Jahrbuch 2003*, Berlin: Sigma.

Kallscheuer, O. (ed.) (1996) *Das Europa der Religionen. Ein Kontinent zwischen Säkularisierung und Fundamentalismus*, Frankfurt/M.: S. Fischer.

Kaufmann, F.-X. (1988) 'Christentum und Wohlfahrtsstaat', *Zeitschrift für Sozialreform*, 34: 65–89.

Kaufmann, F.-X. (1989) *Religion und Modernität. Sozialwissenschaftliche Perspektiven*, Tübingen: Mohr.

Kaufmann, F.-X. (2003) *Varianten des Wohlfahrtsstaats. Der deutsche Sozialstaat im internationalen Vergleich*, Frankfurt/M.: Edition Suhrkamp.

Kaufmann, F.-X., Kuijsten, A., Schulze, H.-J. and Strohmeiner, K.P. (eds) (1997) *Family Life and Family Policies in Europe*, Oxford: Clarendon Press.

Kecskes, R. (2000) 'Religiosität von Frauen und Männern im internationalen Vergleich', in I. Lukatis, R. Sommer and C. Wolf (eds) *Religion und Geschlechterverhältnis*, Opladen: Leske + Budrich.

Keller, B. (2001) *Europäische Arbeits- und Sozialpolitik*, Munich and Vienna: Oldenbourg.

Kelley, J. and de Graaf, N.D. (1997) 'National Context, Parental Socialization, and Religious Belief: Results from 15 Nations', *American Sociological Review*, 42, 4: 639–60.

Kerber, W. (ed.) (1986) *Säkularisierung und Wertewandel. Analysen und Überlegungen zur gesellschaftlichen Situation in Europa*, Munich: Kindt.

Kersbergen, K. van (1997) *Double Allegiance in European Integration. Publics, Nation-States, and Social Policy. Working Paper RSC No 97/15*, Florence: European University Institute.

Kielmannsegg, P. Graf (1996) 'Integration und Demokratie', in M. Jachtenfuchs and B. Kohler-Koch (eds) *Europäische Integration*, Opladen: Leske + Budrich.

Klages, H. (1984) *Wertorientierungen im Wandel. Rückblick, Gegenwartsanalyse, Prognosen*, Frankfurt/M.: Campus.

Kleinmann, M. (2002) *A European Welfare State? European Union Social Policy in Context*, New York: Palgrave.

Klingemann, H.-D. (1999) 'Mapping Political Support in the 1990s: A Global Analysis', in P. Norris (ed.) *Critical Citizens. Global Support for Democratic Government*, Oxford: Oxford University Press.

Kluckhohn, C. (1951) 'Values and Value-orientations in the Theory of Action. An Exploration in Definition and Classification', in T. Parsons and E.A. Shils (eds) *Toward a General Theory of Action*, Cambridge, MA: Harvard University Press.

Knill, C. (2001) *The Europeanisation of National Administrations. Patterns of Institutional Change and Persistence*, Cambridge: Cambridge University Press.

Knöbl, W. (2001) *Spielräume der Modernisierung*, Weilerswist: Velbrück.

Knöbl, W. (2003) 'Theories That Won't Pass Away: The Never Ending Story of Modernization Theory', in G. Delanty and E.F. Isin (eds) *Handbook of Historical Sociology*, London: Sage.

Knudsen, K. and Waerness, K. (1999) 'Reactions to Global Processes of Change: Attitudes Toward Gender Roles and Marriage in Modern Nations', *Comparative Social Research*, 18: 161–95.

Kocka, J. (2002) 'Wo liegt Europa?', *DIE ZEIT*, 49, 28.11.2002: 11.

Kohn, M.L. and Schooler, C. (1982) 'Job Conditions and Personality: A Longitudinal Assessment of their Reciprocal Effects', *American Journal of Sociology*, 87: 1257–86.

Köktas, E.M. (2002) 'Untersuchungen zur Lage der Religiosität in der türkischen Gesellschaft', *Journal of Religious Culture, Journal für Religionskultur*, 56: 1–10.

Kommission der Europäischen Gemeinschaften (2001) *Europäisches Regieren. Ein Weissbuch*, Luxembourg: Amt für Amtliche Veröffentlichungen der Europäischen Gemeinschaften.

Kommission der Europäischen Gemeinschaften (2002a) *Auf dem Weg zur erweiterten Union. Strategiepapier und Bericht der Europäischen Kommission über die Fortschritte jedes Bewerberlandes auf dem Weg zum Beitritt*, Brussels: Kommission der Europäischen Gemeinschaften.

Kommission der Europäischen Gemeinschaften (2002b) *Bericht der Kommission über Europäisches Regieren*, Luxembourg: Amt für amtliche Veröffentlichungen der Europäischen Gemeinschaften.

Kommission der Europäischen Gemeinschaften (2002c) *Die Lissabonner Strategie – Den Wandel herbeiführen. Mitteilung der Kommission für den Europäischen Rat auf seiner Frühjahrstagung in Barcelona. KOM (2002) 14*, Brussels: Kommission der Europäischen Gemeinschaften.

Kommission der Europäischen Gemeinschaften (2002d) *Konsultationsdokument: Hin zu einer verstärkten Kultur der Konsultation und des Dialogs – Vorschlag für allgemeine Grundsätze und Mindeststandards für die Konsultation betroffener Parteien durch die Kommission*, Luxembourg: Amt für amtliche Veröffentlichungen der Europäischen Gemeinschaften.

Kommission der Europäischen Gemeinschaften (2003) *Die Erweiterung fortsetzen. Strategiepapier und Bericht der Europäischen Kommission über die Fortschritte Bulgariens, Rumäniens und der Türkei auf dem Weg zum Beitritt*, KOM (2003) 676 endgültig, Brussels.

Korpi, W. (2001) 'Class, Gender and Inequality: The Role of the Welfare State', in M. Kohli and M. Novak (eds) *Will Europe Work? Integration, Employment and the Social Order*, London and New York: Routledge.

Kowalsky, W. (1999) *Europäische Sozialpolitik: Ausgangsbedingungen, Antriebskräfte und Entwicklungspotentiale*, Opladen: Leske + Budrich.

Künzler, J., Schulze, H.-J. and van Hekken, S. (1999) 'Welfare States and Normative Orientations Toward Women's Employment', *Comparative Social Research*, 18: 161–95.

Lagemann, B. (2001) '"Soziales Kapital" als Kategorie kulturorientierter Transformationsforschung', in H.-H. Höhmann (ed.) *Kultur als Bestimmungsfaktor der Transformation im Osten Europas. Konzeptionelle Entwicklungen – empirische Befunde*, Bremen: Edition Temmen.

Lahusen, C. and Jauß, C. (2001) *Lobbying als Beruf. Interessengruppen in der Europäischen Union*, Baden-Baden: Nomos.

Landes, D. (2000) 'Culture Makes Almost all the Difference', in L.E. Harrison and S.P. Huntington (eds) *Culture Matters. How Values Shape Human Progress*, New York: Basic Books.

Lane, J.-E. (2002) *Substance of EU Law. Working Paper 22*, Singapore: Public Policy Programme of the National University of Singapore. Online. Available HTTP: http://www.fas.nus.edu.sg/ppp/docs/wp/wp22.pdf (accessed 29 September 2004).

Lane, J.-E. and Errson, S. (2002) *Culture and Politics. A Comparative Approach*, Aldershot: Ashgate.

Lane, R. (1992) 'Political Culture. Residual Category or General Theory?', *Comparative Political Studies*, 25: 362–87.

La Porta, R., Lopez-de-Silanes, F., Shleifer, A. and Vishny, R.W. (1997) 'Trust in Large Organizations', *American Economic Review*, 87, 2: 333–8.

Läufer, T. (ed.) (1999) *Vertrag von Amsterdam. Texte des EU-Vertrages und des EG-Vertrages mit den deutschen Begleitgesetzen. Herausgegeben im Auftrag des Presse- und Informationsamtes der Bundesregierung*, Bonn: Europa Union Verlag.

Leggewie, C. (ed.) (2004) *Die Türkei und Europa. Die Positionen*, Frankfurt: Suhrkamp.

Leibfried, S. (1996) 'Wohlfahrtsstaatliche Perspektiven der Europäischen Union. Auf dem Wege zu positiver Souveränitätsverflechtung', in M. Jachtenfuchs and B. Kohler-Koch (eds) *Europäische Integration*, Opladen: UTB.

Leibfried, S. and Pierson, P. (eds) (1995) *European Social Policy. Between Fragmentation and Integration*, Washington: The Brookings Institution.

Leibfried, S. and Pierson, P. (2000) 'Soziales Europa. Bilanz und Perspektiven', in H.-D. Klingemann and Neidhardt, F. (eds) *Zur Zukunft der Demokratie. Herausforderungen im Zeitalter der Globalisierung. WZB-Jahrbuch 2000*, Berlin: Edition Sigma.

Leipold, H. (2003) 'Wirtschaftsethik und wirtschaftliche Entwicklung im Islam', in H.G. Nutzinger (ed.) *Christliche, jüdische und islamische Wirtschaftsethik. Über religiöse Grundlagen wirtschaftlichen Verhaltens in der säkularen Gesellschaft*, Marburg: Metropolis-Verlag.

Lepsius, M.R. (1986) 'Interessen und Ideen. Die Zurechnungsproblematik bei Max Weber', in F. Neidhardt, M.R. Lepsius and J. Weiß (eds) *Kultur und Gesellschaft. Sonderheft 27 der Kölner Zeitschrift für Soziologie und Sozialpsychologie*, Opladen: Westdeutscher Verlag.

Lepsius, M.R. (1990) 'Der europäische Nationalstaat: Erbe oder Zukunft', in R.M. Lepsius (ed.) *Interessen, Ideen, Institutionen*, Opladen: Westdeutscher Verlag.

Lepsius, M.R. (1997) 'Bildet sich eine kulturelle Identität in der Europäischen Union?', *Blätter für deutsche und internationale Politik*, Issue 8: 948–55.

Lepsius, M.R. (2003) 'Eigenart und Potenzial des Weber-Paradigmas', in Gert Albert, Agathe Bienfait, Steffen Sigmund and Claus Wendt (eds) *Das Weber-Paradigama. Studien zur Weiterentwicklung von Max Webers Forschungsprogramm*, Tübingen: Mohr Siebeck.

Lerner, D. (1958) *The Passing of Traditional Society. Modernizing the Middle East*, New York and London: The Free Press.

Lessenich, S. and Ostner, I. (eds) (1998) *Welten des Wohlfahrtskapitalismus*, Frankfurt/ M.: Campus.

Lesthaeghe, R. and Meekers, D. (1986) 'Value Changes and the Dimensions of Familism in the European Community', *European Journal of Population*, 2: 225–68.

Lipset, S.M. (1959) 'Some Social Requisities of Democracy', *American Political Science Review*, 53: 69–105.

Lipset, S.M. (1994) 'The Social Requisites of Democracy Revisited', *American Sociological Review*, 59: 1–22.

Lipset, S.M. (1996) *American Exceptionalism. A Double-Edged Sword*, New York and London: Norton.

Lipset, S.M. (2000) 'Conditions for Democracy', in H.-D. Klingemann and F. Neidhardt (eds) *Zur Zukunft der Demokratie. Herausforderungen im Zeitalter der Globalisierung. WZB-Jahrbuch 2000*, Berlin: Sigma.

Lipset, S.M. and Lenz, G.S. (2000) 'Corruption Culture and Markets', in L.E. Harrison and S.P. Huntington (eds) *Culture Matters. How Values Shape Human Progress*, New York: Basic Books.

McClelland, D.C. (1961) *The Achieving Society*, New York: Free Press.

Maddison, A. (1995) *Monitoring the World Economy 1820–1992*, Paris: Development Centre of the Organisation for Economic Cooperation and Development.

Majone, G. (1996) 'Redistributive und sozialregulative Politik', in M. Jachtenfuchs and B. Kohler-Koch (eds) *Europäische Integration*, Opladen: UTB.

Manow, P. (2002) '"The Good, the Bad, and the Ugly". Esping-Andersens Sozialstaats-Typologie und die konfessionellen Wurzeln des westlichen Wohlfahrtsstaats', *Kölner Zeitschrift für Soziologie und Sozialpsychologie*, 54, 2: 203–25. Online. Available HTTP: http://www.ksg.harvard.edu/inequality/ Summer/Summer04/papers/Manow.pdf (accessed 19 September 2006).

Martin, D. (1978) 'The Religious Condition of Europe', in S. Giner and M. Scotford-Archer (eds) *Contemporary Europe. Social Structures and Cultural Patterns*, London: Routledge and Kegan Paul.

Marwell, G. and Ames, R.E. (1981) 'Economists Free Ride: Does Anyone Else?', *Journal of Public Economics*, 13: 295–310.

Marx, K. (1972) 'Zur Kritik der Hegelschen Rechtsphilosophie (Einleitung)', in *Karl Marx and Friedrich Engels Werke, Band 1*, Berlin: Dietz Verlag.

Marx, K. and Engels, F. (1969) *Die deutsche Ideologie. Werke Band 3*, Berlin: Dietz.

Mau, S. (2002) 'Wohlfahrtsregimes als Reziprozitätsarrangements. Versuch einer Typologisierung', *Berliner Journal für Soziologie* 12: 345–64.

Mau, S. (2003) *The Moral Economy of Welfare States. Britain and Germany Compared*, London and New York: Routledge.

Maurus, W. (1998) 'Die Bedeutung der Kultur für Politik und Gesellschaft. Das Beispiel Europa', in R. Bernecker (ed.) *Kultur und Entwicklung*, Bonn: Dt. Unesco-Kommission.

Mayer, K.U. and Schoepflin, U. (1989) 'The State and the Life Course', *Annual Review of Sociology*, 15: 187–209.

Merkel, W. (1995) 'Theorien der Transformation: Die demokratische Konsolidierung post-autoritärer Gesellschaften', *Politische Vierteljahresschrift*, 26: 38–40.

Merkel, W. (1999) *Systemtransformation. Eine Einführung in die Theorie und Empirie der Transformationsforschung*, Opladen: Leske + Budrich.

Meulemann, H. (1996) *Werte und Wertewandel: Zur Identität einer geteilten und wieder vereinten Nation*, Weinheim/Munich: Juventa.

Meulemann, H. (ed.) (1998) *Werte und nationale Identität im vereinigten Deutschland. Erklärungsansätze der Umfrageforschung*, Opladen: Leske + Budrich.

Meulemann, H. (2000) 'Beyond Belief', *European Societies*, 2: 167–94.

Meulemann, H. (2004) 'Enforced Secularization – Spontaneous Revival? Religious Belief, Unbelief, Uncertainty and Indifference in East and West European Countries 1991–1998', *European Sociological Review*, 20: 47–61.

Meulemann, H. and Birkelbach, K. (2001) 'Biographische Erfahrungen und politische Einstellungen zwischen der Jugend und Lebensmitte. Die Entwicklung von Wertansprüchen an die Politik bei ehemaligen Gymnasiasten im 16., 30. und 43. Lebensjahr zwischen 1969–1997', *Politische Vierteljahreszeitschrift*, 42: 30–50.

Meyer, J.W., Boli, J., Thomas, G.M. and Ramirez, F.O. (1997) 'World Society and the Nation State', *American Sociological Review*, 103: 144–81.

Micklewright, J. and Stewart, K. (2000) *Child Well-Being in the EU and Enlargement to the East. Innocenti Working Papers, ESP No. 75*, Florence: UNICEF Innocenti Research Centre.

Minkenberg, M. (2003) 'Staat und Kirche in westlichen Demokratien', in M. Minkenberg and U. Willems (eds) *Politik und Religion. Sonderheft 33 der Politischen Vierteljahresschrift*, Wiesbaden: Westdeutscher Verlag.

Minkenberg, M. and Willems, U. (eds) (2003) *Politik und Religion. Sonderheft 33 der Politischen Vierteljahresschrift*, Wiesbaden: Westdeutscher Verlag.

Mishler, W. and Rose, R. (1999) 'Five Years After the Fall: Trajectories of Support for Democracy in Post-Communist Europe', in P. Norris (ed.) *Critical Citizens. Global Support for Democratic Government*, Oxford: Oxford University Press.

Mitterauer, M. (1999) 'Europäische Familienformen im interkulturellen Vergleich', in W. Köpke and B. Schmelz (eds) *Das Gemeinsame Haus Europa*, Munich: Deutscher Taschenbuch Verlag.

Mitterauer, M. and Ortmayr, N. (1997) *Familie im 20. Jahrhundert. Traditionen, Probleme, Perspektiven*, Frankfurt/M.: Brandes and Apsel.

Mitterauer, M. and Sieder, R. (1991) *Vom Patriarchat zur Partnerschaft: Zum Strukturwandel der Familie*, Munich: Beck.

Müller, E.N. and Seligson, M.A. (1994) 'Civic Culture and Democracy: The Question of Causal Relationships', *American Political Science Review*, 88: 635–52.

Müller, G. and Batz, H. (eds) (1976) *Theologische Realenzyklopädie*, Berlin/New York: de Gruyter.

Müller, H. (2003) 'Kampf der Kulturen – Religion als Strukturfaktor einer weltpolitischen Konfliktformation?', in M. Minkenberg and U. Willems (eds) *Politik und Religion. Sonderheft 33 der Politischen Vierteljahresschrift*, Wiesbaden: Westdeutscher Verlag.

Müller, O., Pickel, G. and Pollack, D. (2003) 'Wandel religiös-kirchlicher Orientierungsmuster und Verhaltensweisen in Osteuropa', in M. Brocker, H. Behr and M. Hildebrandt (eds) *Religion – Staat – Politik. Zur Rolle der Religion in der nationalen und internationalen Politik*, Wiesbaden: Westdeutscher Verlag.

Müller-Armack, A. (1959) *Religion und Wirtschaft. Geistesgeschichtliche Hintergründe unserer europäischen Lebensform*, Stuttgart: W. Kohlhammer Verlag.

Müller-Graff, P.-C. (ed.) (2000) *Die Europäische Gemeinschaft in der Welthandelsorganisation. Globalisierung und Weltmarktrecht als Herausforderung für Europa. Schriftenreihe des Arbeitskreises Europäische Integration e.V., Bd. 47*, Baden-Baden: Nomos.

Mummert, U. (2001) 'Kulturelles Erbe und marktwirtschaftliche Reformen', in H.-H. Höhmann (ed.) *Kultur als Bestimmungsfaktor im Osten Europas. Konzeptionelle Entwicklungen – empirische Befunde*, Bremen: Edition Temmen.

Mutlu, K. (1996) 'Examining Religious Beliefs among University Students in Ankara', *British Journal of Sociology*, 47: 353–9.

Nauck, B. and Klaus, D. (2005) 'Families in Turkey', in B.N. Adams and J. Trost (eds) *Handbook of World Families*, London: Sage Publications.

Need, A. and Evans, G. (2001) 'Analysing Patterns of Religious Participation in Post-Communist Eastern Europe', *British Journal of Sociology*, 52, 2: 229–48.

Newton, K. (2001) 'Trust, Social Capital, Civic Society, and Democracy', *International Political Science Review*, 22: 201–14.

Niedermayer, O. and Sinnott, R. (eds) (1995) *Public Opinion and Internationalized Governance*, Oxford: Oxford University Press.

Niles, F.S. (1999) 'Toward a Cross-Cultural Understanding of Work-Related Beliefs', *Human Relations*, 52, 7: 855–67.

Norris, P. (2002) *Democratic Phoenix*, Cambridge: Cambridge University Press.

Norris, P. and Inglehart, R. (2002) 'Islamic Culture and Democracy. Testing the "Clash of Civilizations" Thesis', *Comparative Sociology*, 1: 235–63.

Nutzinger, H.G. (ed.) (2003) *Christliche, jüdische und islamische Wirtschaftsethik. Über religiöse Grundlagen wirtschaftlichen Verhaltens in der säkularen Gesellschaft*, Marburg: Metropolis-Verlag.

Obinger, H. and Wagschal, U. (2001) 'Families of Nations and Public Policy', *West European Politics*, 24, 1: 99–114.

O'Connor, J. (1993) 'Gender, Class and Citizenship in the Comparative Analysis of Welfare State Regimes: Theoretical and Methodological Issues', *British Journal of Sociology*, 44: 501–18.

OECD (2001) *OECD Employment Outlook 2001*, Paris: OECD.

OECD (2002) *Society at a Glance*. Online. Available HTTP: http://www.oecd.org/document/24/0,2340,en_2649_37419_2671576_1_1_1_37419,00.html (accessed 29 September 2004).

Opielka, M. (2003a) 'Religiöse und zivilreligiöse Begründungen der Sozialpolitik', in M. Brocker, H. Behr and M. Hildebrandt (eds) *Religion – Staat – Politik. Zur Rolle der Religion in der nationalen und internationalen Politik*, Wiesbaden: Westdeutscher Verlag.

Opielka, M. (2003b) 'Religiöse Werte im Wohlfahrtsstaat', Text on CD-Rom in J. Allmendinger (ed.) *Entstaatlichung und soziale Sicherheit: Verhandlungen des 31. Kongresses der Deutschen Gesellschaft für Soziologie in Leipzig. Part 1*, Opladen: Leske + Budrich.

Orloff, A.S. (1993) 'Gender and Social Rights of Citizenship: State Policies and Gender Relations in Comparative Perspective', *American Sociological Review*, 58: 303–28.

Osgood, C.E. (1960) 'Cognitive Dynamics in the Conduct of Human Affairs', *Public Opinion Quarterly*, 31: 341–65.

Oesterdiekhoff, G.W. (2000) *Familie, Wirtschaft und Gesellschaft in Europa. Die historische Entwicklung von Familie und Ehe im Kulturvergleich*, Stuttgart: Breuninger Stiftung GmbH.

Ostner, I. (1993) 'Geschlechterverhältnisse im Prozeß der europäischen Integration', in B. Schäfers (ed.) *Lebensverhältnisse und soziale Konflikte im neuen Europa. Verhandlungen des 26. Deutschen Soziologentages in Düsseldorf 1992*, Frankfurt/M.: Campus.

Ostner, I. (2000) 'Review-Essay: Auf der Suche nach dem Europäischen Sozialmodell', in Zentrum für Europa- und Nordamerika-Studien (ed.) *Sozialmodell Europa. Konturen eines Phänomens. Jahrbuch für Europa- und Nordamerika-Studien, Folge 4/2000*, Opladen: Leske + Budrich.

Ostner, I. and Lewis, J. (1998) 'Geschlechterpolitik zwischen europäischer und nationalstaatlicher Regelung', in S. Leibfried and P. Pierson (eds) *Standort Europa. Sozialpolitik zwischen Nationalstaat und europäischer Integration*, Frankfurt/M.: Suhrkamp.

Page, B.I. and Shapiro, R.Y. (1983) 'Effects of Public Opinion on Policy', *American Political Science Review*, 77: 175–90.

Pascall, G. and Manning, N. (2000) 'Gender and Social Policy: Comparing Welfare States in Central and Eastern Europe and the Former Soviet Union', *Journal of European Social Policy*, 10: 240–66.

Patterson, O. (2000) 'Taking Culture Seriously: A Framework and an Afro-American Illustration', in L.E. Harrison and S.P. Huntington (eds) *Culture Matters. How Values Shape Human Progress*, New York: Basic Books.

Paxton, P. (2002) 'Social Capital and Democracy: An Interdependent Relationship', *American Sociological Review*, 67: 254–77.

Pejovich, S. (2003) *Understanding the Transaction Costs of Transition: It's the Culture, Stupid. Working Paper Nr. 24/2003*, Turin: International Centre for Economic Research (ICER).

Pfau-Effinger, B. (2000) *Kultur und Frauenerwerbstätigkeit in Europa*, Opladen: Leske + Budrich.

Pharr, S. and Putnam, R.D. (2000) *Disaffected Democracies: What's Troubling the Trilateral Countries*, Princeton, N.J: Princeton University Press.

Pickel, G. (1998) 'Religiosität und Kirchlichkeit in Ost- und Westeuropa. Vergleichende Betrachtungen religiöser Orientierungen nach dem Umbruch in Osteuropa', in D. Pollack (ed.) *Religiöser Wandel in den postkommunistischen Ländern Ost- und Mitteleuropas*, Würzburg: Ergon Verlag.

Pickel, G. (2001) 'Moralische Vorstellungen und ihre religiöse Fundierung im europäischen Vergleich', in G. Pickel and M. Krüggeler (eds) *Religion und Moral. Entkoppelt oder verknüpft?*, Opladen: Leske + Budrich.

Pickel, G. and Jacobs, J. (2001) *Einstellungen zur Demokratie und zur Gewährleistung von Rechten und Freiheiten in den jungen Demokratien Mittel- und Osteuropas. Discussion Paper No. 9/01*, Frankfurt (Oder): Frankfurter Institut für Transformationsstudien.

Pickel, G. and Krüggeler, M. (eds) (2001) *Religion und Moral. Entkoppelt oder verknüpft?*, Opladen: Leske + Budrich.

Pickel, S., Pickel, G. and Walz, D. (eds) (1998) *Politische Einheit – kultureller Zwiespalt? Die Erklärung politischer und demokratischer Einstellungen in Ostdeutschland vor der Bundestagswahl 1998*, Berlin: Peter Lang.

Platzer, H.-W. (1997) *Sozialstaatliche Entwicklungen in Europa und die Sozialpolitik der Europäischen Union: Die soziale Dimension im EU-Reformprozeß*, Baden-Baden: Nomos.

Pollack, D. (2001) 'Modifications in the Religious Field of Central and Eastern Europe', *European Societies*, 3, 2: 135–65.

Pollack, D. (2002) 'Religion und Politik in den postkommunistischen Staaten Ostmittel- und Osteuropas', *Aus Politik und Zeitgeschichte*, B 42–3: 15–22.

Pollack, D. (2003) 'Das Verhältnis von Religion und Politik in den postkommunistischen Staaten Ostmittel- und Osteuropas und seine Auswirkungen auf die Vitalität des religiösen Feldes', in M. Minkenberg and U. Willems (eds) *Politik und Religion. Sonderheft 33 der Politischen Vierteljahresschrift*, Wiesbaden: Westdeutscher Verlag.

Pollack, D. and Pickel, G. (2000) *The Vitality of Religion – Church, Integration and Politics in Eastern and Western Europe in Comparison. Arbeitsberichte Nr. 13/00*, Frankfurt (Oder): Frankfurter Institut für Transformationsstudien.

Pollack, D. and Pickel, G. (2003) 'Deinstitutionalisierung des Religiösen und religiöse Individualisierung in Ost- und Westdeutschland', *Kölner Zeitschrift für Soziologie und Sozialpsychologie*, 55: 447–74.

Porter, M.E. (2000) 'Attitudes, Values, Beliefs and the Microeconomics of Prosperity', in L.E. Harrison and S.P. Huntington (eds) *Culture Matters. How Values Shape Human Progress*, New York: Basic Books.

Przeworski, A. and Teune, H. (1970) *The Logic of Comparative Social Inquiry*, New York: Wiley.

Putnam, R.D. (2000) *Bowling Alone. The Collapse and Revival of American Community*, New York: Simon und Schuster.

Putnam, R.D. (2002) *Democracies in Flux: The Evolution of Social Capital in Contemporary Societies*, New York: Oxford University Press.

Putnam, R.D., Leonardi R. and Nanetti, R.Y. (1993) *Making Democracy Work. Civic Traditions in Modern Italy*, Princeton, NJ: Princeton University Press.

Rat der Europäischen Union (2000) *Europäische Sozialagenda. Amtsblatt der Europäischen Gemeinschaften (2001/C 157/02)*, Luxembourg: Amt für amtliche Veröffentlichungen der Europäischen Gemeinschaften.

Ratzinger, J. and Amato, A. (2004) *Schreiben an die Bischöfe der katholischen Kirche über die Zusammenarbeit von Mann und Frau in der Kirche und in der Welt*. Online. Available HTTP: http://www.vatican.va (accessed 23 September 2004).

Rémond, R. (1998) *Religion und Gesellschaft in Europa. Von 1789 bis zur Gegenwart*, Munich: Beck.

Robbers, G. (1995) 'Staat und Kirche in der europäischen Union', in G. Robbers (ed.) *Staat und Kirche in der europäischen Union*, Baden-Baden: Nomos.

Robbers, G. (2003a) 'Status und Stellung von Religionsgemeinschaften in der Europäischen Union', in M. Minkenberg and U. Willems (eds) *Politik und Religion. Sonderheft 33 der Politischen Vierteljahresschrift*, Wiesbaden: Westdeutscher Verlag.

Robbers, G. (ed.) (2003b) *Religionsrechtliche Bestimmungen in der Europäischen Union*. Online. Available HTTP: http://www.uni-trier.de/~ievr/EUreligionsrecht/eureligion_de.pdf (accessed 2 July 2003).

Rohe, K. (1990) 'Politische Kultur und ihre Analyse. Probleme und Perspektiven der politischen Kulturforschung', *Historische Zeitschrift*, 250: 321–46.

Rohrschneider, R. (1999) *Learning Democracy. Democratic and Economic Values in Unified Germany*, Oxford: Oxford University Press.

Rokkan, S. (2000) *Staat, Nation und Demokratie in Europa. Die Theorie Stein Rokkans aus seinen gesammelten Werken rekonstruiert und eingeleitet von Peter Flora*, Frankfurt/M.: Suhrkamp.

Roller, E. (1992) *Einstellungen der Bürger zum Wohlfahrtsstaat der Bundesrepublik Deutschland*, Opladen: Westdeutscher Verlag.

Roller, E. (1999) 'Staatsbezug und Individualismus: Dimensionen des sozialkulturellen Wertwandels', in T. Ellwein and E. Holtmann (eds) *50 Jahre Bundesrepublik Deutschland. Rahmenbedingungen – Entwicklungen – Perspektiven*, Opladen: Westdeutscher Verlag.

Roller, E. (2000a) 'Ende des sozialstaatlichen Konsenses? Zum Aufbrechen traditioneller und zur Entstehung neuer Konfliktstrukturen in Deutschland', in O. Niedermayer and B. Westle (eds) *Demokratie und Partizipation. Festschrift für Max Kaase*, Opladen: Westdeutscher Verlag.

Roller, E. (2000b) 'Marktwirtschaftliche und wohlfahrtsstaatliche Gerechtigkeitsprinzipien in Deutschland und den USA', in J. Gerhards (ed.) *Die Vermessung kultureller Unterschiede*, Opladen: Westdeutscher Verlag.

Roller, E. (2002) 'Wohlfahrtsstaat', in M. Greiffenhagen and S. Greiffenhagen (eds) *Handwörterbuch zur politischen Kultur der Bundesrepublik*, Wiesbaden: Westdeutscher Verlag.

Roose, J. (2003) *Die Europäisierung von Umweltorganisationen. Die Umweltbewegung auf dem langen Weg nach Brussels*, Wiesbaden: Westdeutscher Verlag.

Rose, R., Mishler, W. and Haerpfer, C. (1998) *Democracy and its Alternatives. Understanding Post-Communist Societies*, Baltimore, MD: Johns Hopkins University Press.

Rosenbaum, H. (1982) *Formen der Familie. Untersuchungen zum Zusammenhang von Familienverhältnissen, Sozialstruktur und sozialem Wandel in der deutschen Gesellschaft des 19. Jahrhunderts*, Frankfurt/M.: Suhrkamp.

Rössel, J. (2000) 'Mobilisierung, Staat und Demokratie. Eine Reinterpretation einer modernisierungstheoretischen These', *Kölner Zeitschrift für Soziologie und Sozialpsychologie*, 52: 609–35.

Rueschemeyer, D., Huber Stephens, E. and Stephens, J. D. (1992) *Capitalist Development and Democracy*, Chicago, IL: University of Chicago Press.

Rueschemeyer, D., Rueschemeyer, M. and Wittrock, B. (eds) (1998) *Participation and Democracy, East and West: Comparisons and Interpretations*, Armonk, NY: Sharp.

Sandholtz, W. and Stone Sweet, A. (1998) *European Integration and Supranational Governance*, Oxford: Oxford University Press.

Schäfer, A. (2002) *Vier Perspektiven zur Entstehung und Entwicklung der 'Europäischen Beschäftigungspolitik'. Discussion Paper 9/02*, Cologne: Max-Planck-Institut für Gesellschaftsforschung.

Scharpf, F.W. (1996) 'Politische Optionen im vollendeten Binnenmarkt', in M. Jachtenfuchs and B. Kohler-Koch (eds) *Europäische Integration*, Opladen: Westdeutscher Verlag.

Scharpf, F.W. (1998) 'Demokratie in der transnationalen Politik', in U. Beck (ed.) *Politik der Globalisierung*, Frankfurt/M.: Suhrkamp.

Schilling, H. (1999) 'Der religionssoziologische Typus Europas als Bezugspunkt inner- und interzivilisatorischer Gesellschaftsvergleiche', in H. Kaelble and

J. Schriewer (eds) *Gesellschaften im Vergleich. Forschungen aus Sozial- und Geschichtswissenschaften* (2nd edn), Frankfurt/M.: Peter Lang.

Schluchter, W. (1988) *Religion und Lebensführung. Volume 2: Studien zu Max Webers Religionssoziologie und Herrschaftssoziologie*, Frankfurt/M.: Suhrkamp.

Schluchter, W. (1991) *Religion und Lebensführung. Volume 1: Studien zu Max Webers Kultur- und Werttheorie*, Frankfurt/M.: Suhrkamp.

Schmähl, W. and Rische, H. (eds) (1997) *Europäische Sozialpolitik*, Baden-Baden: Nomos.

Schmid, J. (1996) *Wohlfahrtsstaaten im Vergleich. Soziale Sicherungssysteme in Europa: Organisation, Finanzierung, Leistungen und Probleme*, Opladen: Leske + Budrich.

Schmid, J. and Niketta, R. (1998) 'Wohlfahrtsstaat. Krise und Reform im Vergleich. Einführung in die Thematik und in den Band', in J. Schmid and R. Niketta (eds) *Wohlfahrtsstaat. Krise und Reform im Vergleich*, Marburg: Metropolis Verlag.

Schmidt, I. and Binder, S. (1998) 'Wettbewerbspolitik', in P. Klemmer (ed.) *Handbuch Europäische Wirtschaftspolitik*, Munich: Vahlen.

Schmidt, M.G. (1997) *Erwerbsbeteiligung von Frauen und Männern im Industrieländervergleich*, Opladen: Leske + Budrich.

Schmidt, M.G. (1998) *Sozialpolitik in Deutschland. Historische Entwicklung und internationaler Vergleich*, Opladen: Leske + Budrich.

Schmitter, P.C. (1996) 'Imaging the Future of the Euro-Polity with the Help of New Concepts', in G. Marks, F.W. Scharpf, P.C. Schmitter and W. Streeck (eds) *Governance in the European Union*, London: Sage.

Schneider, F. (1998) 'Einige grundlegende Elemente einer europäisch-föderalen Verfassung unter Zuhilfenahme der konstitutionellen ökonomischen Theorie', in D. Cassel (ed.) *Europäische Integration als ordnungspolitische Gestaltungsaufgabe. Probleme der Vertiefung und Erweiterung der Europäischen Union*, Berlin: Duncker and Humblot.

Schulte, B. (2001) 'EG-rechtliche Rahmenbedingungen für nationale Sozialpolitik', in W. Schmähl (ed.) *Möglichkeiten und Grenzen einer nationalen Sozialpolitik in der Europäischen Union*, Berlin: Duncker and Humblot.

Schweitzer, M. (2000) 'Sanktionen gegen Österreich: Rechtliche Analyse des Vorgehens auf dem europäischen Parkett', in Euro-Info-Point (ed.) *Background Europe 71, 29. Februar 2000*. Online. Available HTTP: http://www.ooe.gv.at/info_point_europa/ (accessed 29 September 2004).

Schwinger, E. (2003) 'Der "Geist des Kapitalismus" und die Grenzen der Fürsorglichkeit: Zur Moral der Bürgergesellschaft', in M. Brocker, H. Behr and M. Hildebrandt (eds) *Religion – Staat – Politik. Zur Rolle der Religion in der nationalen und internationalen Politik*, Wiesbaden: Westdeutscher Verlag.

Schwinn, T. (2001) *Differenzierung ohne Gesellschaft. Umstellung eines soziologischen Konzepts*, Weilerswist: Velbrück Wissenschaft.

Sieder, R. (1987) *Sozialgeschichte der Familie*, Frankfurt/M.: Suhrkamp.

Silver, B.D. and Dowley, K.M. (2000) 'Measuring Political Culture in Multiethnic Societies. Reaggregating the World-Values-Survey', *Comparative Political Studies*, 33: 517–50.

Simmel, G. (1992) *Soziologie. Untersuchungen über die Formen der Vergesellschaftung. Gesamtausgabe, Volume 11*, Frankfurt/M.: Suhrkamp.

Singh, B.K. (1980) 'Trends in Attitudes Toward Premarital Sexual Relations', *Journal of Marriage and the Family*, 42: 387–93.

Skocpol, T. and Amenta, E. (1986) 'States and Social Policies', *American Review of Sociology*, 12: 131–57.

Smelser, N.J. and Swedberg, R. (eds) (1994) *The Handbook of Economic Sociology*, Princeton, NJ and New York: Princeton University Press and Russell Sage Foundation.

Smith, D.H. (1972) 'Modernization and the Emergence of Voluntary Organizations', *International Journal of Comparative Sociology*, 13: 113–34.

Smith, D.H. (1975) 'Voluntary Action and Voluntary Groups', *Annual Review of Sociology*, 1: 247–70.

Smith, D.H. and Shen, C. (2002) 'A Model of Voluntary Association Prevalence Applied to Data on Larger Contemporary Nations', *International Journal of Comparative Sociology*, 43: 93–133.

Soysal, Y. (2003) 'Kulturelle Standortbestimmung Europas', *Aus Politik und Zeitgeschichte*, 12: 35–8.

Spohn, W. (2000) 'Die Osterweiterung der Europäischen Union und die Bedeutung kollektiver Identitäten. Ein Vergleich west- und osteuropäischer Staaten', *Berliner Journal für Soziologie*, 2: 219–40.

Stark, R. (2000) 'Die Religiosität der Deutschen und der Deutschamerikaner. Annäherung an ein "Experimentum Crucis"', in J. Gerhards (ed.) *Die Vermessung kultureller Unterschiede. USA und Deutschland im Vergleich*, Opladen: Westdeutscher Verlag.

Statistisches Bundesamt (ed.) (2000) *Datenreport 1999: Zahlen und Fakten über die Bundesrepublik Deutschland*, Bonn: Bundeszentrale für politische Bildung.

Stier, H., Lewin-Epstein, N. and Braun, M. (2001) 'Welfare Regimes, Family-Supportive Policies and Women's Employment along the Life-Course', *American Journal of Sociology*, 106: 1731–60.

Stone Sweet, A. (2004) *The Judicial Construction of Europe*, Oxford and New York: Oxford University Press.

Stone Sweet, A., Sandtholtz, W. and Fligstein, N. (eds) (2001) *The Institutionalization of Europe*, Oxford: Oxford University Press.

Stråth, B. (1996) 'Die kulturelle Konstruktion von Gemeinschaften und die Transformation von Gesellschaften', in W. Kaschuba, T. Scholze and L. Scholze-Irrlitz (eds) *Alltagskultur im Umbruch*, Weimar: Böhlau.

Streeck, W. (1998) 'Vom Binnenmarkt zum Bundesstaat? Überlegungen zur politischen Ökonomie der europäischen Sozialpolitik', in S. Leibfried and P. Pierson (eds) *Standort Europa. Sozialpolitik zwischen Nationalstaat und Europäischer Integration*, Frankfurt/M.: Suhrkamp.

Streeck, W. (2001) 'International competition, supranational integration, national solidarity: the emerging constitution of "Social Europe"', in M. Kohli and M. Novak (eds) *Will Europe Work*, London and New York: Routledge.

Svallfors, S. (1997) 'Worlds of Welfare and Attitudes to Redistribution: A Comparison of Eight Western Nations', *European Sociological Review*, 13: 283–304.

Svallfors, S. and Taylor-Gooby, P. (eds) (1999) *The End of the Welfare State? Responses to State Retrenchment*, London: Routledge.

Swatos, W.H. (1992) 'The Problem of Religious Politics and its Impact on World Society', in V. Bornschier and P. Lengyel (eds) *Waves, Formations and Values in the World System*, New Brunswick, NJ: Transaction Publishers.

Tang, H. (ed.) (2000) *Winners and Losers of EU Integration. Policy Issues for Central and Eastern Europe*, Washington, DC: World Bank.

Tessler, M. (2002) 'Do Islamic Orientations Influence Attitudes Toward Democracy in the Arab World? Evidence from Egypt, Jordan, Morocco, and Algeria', *International Journal of Comparative Sociology*, 43: 229–49.

Thelen, K. (1999) 'Historical Institutionalism in Comparative Politics', *Annual Review of Political Science*, 2: S. 369–404.

Therborn, G. (2000) *Die Gesellschaften Europas 1945–2000. Ein soziologischer Vergleich*, Frankfurt/M.: Campus.

Thiel, E. (1996) *Die Europäische Union*, Munich: Bayerische Landeszentrale für politische Bildungsarbeit.

Thome, H. (2003) 'Soziologische Wertforschung. Ein von Niklas Luhmann inspirierter Vorschlag für eine engere Verknüpfung von Theorie und Empirie', *Zeitschrift für Soziologie*, 32: 4–28.

de Tocqueville, A. (2000), *Democracy in America*, trans. and eds, Harvey C. Mansfield and Delba Winthrop, Chicago, IL: University of Chicago Press.

Tomka, M. and Zulehner, P.M. (2000) *Religion im gesellschaftlichen Kontext Ost(Mittel)Europas*, Ostfildern: Schwabenverlag.

Trifiletti, R. (1999) 'Southern European Welfare Regimes and the Worsening Position of Women', *Journal of European Social Policy*, 9: 49–64.

Turek, J. (1997) 'Competition Policy', in W. Weidenfeld and W. Wessels (eds) *Europe from A to Z. Guide to European Integration*, Luxembourg: Office for Official Publications of the European Communities.

UNDP (2000) *Human Development Report*, New York and Oxford: Oxford University Press.

Uslaner, E.M. (2004) 'Trust and Corruption', in J. Graf Lambsdorff, M. Taube and M. Schramm (eds) *Corruption and the New Institutional Economics*, London: Routledge.

Vanhanen, T. (ed.) (1997) *Prospects of Democracy. A Study of 172 Countries*, London: Routledge.

Vaughan-Whitehead, D.C. (2003) *EU-Enlargement versus Social Europe. The Uncertain Future of the European Social Model*, Cheltenham: Edward Elgar.

Verba, S., Schlozman, K.L. and Brady, H.E. (1995) *Voice and Equality. Civic Voluntarism in American Politics*, Cambridge, MA: Harvard University Press.

Vidinlioğlu, I. (2003) 'Gehört die Türkei zu Europa? Ein komparativer Ansatz zur kulturellen Integrierbarkeit der Türkei in die Europäische Union', Magisterarbeit am Institut für Sozialwissenschaften der Universität Stuttgart.

Viennaen, I. (1999) *Impact of Religion on Business Ethics in Europe and the Muslim World. Islamic Versus Christian Tradition*, Frankfurt/M.: Lang.

Voas, D., Olson, D.V.A. and Crockett, A. (2002) 'Religious Pluralism and Participation. Why Previous Research is Wrong', *American Sociological Review*, 67: 212–30.

Vobruba, G. (1989) *Arbeiten und Essen. Politik an den Grenzen des Arbeitsmarkts*, Vienna: Passagen.

Vobruba, G. (1999) 'Währungsunion, Sozialpolitik und das Problem einer umverteilungsfesten europäischen Identität', *Leviathan*, 27: 78–94.

Vobruba, G. (2001) *Integration + Erweiterung. Europa im Globalisierungsdilemma*, Vienna: Passagen Verlag.

Vobruba, G. (2004) 'Globalisation versus the European Social Model. Deconstructing the Contradiction Between Globalisation and the Welfare State', *Czech Sociological Review*, 40: 261–76.

Vogel, J. (1999) 'Der europäische "Welfare-Mix". Institutionelle Konfigurationen und Verteilungsergebnisse in der Europäischen Union und Schweden. Eine Längsschnitt- und vergleichende Perspektive', in P. Flora and H.-H. Noll (eds) *Sozialberichterstattung und Sozialstaatsbeobachtung. Individuelle Wohlfahrt und wohlfahrtsstaatliche Institutionen im Spiegel empirischer Analysen*, Frankfurt/M.: Campus.

Warren, M.E. (2001) *Democracy and Association*, Princeton, NJ: Princeton University Press.

Watson, P. (2000) 'Politics, Policy and Identity: EU Eastern Enlargement and East–West Differences', *Journal of European Public Policy*, 7: 369–84.

Weber, M. (1985) *Wirtschaft und Gesellschaft. Grundriss der verstehenden Soziologie*, Tübingen: Mohr.

Weber, M. (1988) *Gesammelte Aufsätze zur Religionssoziologie I*, Tübingen: Mohr.

Wehler, H.-U. (2002) 'Das Türkenproblem', *Die Zeit*, 38, 12.9.2002: 9.

Weiler, J.H.H. (1991) 'Problems of Legitimacy in Post 1992 Europe', *Außenwirtschaft*, 46: 411.

Weir, M. (2001) 'Welfare State', in N.J. Smelser and P.B. Baltes (eds) *International Encyclopedia of the Social and Behavioral Sciences*. Volume 24, Amsterdam: Elsevier.

Welzel, C. (2000) 'Humanentwicklung, Systemwettbewerb und Demokratie. Gibt es eine demokratische Evolution', in H.-D. Klingemann and F. Neidhardt (eds) *Zur Zukunft der Demokratie. Herausforderungen im Zeitalter der Globalisierung*, Berlin: Sigma.

Welzel, C. (2002) *Fluchtpunkt Humanentwicklung. Über die Grundlagen der Demokratie und die Ursachen ihrer Ausbreitung*, Wiesbaden: Westdeutscher Verlag.

Welzel, C., Inglehart, R. and Klingemann, H.-D. (2001) *Human Development as a General Theory of Social Change: A Multi-Level and Cross-Cultural Perspective*. Discussion Paper FS III 01–201, Berlin: Wissenschaftszentrum Berlin für Sozialforschung.

Wendt, H. (1997) 'The Former German Democratic Republic: The Standardized Family', in F.-X. Kaufmann, A. Kuijsten, H.-J. Schulze and K.P. Strohmeier (eds) *Family Life and Family Policies in Europe*, Oxford: Clarendon Press.

Weßels, B. (1994) 'Von der staatlichen Überorganisation zur freiwilligen Organisierung: Strukturelle Faktoren assoziativen Verhaltens in postkommunistischen Gesellschaften', in W. Streeck (ed.) *Staat und Verbände. Sonderheft 25 der Politischen Vierteljahresschrift*, Opladen: Westdeutscher Verlag.

Weßels, B. (2003) 'Die Entwicklung der Zivilgesellschaft in Mittel- und Osteuropa: intermediäre Akteure, Vertrauen und Partizipation', in D. Gosewinkel, D. Rucht, W. van den Daele and J. Kocka (eds) *Zivilgesellschaft – national und transnational. WZB-Jahrbuch 2003*, Berlin: Sigma.

Wessels, W. (1997) 'An Ever Closer Fusion? A Dynamic Macropolitical View on Integration Processes', *Journal of Common Market Studies*, 35: 267–99.

Westle, B. (2003) 'Universalismus oder Abgrenzung als Komponente der Identifikation mit der Europäischen Union', in F. Brettschneider, J.W. van Deth and E. Roller (eds) *Europäische Integration in der öffentlichen Meinung*, Opladen: Leske + Budrich.

Wilensky, H.L. (1975) *The Welfare State and Equality*, Berkeley, CA: University of California Press.

Willems, U. (2003) 'Religion als Privatsache? Eine kritische Auseinandersetzung mit dem liberalen Prinzip einer strikten Trennung von Politik und Religion', in

M. Minkenberg and U. Willems (eds) *Politik und Religion. Sonderheft 33 der Politischen Vierteljahresschrift*, Wiesbaden: Westdeutscher Verlag.

Williamson, M.R. and Wearing, A.J. (1996) 'Lay People's Cognitive Models of the Economy', *Journal of Economic Psychology*, 17: 3–38.

Wingen, M. (1997) *Familienpolitik. Grundlagen und aktuelle Probleme*, Bonn: Bundeszentrale für politische Bildung.

Winkler, H.A. (2002) 'Wir erweitern uns zu Tode', *Die Zeit*, 46, 7.11: 6.

Winterberg, J.M. (1994) *Religion und Marktwirtschaft. Die ordnungspolitischen Vorstellungen im Christentum und Islam*, Baden-Baden: Nomos.

Wittrock, B. (2001) 'Early Modernities: Varieties and Transitions', in S.N. Eisenstadt, W. Schluchter and B. Wittrock (eds) *Public Spheres and Collective Identities*, New Brunswick, NJ: Transaction Publishers.

Wobbe, T. (2001) 'Institutionalisierung von Gleichberechtigungsnormen im supranationalen Kontext: Die EU-Geschlechterpolitik', in B. Heintz (ed.) *Geschlechtersoziologie. Sonderheft 41 der Kölner Zeitschrift für Soziologie und Sozialpsychologie*, Wiesbaden: Westdeutscher Verlag.

Wuthnow, R. (1994) 'Religion and Economic Life', in N.J. Smelser and R. Swedberg (eds) *Handbook of Economic Sociology*, Princeton, NJ: Princeton University Press.

Yilmaz, H. (1997) 'Democratization from Above in Response to the International Context: Turkey, 1945–1950', *New Perspectives on Turkey*, 17: 1–38.

Yilmaz, H. (1999) 'Business Notions of Democracy: The Turkish Experience in the 1990s', *CEMOTI*, 27: 183–94.

Zapf, W. (ed.) (1971) *Theorien des sozialen Wandels*, Cologne: Kiepenheuer und Witsch.

Zapf, W. (1998) 'Modernisierung und Transformation', in B. Schäfers and W. Zapf (eds) *Handwörterbuch zur Gesellschaft der Bundesrepublik*, Opladen: Leske + Budrich.

Zulehner, P.M. and Denz, H. (1994) *Wie Europa lebt und glaubt. Europäische Wertestudie*, Düsseldorf: Patmos.

Data Sets

European Commission, Hartung, H., EUROBAROMETER 53 – Racism, Information Society, General Services, and Food Labeling, April–May 2000 [Computer file], distributes as ZA No. 3296 (Zentralarchiv für empirische Sozialforschung (ZA) Köln).

European Values Study, EUROPEAN VALUES STUDY, 1999/2000 [Computer file] 2003/Release 1, The Netherlands, Germany: Tilburg University, Zentralarchiv für Empirische Sozialforschung, Cologne (ZA), Netherlands Institute for Scientific Information Services (NIWI), Amsterdam [producer], 2003. Germany: ZA Köln [distributor], 2003.

ISSP 1996 – "Role of Government III", distributed as ZA No. 2900 (ZA Köln).

ISSP 1998 – "Religion II", distributed as ZANo. 3190 (ZA Köln).

World Values Study Group, WORLD VALUES SURVEY, 1995–1997 [Computer file]. ICPSR version. Ann Arbor, MI: Institute for Social Research [producer], 1998. Ann Arbor, MI: Inter-university Consortium for Political and Social Research [distributor], 1998.

Index

accession countries: culture and values
of 4–5; recent growth of 132,
see also Enlargement I countries;
Enlargement II countries
achievement orientation, economic
16–17, 70, 71–4, 85, 89
Alber, J. 105
Alesina, A., and Angeletos, G.M. 88
Allensbach Institute for Public Opinion
143
Almond, G.A., and Verba, S. 9, 14, 143
Ambrosius, G., and Kaelble, H. 145
Amsterdam, Treaty of 53, 54, 107, 109
assembly and association, freedom of
109
attendance, at religious services 29–31,
33–4, 102, 144
Aust, A., *et al.* 93
authoritarianism 112, 117, 118, 126,
129–30

Bach, M. 3
Barbier, M. 46
behaviour, and value orientations 13–14
Bell, D. 16, 17, 85, 86
"benchmark countries" 40–3, 82–5,
128–30
Berger, P.L. 16, 67
Berglund, S., *et al.* 116
Bergmann, K. 53
Bertelsmann Stiftung 3
Berthold, N., and Hilpert, J. 68
Bible, interpretations of 44, 61
Blekesaune, M., and Quadagno, J. 101,
103
blueprint: and concepts of democracy
and civil society 108–9, 120–1,
128–30, 134, 137; economic
67–71, 81–2, 91, 134, 136; for

family values and gender roles
52–4, 55, 134, 135–6; as normative
reference point 4, 9–12; as object
of content analysis 18; for religion
26–8, 40, 49–50, 134, 135–6; for
welfare state 93–5, 134, 136, *see
also* values
Bornschier, V. 145
Brague, R. 10
Bretherton, C. 63
Bundesamt für Statistik 145
Burgsdorf, W. 11
Busch, K. 104, 106
Buss, A. 87

Campenhausen, A. F. von 49
capital: free movement of 69; social
119, 122–4, 128
capitalism: and economic beliefs 88;
and Protestantism 86
Carson, M. 52
"Cassis de Dijon" verdict 69
Catholicism/Catholic countries 26–7,
29, 36; and attitudes to welfare state
102–3; and gender roles 62
Charter of Fundamental Rights 27, 52,
53
Chaves, M., and Cann, D. 46
childcare: availability of 54; education,
and achievement orientation 71;
and familial roles 55, *see also*
motherhood
childhood, definition of 52
Christian democratic model, of welfare
state 92
Christianity/Christian countries
26–7, 29, 38, 44–5; and attitudes
to welfare state 102–3, 105;
and cultural identity 10, 17; and